# Altamaha River User's Guide

MORNING AND WILLOW, APPLING COUNTY

# Altamaha River User's Guide    Joe Cook

GEORGIA RIVER NETWORK GUIDEBOOKS

The University of Georgia Press    Athens

A Wormsloe
FOUNDATION
*nature book*

GEORGIA
RIVER
NETWORK
GUIDEBOOKS

© 2024 by the University of Georgia Press
Athens, Georgia 30602
www.ugapress.org
Photographs © 2024 by Joe Cook
All rights reserved
Designed by Omega Clay
Set in 9/11.5 Quadraat OT by Kaelin Chappell Broaddus
Printed and bound by Reliance Printing

The paper in this book meets the guidelines for permanence
and durability of the Committee on Production Guidelines for
Book Longevity of the Council on Library Resources.

Most University of Georgia Press titles are
available from popular e-book vendors.

Printed in China
28 27 26 25 24 P 5 4 3 2 1

Library of Congress Cataloging-in-Publication Data

Names: Cook, Joe, 1966– author.
Title: Altamaha River user's guide / Joe Cook.
Description: Athens : The University of Georgia Press, 2024. | Series: Georgia river network guidebooks
Identifiers: LCCN 2022061349 | ISBN 9780820364261 (paperback)
Subjects: LCSH: Boats and boating—Georgia—Altamaha River. | Outdoor recreation—Georgia—Altamaha River. | Altamaha River (Ga.)—Guidebooks.
Classification: LCC GV776.G42 A574 2024 | DDC 797.109758/7—dc23/eng/20230216
LC record available at https://lccn.loc.gov/2022061349

# Contents

## THE RIVER

### ALTAMAHA

### OHOOPEE

# Acknowledgments

The information in this book was gathered from numerous print and online sources as well as interviews with local residents, historians, outfitters, scientists, and river lovers.

During the writing of the book, I drew from the following publications: *Running the River: Poleboats, Steamboats and Timber Rafts on the Altamaha, Ocmulgee, Oconee and Ohoopee* by Carlton A. Morrison; *The Natural Communities of Georgia* by Leslie Edwards, Jonathan Ambrose, and L. Katherine Kirkman; *Major Butler's Legacy: Five Generations of a Slaveholding Family* by Malcolm Bell Jr.; *The Rambler in Georgia*, edited by Mills Lane; *Drifting into Darien: A Personal and Natural History of the Altamaha River* by Janisse Ray; *T. Ross Sharpe's Tales of the Altamaha*, edited by Roger G. Branch and Fred W. Brogdon; *Men of Mark in Georgia*, edited by William J. Northen; *Footprints along the Hoopee* by James E. Dorsey; *Annals and Statistics of Glynn County, Georgia* by Charles S. Wylly; *Footprints in Appling County*, compiled by Ruth T. Baron; *Wayne County, Georgia: Its History and Its People*, edited by Bobby M. Martin; *Water Powers of Georgia*, published by the Geological Survey of Georgia in 1896, 1908, and 1921; *The Georgia and South Carolina Coastal Expeditions of Clarence Bloomfield Moore*, edited by Lewis Larson; *Georgia Place-Names* by Kenneth K. Krakow; *Placenames of Georgia: Essays of John H. Goff*, edited by Francis Lee Utley and Marion R. Hemperley; numerous reports written for Congress by the secretary of war between the 1870s and the 1940s; multiple issues of the *Georgia Historical Quarterly*, published by the Georgia Historical Society; the archives of the *Tattnall Journal*, *Baxley News-Banner*, and *Lyons Progress* newspapers; *River Rogue* by Brainard Cheney; *The War of Rebellion: A Compilation of the Official Records of the Union and Confederate Armies*; *History of the Savannah District 1829–1968* by M. L. Granger; *Encyclopedia of Southern Culture*, edited by Charles Reagan Wilson and William Ferris; *Memoirs of Georgia*, compiled by the Southern Historical Association; *Pioneers of Wiregrass Georgia*, compiled by Folks Huxford; *A Standard History of Georgia and Georgians* by Lucian Lamar Knight; *Early Days on the Georgia Tidewater* by Buddy Sullivan; *The Darien Journal of John Girardeau Legare, Ricegrower*, edited by Buddy Sullivan; and *Bringing Nature Home* by Douglas W. Tallamy.

Important online resources included www.newspapers.com, with historic records of the *Atlanta Constitution* and the *Macon Telegraph*; the Georgia Archives (www.georgiaarchives.com), with historic county maps; Georgia Historic Newspapers at the Digital Library of Georgia (www.gahistoricnewspapers.galileo.usg.edu), with historic records of the *Darien Timber Gazette*, the *Savannah Morning News*, the *Brunswick News*, and many other newspapers; the New Georgia Encyclopedia (www.georgiaencyclopedia.com); the digital library JSTOR (www.jstor.org), which provides access to countless scholarly journals; GenealogyBank (www.genealogybank.com); and multiple web pages of the Georgia Department of Natural Resources and its Environmental Protection Division found at www.gadnr.org.

Additionally, many local historians and river enthusiasts lent their knowledge and expertise to the book, including Campbell Dixon, Dink Nesmith, Lindsay

Thomas, Vince Stanley, Tim Keyes, Steve Friedman, Roger Branch, Christi Lambert, Eric Kauffman, Michael Gowens, Mike Moody, Don Ream, Janisse Ray, Missy Elder, Cricket Mobley, and Janet Fields.

Compiling this book involved traveling every mile of the Altamaha and Ohoopee Rivers on foot, by car, or, most especially, by canoe. Many friends assisted in this endeavor, accompanying me on paddle trips and providing shuttle services and other support. These friends include Kit Carson, Cary Baxter, Barry O'Neill, Ben Thompson, and Ramsey Cook.

A special thanks to those individuals, businesses, and foundations that funded the production of this book, including Rayonier Advanced Materials, Georgia Power Company, Oaks on the River Luxury Boutique Resort in Darien, the Waterfall Foundation, and Cary Baxter.

## Map Legend

★   **Point of Interest**

◎   **Shoal/Rapid**

⊠   **Fish Weir**

⊗   **Water Intake/Discharge**

•   **River Mile Marker**

■   **River Gauge**

—   **Dam**

⬓   **Campground**

⊥   **Marina**

⊙   **Outfitter**

▬   **Take Out/Launch Site**

▨   **Public Land**

The map on the next page provides an overview of the length
of the river, detailing sections covered on the individual
maps later in this book. The legend above explains
the symbols used on the maps.

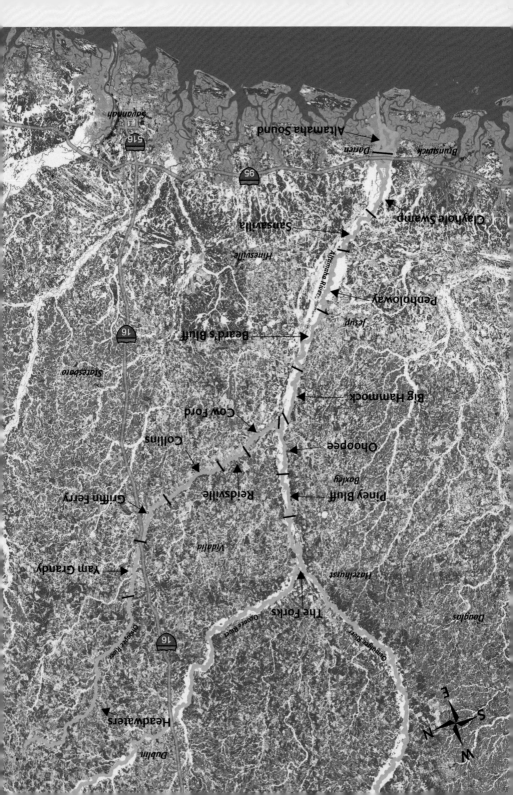

# Altamaha River User's Guide

SOUTH BRANCH OF ALTAMAHA RIVER, GLYNN COUNTY

# Introduction

Georgia's Altamaha River (pronounced ALL-ta-ma-haw) is but 137 miles long, a tri-
fling distance when compared with the Chattahoochee, the state's longest river at
434 miles.

Don't be misled by its length, however: the Altamaha, in the sum of its tributary parts—the Oconee, the Ocmulgee, the Ohoopee, and countless other streams
both named and unnamed—is massive. It is Georgia's largest river, draining nearly a
quarter of the state—some 14,000 square miles. Its headwater streams have inauspi-
cious starts—piped beneath the concrete and asphalt of the city of Atlanta, dammed
to create amenity ponds in suburban neighborhoods—but hundreds of miles downstream, those small, seemingly insignificant streams gather to create a mighty river
that is something to behold.

The Altamaha's winding wildness through Georgia's Coastal Plain is filled
with soaring bluffs, football-field-sized sandbars, vast and haunting river bottom
swamps, enchanting oxbow lakes, and, upon reaching the coast, tens of thousands
of acres of salt marshes and barrier islands.

Someone once described the Altamaha as Georgia's "Little Amazon" in an attempt to quantify its magnitude, and that seems to fit. Though its two major tributaries are dammed, the Altamaha itself is considered the largest free-flowing river
and third-largest river in terms of flow volume on the East Coast. Each year it delivers
on average some 3.2 trillion gallons of water to the Atlantic Ocean, or about 100,000
gallons each second.

It is big—and bigly important to biodiversity. The Georgia Department of Natural
Resources has identified 159 rare plants and animals within the Altamaha River basin. In addition, there are 41 species of amphibians and 59 species of reptiles roam-
ing the Altamaha's land and water. In the same corridor, researchers have found 160
bird species, and beneath the wa-
ter's surface are more than 100
species of fish and 18 species of
freshwater mussels.

Among the river's fauna are
the ancient shortnose sturgeon,
a prehistoric, federally protected
fish highly prized for its meat
and roe; the Altamaha spinymussel, a freshwater mussel with odd
spikes on its shell that give it the
appearance of an alien spaceship;
the common rainbow snake, a
beautifully black and red-striped
dweller of the river's

BROWN WATER SNAKE, McINTOSH COUNTY

OYSTERCATCHER ON OYSTER BED, McINTOSH COUNTY

vast swamps; the American oystercatcher, whose black head contrasts dramatically with its red eyes and its matching red chisel-like bill that it uses to open oysters and other shellfish; and the gopher frog, a 2-to-4-inch habitat specialist of Georgia's once-vast longleaf pine savannas and isolated wetlands.

The Amazon and the Altamaha also have in common the fact that many of their critters remain a mystery to us. For instance, we're just now beginning to understand the life cycle of the river's freshwater mussels. These immobile river bottom dwellers propagate and migrate by having their larval young hitchhike on fish, and recent studies have pointed to the likelihood that specific varieties of mussels depend on specific species of fish to survive. Then there's the American eel, a river dweller that, even after centuries of speculation and research, is still something of an enigma. We know it travels thousands of miles to the Sargasso Sea in the Atlantic Ocean to spawn, but the exact mechanism that triggers this epic journey remains poorly understood.

The plant life of the Altamaha is equally mysterious. Consider the fabled *Franklinia alatamaha*. First identified by John and William Bartram in 1765 in the bottomlands along the river not far from Fort Barrington, it has not been seen in the wild since 1803. The Bartrams, however, did modern mankind a favor by collecting and propagating the tree's seeds, and today all existing *Franklinia* are descended from those collections. There's also Radford's dicerandra, a plant so rare that it exists in only two known locations . . . both in McIntosh County. If you are lucky, you can spot the herb's showy pink blooms along river bluffs there in the early fall.

Humankind's interaction with this mysterious and wild garden dates back thousands of years. Along the river's route through the Coastal Plain, archaeologists have uncovered dozens of burial mounds and shell middens, attesting to the presence of

Native people long before Spanish explorers and missionaries set up shop in what would become Georgia's Golden Isles and then plied upriver into the interior in the late 1500s.

The English soon arrived, hoping to establish a buffer between their settlements in modern-day South Carolina and Spanish Florida to the south. Into this "debatable land" came General James Oglethorpe and his Georgia colonists in 1733, with high-minded ideals for economic equity, temperance, and Christian living. As such, in those early days both rum and slavery were prohibited, and individual land grants were limited to 500 acres.

But as the Carolinians moved in, they brought with them an economic system that depended on slavery. As the Carolina model consolidated land, wealth, and power, Oglethorpe's utopian vision faded, and by the mid-1700s, the Altamaha delta had been forever changed, the barrier and marsh islands ditched and diked to grow rice and cotton. To this day, you can still float your boat through the cross-hatched "rice canals" dug by enslaved people more than 200 years ago.

The colony's push inland was aided by "the Pocahontas of Georgia," Mary Musgrove, the daughter of an English trader and a Creek Indian mother who served as translator and counselor to Oglethorpe in the English colony's dealings with Native Americans. By the mid-1700s, Musgrove, with her second and third husbands, had established trading posts along the Altamaha, first at Sansavilla Bluff and then at the Forks, where the river begins.

For a time in the late 1700s and early 1800s, the river served as the boundary between Creek Indian lands to the south and west and the territory of the newly minted United States to the north and east. It was during this time that the pilots of pole boats and timber rafts began using the terms "bow injun" and "bow white" to direct their oarsmen as to which side of the river to pull the boat.

Darien, established in 1736 at the mouth of the river, would over the next 170 years become one of the most important seaports on the East Coast, as settlers pushed up the Altamaha, Oconee, and Ocmulgee Rivers and began felling the vast forests of longleaf pine that once stretched across South Georgia.

Hauled to the riverbanks and crafted into massive rafts or tapped to produce barrels of rosin and turpentine, the region's pine forests floated downriver, spawned the port at Darien and its sawmills, filled the holds of seagoing vessels, and birthed a timber rafting and steamboat culture that today still echoes off bluffs and across sandbars in place-names like Rag Point, Hell Shoals, Steamboat Eddy, the Sweatbox, and Alligator Congress. Trace the course of the Altamaha on a map, and you'll find seemingly every bluff and bend named—a product of this river being a highway of commerce for nearly two centuries.

The commercial importance of the river also brought decades of state and federal "river improvement" projects. Between the mid-1800s and the 1940s, workers dynamited rock shoals, dredged the river bottom, hauled away snags, and built extensive wooden dikes to constrict, deepen, and direct the river's flow. At low water, some of these century-old structures can still be seen.

As the pines played out, however, so did the river's importance as a highway for the products of the state's forests and fields. By the 1930s, the timber rafts had all but

3

ceased floating to Darien, and railroads, automobiles, and improved roads had rendered the venerable steamboats obsolete.

But that didn't stop local boosters from continuing to call for federal intervention to tap the river's "unrealized" potential. Plans to build multiple locks, dams, and canals on the river to create a barge superhighway persisted until the 1980s, when it became clear the meager returns of such projects could not justify the cost to taxpayers and the environment.

The second half of the 20th century did, however, bring industrial development to the Altamaha: a Rayonier pulp mill opened in Jesup in 1954, and a Georgia Power Company nuclear power plant began operations in Baxley in the early 1970s. The latter still pumps water from the river to cool its reactors. The former still uses the river as a repository for treated industrial waste, and that facility's history tracks the environmental awakening that has played out on every river across the state since the 1950s.

The mill in Jesup was initially hailed as an economic savior for the area; for once, high-paying jobs were available locally. But as untreated waste poured into the river in an era before environmental regulations, the Altamaha's commercial and recreational fisherman revolted. A newspaper headline of the era read "Pay Rolls vs. Fish Up for Georgia Debate"—and indeed, the conventional thinking at the time was that you could have one or the other, but not both. As an industrial executive remarked in an address to Georgia industry members in 1955: "Industry has not yet reached the millennium where there will be no odors, noises, or waste disposal problems."

But as the country hurtled toward a new millennium, America's attitude toward its rivers began to change, and citizens—the Altamaha's shad fisherman among the

RAYONIER ADVANCED MATERIALS, WAYNE COUNTY

loudest of them—began demanding change. In the 1960s, Georgia began forcing municipalities and industries to install wastewater treatment systems. Then in 1972, Congress passed the Clean Water Act, overriding a veto by President Richard Nixon. Over the next 40 years, citizen-based river protection groups organized to persuade, cajole, embarrass, and litigate state leaders and industrial polluters into abiding federal law.

On the Altamaha, that struggle played out well into the 21st century, as the grassroots environmental organization Altamaha Riverkeeper repeatedly challenged state pollution control permits issued to the Jesup mill, demanding a higher level of treatment to protect the river. Today, questions and conflicts linger over just how much pollutant removal is enough, but the jobs versus fish debate has been relegated to the previous century, and the river has seen marked improvements over the past several decades.

Recognition of the river's biological importance also led over the past three decades to the protection of more than 100,000 acres along the river corridor. Spearheaded by the Nature Conservancy, which was instrumental in protecting Altamaha Sound's barrier islands in the late 1960s, the effort has created a 42-mile corridor running from near Jesup to Darien in which both banks of the river are protected as state-owned wildlife management areas.

No narrative of the Altamaha would be complete without a nod to its major tributary, the Ohoopee River—referred to locally as simply the "Hoopee" (think short "oo" sound, as in "look," followed by a long "e" on the end). This stream flows in stark contrast to the alluvial Altamaha, which carries sediment from as far away as Georgia's Blue Ridge. Originating in Washington County in the Coastal Plain and winding more than 100 miles to its confluence with the Altamaha, the Ohoopee is a true blackwater river, collecting the tannins from decaying organic matter and flowing the color of black tea between white sandbars and cut banks.

The Ohoopee corridor is home to one of the state's more unique natural communities, the Ohoopee Dunes. Created by river sands blowing up along the eastern and northern banks of the Little Ohoopee and Ohoopee Rivers, this habitat is characterized by infertile sandy soils that lead to elfin forests of stunted oak and longleaf pine and harbor a host of rare species, such as gopher tortoises and eastern indigo snakes.

It is also home to communities like Wrightsville, Swainsboro, and Reidsville, for which the river has served as a primary recreation destination and gathering place. Through the years, places like Idylwild, the Rocks, Coleman Bridge, Ryals Bridge, and Tattnall County Landing have hosted everything from church picnics to political rallies. Such gatherings were dutifully reported in local newspapers, as epitomized by this account from a 1924 issue of the *Tattnall Journal*: "The Ohoopee River . . . will be a mecca for hundreds of people of this and adjoining counties on the fourth of July when the big pavilion will be opened to the public and a big band from Savannah will furnish music for the revelers."

Those locals who have long gathered at the Ohoopee and the Altamaha are now marketing their hometown play place. In 1998, a coalition of state, regional, and local representatives formed the Altamaha River Partnership to promote nature-based

5

SANDBAR CAMP, WAYNE COUNTY

tourism and associated economic development. This organization has worked to develop river-based special events ranging from catfish tournaments to paddle trips and promoted the development of the Altamaha River Water Trail, a boating route stretching from the confluence of the Ocmulgee and Oconee Rivers to Darien. The most recent push involves creating an environmental education center and associated amenities at Jesup's Jaycee Landing.

Today, the Altamaha, with its wild bottomland swamps, oxbow lakes, and backwater sloughs, remains a recreational mecca, attracting paddlers, motorboaters, jet skiers, hunters, and anglers who flock to the river's wide sandbars, which are ideally suited for overnight camps.

Owing to the river's wide floodplain (more than five miles wide at times), no towns—with the exception of Darien—ever grew up and stayed along its banks, and today, riverfront development is restricted to small neighborhoods situated on the river's high bluffs. The river corridor is sparsely populated and—with these few exceptions—presents a decidedly wild vibe.

In fact, while the Altamaha River basin spans over 2,850 square miles, the population of 15 counties lying within that watershed sits at around 360,000—less than 125 people per square mile! That's about half the number of people living in just a 525-square-mile area around the Altamaha's upstream tributary, the South River in Atlanta.

To take that comparison further, some 20 percent of the South River watershed is covered by concrete, asphalt, and buildings; the Altamaha watershed has less than 2 percent urban land cover. A whopping 61 percent of the lands draining directly into the Altamaha are classified as either forests or wetlands.

From 30,000 feet, the Altamaha presents a wide green swath across the state's Coastal Plain, and with some 165,000 acres of state-protected land along its flanks, a healthy future would seem to be secure for Georgia's largest river. But that conclusion would belie the reality that the Altamaha is the sum of its parts.

The water filling the Altamaha begins its journey on the streets of Atlanta, Decatur, Lawrenceville, Winder, Athens, and Commerce. Along that water's path to the Georgia coast, nearly 200 municipalities and industries discharge treated wastewater into the river system; another 96 spread treated wastewater on land within the basin. About 3 million people live within the wider basin's 14,000 square miles. Those people depend on the Altamaha's tributaries to supply drinking water and rely on those same streams to carry away their waste. And what those people do to the land around them accrues to the Altamaha. Fill a wetland here, dam a stream there, and the negative impacts roll downstream.

Because the Altamaha River basin lies wholly within Georgia and encompasses such a wide range of communities—from Atlanta's urban streets to Appling County's rural backroads—it, better than any other Georgia river, reflects the values of Georgia's populace. A healthy Altamaha suggests that residents upstream value not just the Altamaha but also Shoal Creek in Decatur, No Business Creek in Snellville, and Trail Creek in Athens.

Standing on the docks in Darien and looking upstream, you will see one wide river, but a better perspective is to view the Altamaha not as a single body of water but as the sum of thousands of tiny streams. We'd do well to think of ourselves likewise. Alone, we may seem insignificant, but like the streams that feed a river, our cumulative actions create mighty movements.

## Safety

Like all rivers, the Altamaha is not without its dangers. Rivers are unforgiving of our carelessness. Being properly prepared for your excursion and abiding by safe boating practices (including state boating laws) will reduce your risk of mistakes and keep you coming back to the river time after time.

### Wear Your Life Jacket

This is the No. 1 rule of boating safety. PFDs—personal flotation devices—are known as "life jackets" for a reason: they save lives. Georgia state law requires that all vessels have at least one U.S. Coast Guard–approved Type I, II, III, or V PFD for each person on board. However, Type V PFDs are acceptable only when worn and securely fastened. Children under the age of 10 must wear a life jacket at all times on a moving vessel.

Though state law doesn't require it, wearing your life jacket at all times is the best practice.

### Know Your Boat

Whether you are in/on a canoe, kayak, paddleboard, or motorized boat, you should know how to operate your vessel. Canoeing and kayaking classes are taught by nu-

KAYAKER AND SHRIMP BOAT NEAR EGG ISLAND BAR,
McINTOSH COUNTY

merous organizations. The Georgia Canoeing Association (www.gapaddle.com) and Georgia River Network (www.garivers.org) teach regular classes on paddling and boating safety. Additionally, the American Canoe Association (www.american canoe.org) is an excellent resource for online boating safety information.

The Georgia Department of Natural Resources (DNR) also provides extensive information on safety practices in motorized vessels (www.georgiawildlife.com /boating/boater-resources). Anyone born on or after January 1, 1998, must complete a boating education course approved by the DNR prior to operating a motorized vessel.

## Know the River and Prepare for Your Trip

If you are reading this, you've taken the first step toward a safe river trip—knowing the section of river that you plan to travel and understanding its unique dangers. For example, the coastal portions of the Altamaha River are tidally influenced; thus, tide charts should always be consulted before planning a trip on these sections. And on the Ohoopee River, there is a lowhead dam that, depending on water levels, can create a serious hazard. Before embarking on a trip, leave your itinerary with someone who can notify authorities if you don't return as planned. Remember: what you take on the trip is all that you have to survive and rescue yourself. Carry appropriate food, water, clothes, and rescue equipment. While no section of the Altamaha or Ohoopee River is far from "civilization," expect the unexpected and plan accordingly.

## Wear the Right Clothes

Wear the appropriate clothes to protect from sun, heat, rain, and cold. Cold water is especially dangerous, as extended contact with cold and wet can lead to hypothermia

DARIEN BOAT LANDING, McINTOSH COUNTY

and death. During cool weather, dress in layers using clothing made of synthetic fabrics such as polypropylene, nylon, neoprene, and polyester fleece. Always bring extra clothing protected in a waterproof container. When temperatures are below 60 degrees Fahrenheit, or combined air and water temperatures are below 120 degrees Fahrenheit, wear a wet suit or dry suit. Waterproof shoes, socks, and gloves are also recommended. Always wear secure-fitting river shoes to protect your feet. Helmets should always be worn when paddling whitewater.

## Watch for Other Boaters

The Altamaha is a wide river, providing plenty of space for boaters of all kinds to coexist. Nevertheless, those in person-powered vessels should be mindful of motorboat traffic. Waves created by motorboats are best navigated by turning the bow (nose) of the boat into the wave rather than taking the wave broadside. When paddling at night, a white light must be shown toward oncoming traffic.

BOATER'S CHECKLIST

- ☐ Spare Paddle . . . because paddles break and motors die
- ☐ Hat or Helmet . . . a hat for sun protection and/or warmth; a helmet for whitewater paddling
- ☐ Whistle or Signaling Device . . . three sharp blows on a whistle are a universal distress signal
- ☐ Throw Bags (ropes) and Other Rescue Gear . . . especially important in whitewater

9

- ☐ "River" Knife . . . a safely and easily accessible knife can save a life when entangled in rope or other hazards
- ☐ Bilge Pump or Bailer . . . because holes in boats do happen
- ☐ Extra Clothing in Dry Bag . . . dry clothes keep you warm; wet clothes, not so much
- ☐ Sunscreen
- ☐ Compass and Map
- ☐ First-Aid Kit
- ☐ Matches in Waterproof Container
- ☐ Small-Boat Repair Kit with Duct Tape

# Boating Etiquette

## Practice No-Trace Travel

Practicing no-trace travel is simple: just remember to leave your route so that those who come behind would never know that someone passed before them. Never litter, and always pack out trash (including the trash of those less considerate).

Conduct all toilet activity at least 200 feet from any body of water. Bury your waste in a cathole 6–8 inches deep or pack it out. Be conscious of private property and do not conduct your toilet activity in someone's backyard.

Additionally . . .

- Avoid building campfires, except in established fire rings or in emergencies.
- Minimize impacts to shore when launching, portaging, scouting, or taking out.
- Examine but do not touch cultural or historic structures and artifacts.
- Leave rocks, plants, and other natural objects as you find them.
- Do not disturb wildlife.

## Respect Others

The Altamaha and Ohoopee Rivers and their tributaries are traveled by many, and many people make their home along these waterways. Always be respectful of other river users and of riverfront property owners. Poor behavior by some river users can adversely impact other users through increased regulation and fees, limitations on access, and damage to the environment. Much of the property along the Altamaha and its tributaries is privately owned. While Georgia law allows boaters the right of passage on navigable streams, the law does not extend the right to travel on private property. Remain in the river channel, except in cases where you know public land exists or where you know that property owners allow boaters access.

Additionally . . .

- Know and obey all rules and regulations.
- Be courteous and polite when communicating with others.
- Avoid interfering with the recreational activities of others.
- Never engage in loud, lewd, or inappropriate behavior.

DAVIS LANDING, APPLING COUNTY

- Take care to avoid paddling near areas of heightened security.
- Control pets or leave them at home.
- Do not operate your vessel while under the influence of alcohol or drugs. Georgia law prohibits operating both motorized and nonmotorized vessels while under the influence of alcohol or drugs.

## A Note on Parking at Launch Sites and Take Outs

While many popular launch and take out sites have designated parking areas or pull-offs on rights-of-way, some river access locations identified in this guide do not have developed and designated, or even adequate, parking. Care should be taken when parking vehicles and unloading boats. Avoid parking on roadsides whenever possible.

## Outfitters

Numerous private outfitters provide services on the Altamaha and its tributaries, offering boat rentals, parking, shuttles, and other services. These businesses are listed here as well as in the chapters covering river sections in which they commonly operate.

### Three Rivers Outdoors

612 McNatt Falls Rd., Uvalda, Ga. 30473, 912-594-8379,
www.explorethreerivers.com

11

Located near the confluence of the Ocmulgee and the Oconee along the Altamaha River, Three Rivers Outdoors provides canoe and kayak rentals and shuttle service on the Altamaha, as well as on portions of the Ocmulgee and Oconee Rivers.

## Southeast Adventure Outfitters

313 Mallery St., St. Simons Island, Ga. 31522, 912-638-6732, www.southeastadventure.com

Located on St. Simons Island, Southeast Adventure Outfitters provides kayak tours, shuttle service, and boat charters, working primarily between Altamaha Regional Park and the coast.

## Altamaha Coastal Tours

85 Screven St., Darien, Ga. 31305, 912-437-6010, www.altamaha.com

Located in Darien, Altamaha Coastal Tours provides guided kayak trips as well as boat rentals and shuttle service, working primarily between Altamaha Regional Park and the coast.

## Ohoopee River Campground

1449 John Trull Cir., Lyons, Ga. 30436, 833-646-6733, www.ohoopeerivercampground.com

Located on the river near Lyons, Ohoopee River Campground provides canoe and kayak rentals as well as shuttle service. The campground features RV and tent sites as well as rental cabins.

## Stanley Southern Traditions

251 Bud Clifton Rd., Lyons, Ga. 30436, 256-684-6735, www.stanleysoutherntraditions.com

Located near Lyons, this lodge and event space also provides canoe and kayak rentals and shuttle service on the Ohoopee River in the Reidsville area.

# How to Use This Book

Each chapter presents a portion of the river that can generally be paddled in a canoe, kayak, or other nonmotorized vessel within a single day and provides essential information about the estimated length of the run (both in hours and miles), recommended water levels, the location for current water level information, and directions to launch and take out sites. Alternative launch sites and take out sites are noted where available. When determining travel time, we have estimated an average pace of 2 miles per hour. This pace will vary based on water levels and the effort of the paddler. The largest portion of each chapter presents, by miles and GPS coordinate, points of interest along the river. The map accompanying each chapter is intended for use as a reference while on the river. For that reason, all the maps are oriented from upstream to downstream rather than from north to south, and they present only the most important roads for reference. Drivers should, in conjunction with the written directions to launch and take out sites, use road maps and/or a GPS.

## Georgia River Guide App

In addition to the information contained in this printed guidebook, Georgia River Network provides information about dozens of recreational boating trails across Georgia through the Georgia River Guide, a smartphone app. Using the app, anyone looking to recreate on Georgia's rivers can, in a few simple taps, discover nearby water trails and learn about safe public access points, river mileage between accesses, points of interest, nearby shuttle services, and more. The app also provides details about river difficulty and potential hazards and rapids, as well as real-time access to river gauges and recommended runnable levels. The app is available through Google Play and the Apple App Store, or you can use the QR code below to download the app to your phone.

WATERMELON CREEK/BLUFF LAKE, TATTNALL COUNTY

# An Altamaha and Ohoopee Rivers Fishing Primer

The Altamaha and Ohoopee Rivers, free from dams that block fish migration, are blessed with an abundance of both year-round and migratory sport fish species, while the river's estuary on the coast provides opportunities to land a host of saltwater sport fish. The river has a long history of both commercial and recreational fishing, though some species that were overharvested in the past (such as Atlantic and shortnose sturgeon) are now protected under the Endangered Species Act.

## Freshwater Sport Fish

### Catfish

Considered one of the premier catfish rivers in Georgia, the Altamaha is home to two state records as of 2022: an 83-pound flathead catfish caught in 2010 and a 44-pound, 12-ounce channel catfish landed in 1972. Introduced illegally into the river system in the 1970s, flatheads have since adapted well to the Altamaha, and 30-to-50-pound fish are commonly taken. Large flatheads are not scavengers; they are top-tier predators, and as such they are best caught on live bait such as bream, shad, shiners, and large worms. Though they can be caught year-round, summer is prime catfish time in the Altamaha.

SANDBAR GATHERING, LONG COUNTY

Big blue catfish can also be taken in the Altamaha, though they are not as abundant as flatheads. Like the flathead, the blue catfish is a top predator that prefers live bait and can be targeted using bream, shiners, or shad. Typical catches in the Altamaha weigh in at 5 pounds, though fish above 20 pounds are not uncommon. The state record for blue catfish as of 2022 was a 110-pound, 6-ounce behemoth caught in the Chattahoochee River in 2020; the Altamaha River record is a 93-pounder caught in 2017. For both blue and flathead catfish, look to the deep holes where cover is available along the outside bends in the river, and come equipped with 30-pound test line and large 3/0 to 8/0 hooks.

Smaller than blues and flatheads, channel catfish are more opportunistic feeders, taking both live and dead bait. And because they rely heavily on their sense of smell to locate food, they are easily attracted to stink bait—the smellier the better. Chicken parts (including gizzards, hearts, and livers), cut bait, and commercially available stink bait are all good choices. Medium-sized hooks and 14-pound line are recommended. If it's trophy channel cats you are after, consider live bait such as bream or shad.

## Largemouth Bass

Altamaha River bass typically top out at 12 to 16 inches in length, but larger fish can be found. It's a big river, so finding them is half the challenge. In the cooler months, bass tend to migrate to the warmer water of the river's oxbow lakes and backwater sloughs, but as water temperatures move toward 60 degrees Fahrenheit, the bass begin moving to the river's main channel and will reside there throughout the summer.

In the oxbow lakes and sloughs, anglers should target areas with wood, overhanging willows, and other cover such as lily pads. Artificial lures mimicking frogs, crayfish, and shad are effective—the frog lures in the lily pads, and the crayfish and shad lures around other underwater structure. Crankbaits and spinner baits are also effective.

Once summer comes, the fish move to the mainstem of the river, seeking structure where they can rest in an eddy and ambush prey. Wood cover and eddies on the backside of sandbars are likely spots to find them.

The tidally influenced portion of the river from just upstream of Altamaha Regional Park to Darien is a largemouth bass hot spot, with multiple oxbow lakes and creeks that hold big bass, especially in March and April. Paying attention to the incoming and outgoing tides is important, as bass and the fish they feed on move with the tides. The last two hours of the outgoing tide and the first two hours of the incoming tide are the best times to fish for bass. One method is to fish the creek mouths during these periods.

While there are plenty of 1-to-2-pound bass in the river, 5-pound fish are not uncommon. It should be noted that the world-record largemouth bass was landed on Montgomery Lake, an oxbow lake on the Ocmulgee River not far upstream from where that river meets the Oconee River to form the Altamaha; caught by George Perry in 1932, the record-setting fish weighed in at 22 pounds, 4 ounces. The Altamaha River record is a 12-pounder caught in 1974.

## Bream

As with the Altamaha's other sport fish species, the abundance and size of the river's bream species (redbreasts, bluegills, and redears) are contingent on winter and spring floods. When the river stays high and spreads into the floodplain, it introduces more nutrients into the system and provides more habitat for fish. Thus more fish survive, and they grow larger. Hitting the river as it drops after a prolonged period of high water—regardless of the time of year—improves your chances of bringing home a stringer of panfish.

The peak season for targeting panfish on the Altamaha is between April and June, the very same time when river levels begin dropping and water temperatures begin rising. Redbreasts can typically be found in deep holes located along the main river channel where wood and other cover break the current and create eddies. Fishing with crickets and worms under a bobber is the traditional way to land these hand-sized fish; spinner baits and rooster tails are effective artificial lures.

Larger than the redbreasts, bluegills and redear sunfish—also called shellcrackers—like slower-moving water and thus can best be taken in the river's many oxbow lakes and backwater sloughs off the river's main channel, using the same baits as you would when casting for redbreasts.

As of 2022, the state record redbreast stood at 1 pound, 11 ounces; the redear sunfish at 4 pounds, 2 ounces; and the bluegill at 3 pounds, 5 ounces. When casting for these smaller fish, you are better off using light to medium rods with light spincast or spinning reels outfitted with 6-to-8-pound line. If you want to go old school, simple cane or fiberglass poles will do the trick as well.

## Crappie

Crappie fishing on the Altamaha cranks up in March and April when crappie begin spawning beneath the cover of willows and other trees along the banks of the river and its tributaries. Slack water found at the mouths of creeks and sloughs can be hot spots as the fish seek cover out of the main current.

In the tidal sections of the lower Altamaha, the mouths of rice canals cutting into the river's numerous islands as well as the mouths of creeks like Lewis, Stud Horse, and Big and Little Buzzard Creeks are likely spots to land crappie during the spring spawn.

Live minnows fished beneath bobbers and jigs are effective at fooling crappie.

The most recent state record black crappie was caught in 1975 and weighed in at 4 pounds, 4 ounces; the white crappie record was landed in 1984 and weighed 5 pounds.

## Shad

Historically, shad were among the most important species for commercial fishermen on the East Coast, including along the Altamaha River. Prized for their savory meat, shad were harvested in abundance through the late 1800s, when as much as 50 million pounds were harvested annually, but during the first half of the 20th century, landings declined precipitously. Georgia's harvest dropped by 85 percent between

1908 and 1981 and has not topped 60,000 pounds since the late 1990s. Commercial fishing using drift and set nets is still permitted on specific sections of the Altamaha and Ohoopee Rivers between January 1 and March 31.

Recreational fishermen can take shad on hook and line throughout the year, but you'll find the fish in the river during their late winter/spring spawning runs. Look for eddies where the shad may congregate and cast plastic grubs or flies that are colorful and flashy.

Lightweight tackle makes these fierce fighters and jumpers fun to catch, but be sure to bring along a long-handled net. Shad have notoriously thin skin around their mouths and can easily be lost off the hook when being pulled into shore or onto a boat.

## Mullet

Like shad, mullet have long been prized for their tasty meat—and for their roe. Unlike shad, however, mullet go to sea to spawn; yet they still spend much of their time venturing up coastal rivers. The hot summer months between July and September are prime time to target these fish that are often seen making impressive leaps from the water.

As omnivores, mullet feed mostly on algae, small insects, and insect larvae, so finding the right bait to fool these fish is challenging. In fact, it has led to one of the more unusual fishing techniques used on the Altamaha: simply place a salt block and a chum bag filled with farm feed like rabbit chow in the eddy of a sandbar and mark the spot. This will attract the fish, and they can then be taken using small hooks baited with red wiggler worms, bread, cheese, or meal worms.

JAYCEE LANDING, WAYNE COUNTY

Typically a mullet will weigh in at 1 to 3 pounds, though 5-pounders are common. The state record mullet weighed 9 pounds, 3 ounces, and was landed in 1994 along Cathead Creek, a tributary of the Altamaha near Darien.

# Marine Sport Fish

## Spotted Seatrout

Considered the most targeted marine sport fish in Georgia, spotted seatrout can be taken year-round in the Altamaha River estuary.

Cast live shrimp below floats to shallow water near the mouths of creeks, over oyster beds, or along sandbars—wherever structure on the bottom creates areas in which shallows drop to deep water. This is where seatrout tend to congregate. The best times to catch these fish are during low tides—the last two hours of the outgoing tide and the first two hours of the incoming tide. Jigs imitating minnows or shrimp also can be effective.

Seatrout can range up to 6 pounds, with the state record, landed in 1976, topping out at 9 pounds, 7 ounces. The daily limit on seatrout is 15 per angler, with a 14-inch minimum size.

## Red Drum

One of the most highly sought after sport fish of Altamaha Sound, red drum—also known as redfish—can be found in the sound year-round. Adult drum will migrate offshore during the winter months and then inshore during the spring while spawning in the estuary during the late summer and early fall. The offspring of these breeding fish, however, stay in the estuary, making it possible to catch small 14-inch yearlings year-round as well as massive "bull reds" of 25 pounds or more.

To land yearling red drum, cast live shrimp to shallow water near the mouths of creeks, over oyster beds, or along sandbars where shallows drop to deep water. Jigs imitating minnows also can be effective. The best times to catch these fish are during low tides—the last two hours of the outgoing tide and the first two hours of the incoming tide.

Older, larger drum can be taken when high tides flood the marshes, allowing the redfish access to the marsh grass, where they will forage on fiddler crabs. Look for tails topping the water, indicating that the fish are present and feeding, and then cast hooks baited with cut mullet or crabs to the marsh grasses. Artificial lures mimicking shrimp or crab can also be effective. Shallow draft vessels are needed to access the flooded marshes.

Finally, in the late summer and early fall, mature redfish move into the estuary to spawn. In the Altamaha estuary, look for the big bull reds in shallow water along shoals and sandbars. Fishing with live or cut bait or shrimp beneath a float is effective, as are jigs. Spawning redfish average 15 to 20 pounds, but the Georgia record, caught in 1986, is 46 pounds, 7 ounces.

To assure that mature, spawning red drum are not taken, state regulations limit each angler to a daily take of five redfish, each of which must measure between 14 and 23 inches.

## Tarpon

While red drum and seatrout are targeted for fun and food, bony—but big—tarpon are all about the fun, and the Altamaha River estuary is considered a world-class tarpon fishery by many.

Tarpon ascend Altamaha Sound periodically between July and September chasing menhaden and mullet. If those species are present in abundance, monster tarpon weighing from 40 to more than 200 pounds are not far behind. Thus whole, freshly netted menhaden or mullet make excellent bait, as does cut bait. Rig the bait so that you reach all parts of the water column, from near the surface to the depths. Large jigs and topwater lures can also be effective.

The state record was caught in Buttermilk Sound, the southern arm of the Altamaha River estuary, in 1995. It weighed in at 161 pounds and was more than 6 feet in length.

For additional and updated information about fishing trends on the Altamaha River, visit the Fishing Forecasts page of the Georgia Department of Natural Resources website: www.georgiawildlife.com/fishing-forecasts. Georgia River Fishing (www.bassblog.org/georgia-fishing) and Georgia Outdoor News (www.gon.com) are also useful resources for learning more about fishing on the Altamaha.

Remember: to fish in Georgia, all anglers must first obtain a state fishing license. Licenses can be purchased online at www.gooutdoorsgeorgia.com. The state is required to spend 100 percent of your license fee to support sport fish and wildlife management for the benefit of hunters and anglers. In doing so, the state receives a portion of federal taxes levied on guns, ammunition, fishing equipment, and motorboat fuel that annually amounts to about $20 million. Those funds are also invested in sport fish and wildlife management in Georgia. The amount of the annual federal appropriation is based in part on how many hunting and fishing licenses are sold in the state.

TAMA ISLAND, McINTOSH COUNTY

# ALTAMAHA

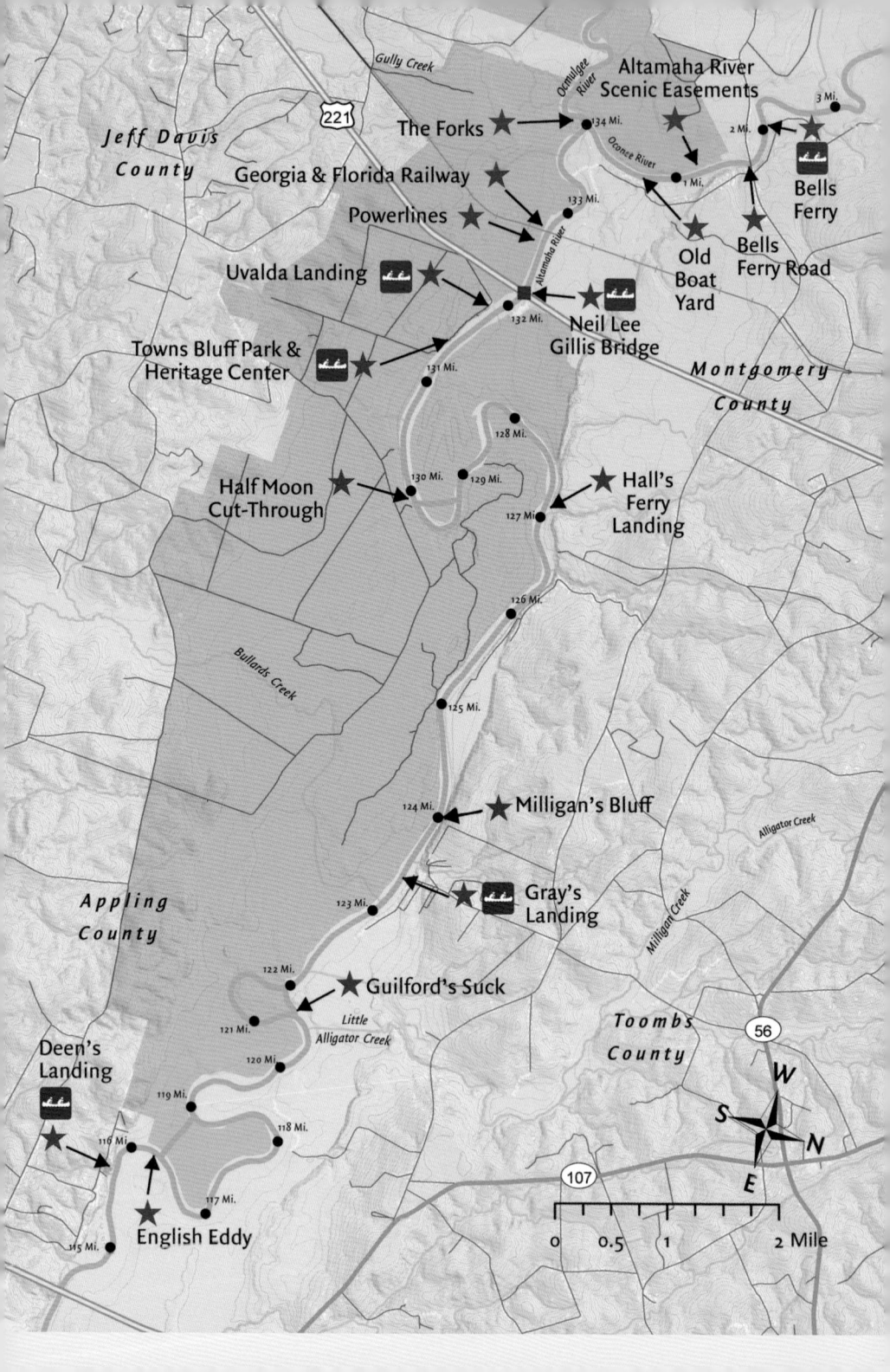

# The Forks

Length   17 miles (Bells Ferry on Oconee River to Deen's Landing)
Class   Flatwater/I
Time   6–9 hours
Minimum Level   Navigable year-round

River Gauge   The nearest river gauge is located at U.S. 221, 2 miles downstream from the confluence of the Oconee and Ocmulgee Rivers: https://waterdata.usgs .gov/ga/nwis/uv?site_no=02224940.

Launch Site   The launch site is located at Bells Ferry on the Oconee River, with a boat ramp and parking area off Dead River Road.

Directions   From the intersection of U.S. 221 and Ga. 56 in Uvalda, travel south on U.S. 221 3.4 miles. Turn right onto Old River Road and proceed 1.3 miles. At the fork, bear left onto Bells Ferry Road and proceed 0.9 mile. Turn right onto Dead River Road and proceed 0.4 mile. Turn left onto the road to the boat ramp.

Take Out Site   The take out site is on river right 1 mile upstream of the U.S. 1 bridge, with a boat ramp, parking area, and restrooms.

DIRECTIONS   From the Bells Ferry boat ramp, return to Dead River Road. Turn right and proceed 0.4 mile. Turn left onto Bells Ferry Road and proceed 0.9 mile, cross U.S. 221, and continue for another 9.5 miles. Turn right onto Cedar Crossing Road and proceed 1.5 miles. Turn right onto U.S. 1 and travel 2.8 miles. Turn right onto West River Road and proceed 0.9 mile. Turn right onto Deen's Landing Road and proceed 0.9 mile to the entrance to the boat ramp on the right.

Alternative Take Out Sites   Trips of 4, 5, or 13 miles can be created by taking out at the U.S. 221, Towns Bluff, or Gray's Landing boat ramps, respectively.

DIRECTIONS   The U.S. 221 and Towns Bluff take outs are easily reached by returning to U.S. 221 from Bells Ferry and turning right. The entrance to the U.S. 221 boat ramp is located 1.9 miles south on the left. To reach the Towns Bluff boat ramp, continue 0.8 mile further south and follow the signs to Towns Bluff Park and Heritage Center located off Uvalda Landing Road. To reach Gray's Landing, from Bells Ferry return to U.S. 221 via Old River Road. At U.S. 221, continue straight on Old River Road and proceed 5.1 miles. Turn right onto Gray's Landing Road and proceed 1.4 miles to the boat ramp.

Outfitters   Three Rivers Outdoors offers canoe and kayak rentals and shuttle service.

Three Rivers Outdoors, 612 McNatt Falls Rd., Uvalda, Ga. 30473, 912-594-8379, www.explorethreerivers.com

Description This section begins on the Oconee River 2 miles upstream from its collision with the Ocmulgee River at the Forks, where the Altamaha starts its fluid

ENTRANCE TO OXBOW LAKE AT GUILFORD SUCK, APPLING COUNTY

march to the sea, and that junction is undoubtedly the section's highlight. The 17-mile run also features numerous oxbow lakes, the former main channels of the river, which provide scenic off-the-main-channel exploration opportunities. Cut banks and sandbars are numerous. On the river's south bank, land is protected as the state-owned Bullard Creek Wildlife Management Area, which includes the Towns Bluff Park and Heritage Center, with multiple amenities for river travelers. The north bank is unique in that at Gray's Landing, river sojourners can stop for dinner at Benton Lee's Steakhouse, a fixture on the river for decades.

## Points of Interest

OCONEE MILE 2.1 (31.981561, -82.551419) Bells Ferry. The launch site for this section marks this historic river crossing. In the late 1700s and early 1800s, a ferry was established at this location, long used as a crossing by Native Americans. In January 1815, the site was used as a crossing by General David Blackshear and his 800 men as they raced to the Georgia coast to prevent invasion by British troops in the waning days of the War of 1812. The Oconee played an important role in supplying the American army. In a letter to Georgia governor Peter Early, Blackshear urged him to employ the river in delivering necessities to this location: "We have been much neglected by that department in small rations. Provisions and forage might be sent down the Oconee, and for which we shall suffer if we do not get a supply in a few days." Unbeknownst to Blackshear and Early, the Treaty of Ghent, which settled the war, had been signed more than a month earlier in Belgium. By the time Blackshear and his men reached the coast in February, word of peace had reached the soldiers in the field, and the British troops withdrew. Nevertheless, letters from Blackshear during his march paint a picture of the rough and rudimentary roads of the era: "I . . . am extremely sorry to have to state that from the great number of small streams bordered by extensive swamps rendered almost impassable by the multitude of wagons flying from the horrors of invasion and insurrection, my march to Barrington [Fort Barrington on the Altamaha River] is much retarded."

OCONEE MILE 1.7 (31.981033, -82.546269) Bells Ferry Road.

OCONEE MILE 1.4 (31.975900, -82.543716) Altamaha River Scenic Easements. On river right is the beginning of a 300-foot-wide conservation easement that preserves the river corridor for more than a mile to the Oconee's confluence with the Ocmulgee, where the rivers become the Altamaha. This is one of many parcels encompassing more than 165,000 acres of land that public and private efforts have placed under permanent protection along the Altamaha River since the 1970s. The goal is to protect the scenic view from the river itself and protect the more than 150 rare or endangered plant and animal species that are found in the Altamaha River basin. This parcel was acquired by the state in 1999 using Rivercare 2000 funds set aside during Governor Zell Miller's administration.

OCONEE MILE 0.7 (31.968546, -82.539253) Old Boat Yard. Where today fish camps, cabins, and homes line the land between Three Rivers Road and the river (on river left), in the 1800s a boatyard could be found here . . . and, on occasion, the U.S. Army Corps of Engineers (USACE) snag boats. Between 1890 and 1894, the USACE spent thousands of dollars here driving a line of more than 1,000 feet of wooden posts into the riverbed and filling the voids between the posts with brush and stone. The work was an attempt to constrict the river and increase the depth of the navigable channel at low water in front of the boatyard.

MILE 134.0 (31.959517, -82.543373) The Forks. At this spot, the Oconee collides headlong with the Ocmulgee, forming Georgia's largest river—the Altamaha. The Altamaha is the third-largest contributor of freshwater to the Atlantic Ocean on North America's eastern shore. It flows more than 130 miles from here to its mouth between Wolf Island and Little St. Simons Island. As the rivers gather at the Forks, so have people. Among the most famous to reside or do business near here is Mary Musgrove, often referred to as "the Pocahontas of Georgia." Around 1745, Musgrove and her third husband, the Reverend Thomas Bosomworth, established a trading post in this vicinity. By that time, Musgrove, the daughter of an English trader and a Creek Indian woman, had already made a name for herself serving as an intercessory and interpreter for General James Oglethorpe and the Creek Indians. As such, she played a pivotal role in the new colony, keeping the Creeks loyal to the English and limiting Spanish influence. In her later years, she became embroiled in a bitter legal battle with England over debts owed to her for serving as interpreter and over her claim of ownership of several barrier islands granted to her by a Creek leader. In the end, the colonial

THE FORKS, JEFF DAVIS COUNTY

government granted her some back payments and title to St. Catherine's Island, where she died in 1763.

The Ocmulgee, like its sister river the Oconee, has its origins in Georgia's Piedmont. The South River, which rises near downtown Atlanta, and the Alcovy and Yellow Rivers, which begin in Atlanta's northeast suburbs, join near Jackson to form the Ocmulgee, which flows 241 miles to the Forks. In the days when raft hands floated timber rafts from the upper reaches of the Ocmulgee and the Oconee, the Forks came to be known as "Sunday," for the wider, less treacherous Altamaha brought a measure of rest to the hands who had been navigating the twisting, narrow passages of the smaller rivers for several days. Janet Mauney, in a May 1940 issue of the *Atlanta Constitution*, documented the memories of old raft hands: "On approaching the 'forks' the colored raft hands always sang a song of their own composition entitled, 'I See Sunday.'"

MILE 132.8 (31.958661, -82.526829) Georgia & Florida Railway. This now-abandoned railroad bridge was built in 1909 at a cost of about $140,000 to carry freight and passengers on the Georgia & Florida Railway. On river right is visible the bascule drawbridge mechanism that allowed the passage of river steamers. This type of drawbridge was known as the Scherzer rolling lift bridge, a concept developed and patented by William Scherzer. When engaged, counterweights on the end of the bridge would lift the 102-foot-long rail span to a vertical position. Sadly, Scherzer died in 1893 at age 35 from complications of typhoid fever, but his brother continued Scherzer's work, building 175 rolling lift drawbridges, including this one, before 1916.

GEORGIA & FLORIDA RAILWAY, JEFF DAVIS COUNTY

MILE 132.7 (31.958379, -82.524790) Powerlines.

MILE 132.1 (31.957883, -82.517178) Neil Lee Gillis Bridge. In 2021, the latest version of this bridge was completed, and the original circa-1952 bridge was dismantled. The structure carrying U.S. 221 / Ga. 135 spans a half mile across the Altamaha and its expansive floodplain. On river left is the first public boat ramp on the Altamaha. The bridge is named for the patriarch of one of south Georgia's most influential political families. Neil Lee Gillis is known as the father of Treutlen County, as he campaigned tirelessly for its creation in 1917. Voters rewarded him for his efforts by electing him state senator, the first to represent the newly created county. Gillis's son, Jim L. Gillis Sr., served as chairman of the State Highway Board during the 1950s and 1960s; in turn, Jim Gillis's son Hugh Gillis served 56 years in the General Assembly. And in 2007, Governor Sonny Perdue appointed Hugh's son Donald W. Gillis a superior court judge in the state's Eighth District Court in Dublin. Prior to construction of the bridge, the Towns Bluff Ferry moved travelers across the river here. The ferry was described by Florence M. Pettee in a 1920 issue of *Motor Travel* magazine: "Long festoons of swaying Spanish moss hang from the arching trees, adding an exotic touch to the landscape. . . . The ferry resides on the south side and is summoned by making the woods resound by great ax blows against the inviting saw blade hanging from a sentinel tree. A wholly river-worthy raft towed by a gamey little motorboat holds its course across this ambitious river by the aid of a long steel cable."

MILE 131.8 (31.954427, -82.513519) Uvalda Landing. This landing, located on river right, borrows its name from the town of Uvalda, located 6 miles north of the river in Montgomery County. Incorporated in 1910, the town was laid out

29

in 1909 as a stop on the Georgia & Florida Railway. J. J. Moses, who originally owned the land on which the city was built, is said to be responsible for the unusual name, suggesting it after finding Uvalde, Texas, in a book. That city is named for a Spaniard who served as governor of portions of Spanish colonial territory, including Texas, in the late 1700s.

MILE 131.4 (31.951028, -82.507069) Towns Bluff Park & Heritage Center. On river right is a boat ramp providing access to the Jeff Davis County–maintained Towns Bluff Park and Heritage Center, which offers camping, RV sites, yurt and RV rentals, a bathhouse, walking trails, a playground, a museum, and a meeting space. The facility sits within the 14,000-acre Bullard Creek Wildlife Management Area, which stretches along the south bank of the Ocmulgee and Altamaha Rivers. From this boat ramp, the WMA borders the river for the next 12 miles. It was first protected in 1961. Beginning in 1881, a "shoal" at Towns Bluff was targeted for excavation by the U.S. Army Corps of Engineers (USACE) to improve steamboat navigation on the river. Described as a "ledge of rocks running nearly across the river," the obstacle was eliminated by 1883, with the USACE removing 319 cubic yards of material.

MILE 129.9 (31.953538, -82.482868) Half Moon Cut-Through. On river left is a cut-through that provides a shortcut, eliminating an oxbow to the east known as Half Moon Bluff. On January 9, 1866, near this site, the steamer *Asher Ayres*, loaded with more than 1,000 bales of cotton and some 60 passengers on its first journey downriver from Hawkinsville, caught fire and was destroyed. The *Savannah Republican* newspaper carried eyewitness accounts of the harrowing fire: "As soon as it was discovered there was no hope of saving the steamer, the passengers busied themselves by throwing overboard bales of cotton and jumping in the river after them. In this way many lives were saved. . . . Mothers frantic with

HALF MOON BLUFF, JEFF DAVIS COUNTY

despair sought some avenue of escape for terrified children. Devoted husbands, blanched with fear, struggled to protect their horror stricken wives." Seven people died in the disaster: "One negro woman, with her three children, two negro men and a Portuguese boy, named Johnny, deck hand, were lost," reported the *Daily Constitutionalist* in Augusta. Embedded in the riverbanks near here, and visible at low water, are the rusted remains of what appears to be part of a steam engine. Whether the engine belonged to the *Asher Ayres* is anyone's guess.

MILE 127.1 (31.970801, -82.481225) Hall's Ferry Landing. On river left is this historic landing that was originally the site of a ferry. In 1820, Lewis Hall Jr. secured from the Georgia General Assembly the right to establish a ferry near this location at what was then known as Berry-hill Bluff. Ferriage privileges were highly valuable in this era; though authorized by the state, ferry operators kept the tolls, which in 1820 were set at $1 for a wagon pulled by four horses—the equivalent of an $18 toll today. A Revolutionary War veteran who was held prisoner during the conflict, Hall, along with his family, had moved from North Carolina to Georgia in the late 1790s. According to a family history, Hall is notable for siring 18 children by two wives in his 68 years—the last one born just two years before his death in 1821. Hall was buried on the bluff here overlooking the river.

MILE 124.0 (31.967897, -82.438595) Milligan's Bluff. On river left is a high bluff that in the early 1840s was the site of a fantastical tale of treasure. The *Macon Messenger* reported on the incident, the veracity of which remains in question: "The circumstances are related that a man by the name of John Mazo discovered three dollars, which had become exposed by the blowing up of a tree. He commenced examining the earth below, and the coin continued to appear, un-

SUNSET, TOOMBS COUNTY

til he had exhumed the handsome amount of Forty-five Thousand Spanish Dollars . . . the latest date on the coin was over 160 years since. The place where they were found had the appearance of an ancient fortification, such as are common in many parts of Georgia . . . The money, we understand, was found on the land of Mrs. Gray, a widow, in needy circumstances, and a relative of the fortunate discoverer, who has shared it with her." Spanish missionaries were known to have traveled up the Altamaha from the coast in the late 1500s.

MILE 123.4 (31.966315, -82.428972) Gray's Landing. This landing on river left traces its name to Daniel Levi Gray, who was among the earliest settlers of what was then Tattnall County. According to 1820 census data, Gray and his wife, Rebecca, farmed land in this area with a large family. Gray and many of his descendants are buried in the Gray Partin Cemetery, located 1 mile north of this boat ramp. Though the Gray name has stuck to this landing, the Mann family also played a prominent role in the history of this locale. William Mann Sr. and his family came to the region in the first decade of the 1800s, establishing a ferry and later a sawmill. In 1890, the landing was home to "Henry Mann's Sawmill," as well as a gristmill and store.

Over the years the spot has been the scene of much tragedy and drama. In 1893, during the height of the river's log-rafting days, Charley Johnson, a fugitive, hitched a ride from here on a log raft after murdering a rival for a woman's affection. He rode the raft all the way to Darien but was ultimately captured, tried, and sentenced to death, a verdict that, according to newspaper accounts of the day, was carried out in front of 6,000 people in Midville. The execution attracted a crowd in part because the doomed man was an itinerant preacher who was per-

ENTRANCE TO OXBOW LAKE AT GUILFORD SUCK, APPLING COUNTY

mitted to preach his own funeral sermon and lead the crowd in singing "Canaan's Happy Shore" in the moments before he was hanged. In 1930, 70-year-old S. S. Mincey, a Black leader of the Republican Party in nearby Mt. Vernon, was dragged from his home by "a band of masked and robed men" and carried near Gray's Landing, where he was beaten, whipped, and left to die. Newspaper accounts reported that "most of the skin was lashed off the negro's back." Mincey died the next day. Though there was public outcry, no one was ever prosecuted for the lynching. Finally, in 1956, five people on a picnicking excursion drowned here when their boat capsized. Among the victims were three children. A monument overlooking the river at the landing memorializes the dead from this tragedy.

Today, the landing is perhaps best known as the home of Benton Lee's Steakhouse, a fixture on this part of the river for decades and the only restaurant located on the river upstream of Darien. Benton Lee's is famous for its mammoth steaks, but local fare like gator tail, quail, and frog legs is also on the menu. On the south side of the river, opposite the landing, is the Jeff Davis–Appling County line. The river forms the northern border of Appling County for the next 34 miles.

MILE 120.6 (31.955860, -82.405467) Guilford's Suck. On river right is a short slough that marks the spot of a former mile-long oxbow to the south. A narrow oxbow lake hidden beyond the riverbank is all that remains of the river's former main channel, where the 19th-century boat landing called Barcklay's was located. In 1890, U.S. Army Corps of Engineers surveyors noted a cut-through forming here and beginning to cut off the oxbow, and they dubbed it Guilford's Suck. (Locations where the river's main flow was being "sucked" into a new channel were commonly referred to as "sucks" by boaters of that era.)

MILE 116.2 (31.947034, -82.378534) English Eddy. On river left is an off-river slough that is a testament to the changing nature of the Altamaha and the communities that have relied on it. This is the tail end of a former oxbow known as English Eddy—the upstream mouth having long since been cut off by the new channel—that wound north for nearly 3 miles. During the latter half of the 20th century, the river determined to cut a straighter path to the sea and cut off the oxbow. Before being abandoned first by changing modes of transportation and then by the river itself, the riverside community of English Eddy was small but thriving.

NEAR ENGLISH EDDY, TOOMBS COUNTY

WILLOW SEEDS ON OXBOW LAKE, APPLING COUNTY

In the late 1800s and early 1900s, the J. K. Clark Lumber Company operated a lumberyard here. In 1900 the community included a post office and school and had a population of 41, and it was still connected to the larger world via a steamboat landing known in the late 1800s as Henry Mann's Landing. In the late 1870s, the *Darien Timber Gazette* reported on England-bound ships loaded with thousands of feet of Clark Company lumber. As railroads gained favor over river steamers and the stands of pine petered out, the English Eddy community faded into history. The oxbow, owing to the shifting ways of the Altamaha, followed its path.

MILE 115.8 (31.941488, -82.374188) Deen's Landing. On river right is this boat ramp and parking area with restroom facilities and a private campground with tent and RV sites located 0.1 mile from the boat ramp. The many generations of the Deen family (there are three family cemeteries in Appling County, including one on Deen's Landing Rd.) have played prominent roles in the region's history. Most notably, Columbus William Deen was a naval stores baron in the late 1800s and early 1900s, when the county earned the reputation as the "Turpentine Capital of the World." Orphaned when he was just two years old in a family of eight children, Deen grew into what regional history books call a "self-made" man. He rose from farmer to merchant to owner of an expansive lumber and naval stores empire before moving to Lakeland, Florida, where he invested in land and banks. The success of his naval stores business depended on the Altamaha River—for transport of rosin and turpentine to the coast—and on Georgia's convict lease system—for cheap labor. The practice of convict leasing was highly controversial, though also highly profitable for both the state and the businesses that leased the convicts. In the system, businesses paid the state for use of the prisoners and were required to provide the workers with proper food, housing, and care. In practice, many businesses kept their workers in deplorable conditions. Whippings and deaths were common, and in 1898, C. W. Deen & Company and its "whipping master" were accused of killing an inmate. Though charges were never brought, stories of this nature ultimately led to the state ending the prison lease system in 1908.

C. W. Deen's Queen Anne–style home, completed in 1897, still stands along North Main Street in Baxley and is on the National Register of Historic Places. Other notable Appling County Deens include Braswell Deen, a congressman from the region during the 1930s, and Bill and Green Deen, twins born in 1891 who worked on timber rafts and steamboats on the river. In fact, at age 90, Bill Deen became known as the "last timber raft pilot" when in 1982 he participated in Project RAFT (Restoring Altamaha Folklife Traditions), in which organizers constructed a replica timber raft and floated it from Lumber City to Darien in celebration of the region's cultural ties to the river. Deen, having piloted his first raft at age 17, served as advisor and pilot on the commemorative journey, telling the *Athens Observer* newspaper, "I've known the river from birth. From right up since I was ten years old, I've known every durn scratch in here." Deen died in 1988 at age 97.

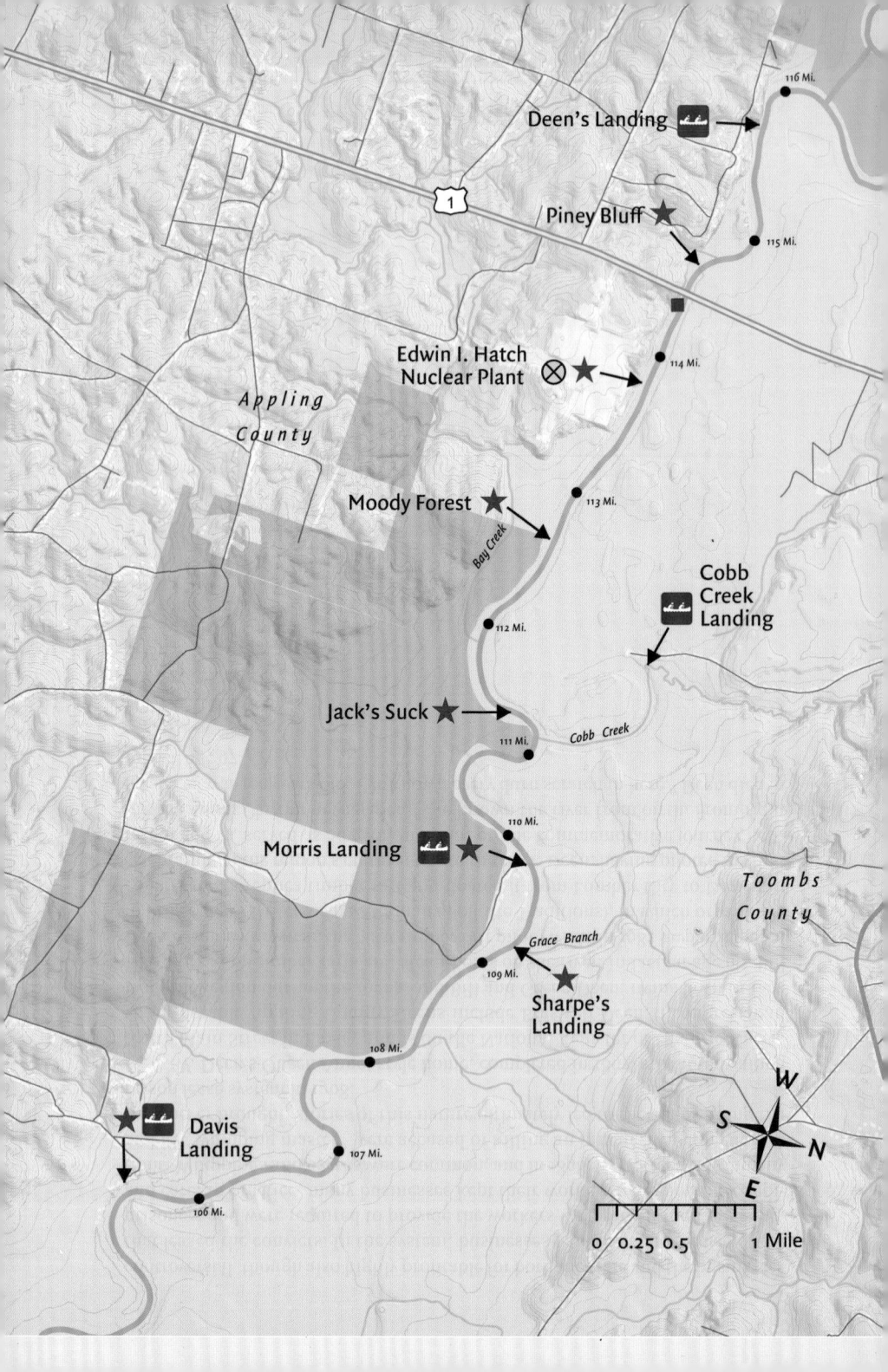

Deen's Landing

116 Mi.

1

Piney Bluff

115 Mi.

Edwin I. Hatch
Nuclear Plant

114 Mi.

*Appling
County*

Moody Forest

113 Mi.

*Bay Creek*

Cobb
Creek
Landing

112 Mi.

Jack's Suck

111 Mi.

*Cobb Creek*

110 Mi.

Morris Landing

*Toombs
County*

*Grace Branch*

109 Mi.

Sharpe's
Landing

108 Mi.

Davis
Landing

107 Mi.

106 Mi.

W

S

N

E

0   0.25  0.5        1 Mile

# Piney Bluff

**Length**  10 miles (Deen's Landing to Davis Landing)

**Class**  Flatwater/I

**Time**  4–7 hours

**Minimum Level**  Navigable year-round

---

**River Gauge**  The nearest river gauge is located at U.S. 1, 1.2 miles downstream from the launch site: https://waterdata.usgs.gov/ga/nwis/uv?site_no=02225000.

**Launch Site**  Deen's Landing is located on the south side of the river off Deen's Landing Road, with a boat ramp, parking area, restroom, picnic area, and nearby campground.

DIRECTIONS   From the intersection of U.S. 341 and U.S. 1 in Baxley, proceed north on U.S. 1 10.7 miles. Turn left onto West River Road and proceed 0.8 mile. Turn right onto Deen's Landing Road and travel 0.9 mile to the entrance to the landing on the right.

**Take Out Site**  The take out site is on river right, with a boat ramp and parking area.

DIRECTIONS   From Deen's Landing, turn left onto Deen's Landing Road and proceed 0.9 mile. Turn left onto West River Road and proceed 0.8 mile. Turn right onto U.S. 1 and proceed 2 miles. Turn left onto East River Road and proceed 2.8 miles.

DEEN'S LANDING, APPLING COUNTY

At the fork, bear left, continuing on East River Road 1 mile to another fork. At that fork, bear left, continuing on East River Road another mile to the next fork. Bear right, continuing on East River Road 1.7 miles. Turn left onto Davis Landing Road and travel 1.4 miles to the parking area and boat ramp.

Alternative Take Out Sites   Trips of 5.5 or 6 miles can be created by taking out at Cobb Creek Landing or Morris Landing, respectively.

DIRECTIONS   Located on an oxbow lake on the north side of the main channel of the river, Cobb Creek Landing is reached by turning left onto U.S. 1 from West River Road and traveling 2.8 miles north across the river to Ga. 147 (Cedar Crossing Road). Turn right and proceed 1.8 miles. Turn right onto Old Dead River Road and proceed 2 miles to the boat landing. Morris Landing is reached by turning right onto U.S. 1 from West River Road and traveling 2 miles south. Turn left onto East River Road and proceed 2.8 miles. At the fork, bear left, continuing on East River Road 1 mile to another fork. At that fork, bear left, continuing on East River Road another mile to the next fork. Here, bear left onto Morris Landing Road and proceed 3.2 miles to the parking area and landing.

Outfitters   Three Rivers Outdoors offers canoe and kayak rentals and shuttle service.

Three Rivers Outdoors, 612 McNatt Falls Rd., Uvalda, Ga. 30473, 912-594-8379, www.explorethreerivers.com

Description   While short in distance, this 10-mile run of river dishes out diverse scenery. After flowing beneath the U.S. 1 bridge, the river passes by the hulking Edwin I. Hatch Nuclear Plant, only to descend immediately into the wildness of the Moody Forest Wildlife Management Area, home to stands of old-growth longleaf pine. Cut banks and expansive sandbars are numerous, while Cobb Creek, a blackwater tributary flowing through Toombs County, offers scenic off-the-main-channel exploration.

## Points of Interest

MILE 114.6 (31.939589, -82.358203) Piney Bluff. On river right here, where powerlines span the river, begins this bluff, which has played an important role in the region's cultural history. The bluff extends downriver to the Plant Hatch water intake. In the 1800s, it was home to Melton's sawmill and Piney Bluff Ferry. In the 1920s it became the site of an important highway bridge, and then in the 1970s the bluff became home to Georgia's first nuclear power plant. The scene here might look very different had the peculiar vision of a Baxley capitalist come to fruition in the early 1900s. Alexander Legler, a Russian immigrant who made a name for himself establishing "colonies" for European immigrants in the American West and Mexico, announced in 1903 his plans for an Altamaha colony. The project hinged on the construction of a railroad running from Reidsville through Baxley and on south toward the Satilla River and included a plan to create a city called Port Alexander by developing "63,000 acres of hardwood and agricultural land" along the river. Legler's plan, however, never gained legs.

Nevertheless, momentum to build a bridge here grew in the first two decades of the 1900s, culminating in 1927 with the completion of the Altamaha's third highway bridge—the Piney Bluff Bridge, a $275,000 steel truss structure that was a novelty in these parts. Newspapers reported that 20,000 people witnessed its dedication, feasting on "immense kettles of Brunswick stew" and some "16,000 pounds of barbecue." The crossing, as it had been during the days of the ferry, was something of a destination for both locals and tourists. Belltona Park, operated by the Bell family, offered a dozen cottages and a campground for overnight guests, as well as a gas pump and a restaurant specializing in (of course) fried catfish. Among the other amenities were slot machines—very popular during the 1920s—a dance floor with a jukebox, and even an ice-making machine. Of course, the bridge brought an end to the old Piney Bluff Ferry, which, even as late as 1925, ran full-page ads in the *Baxley News-Banner* extolling the virtues of ferry travel: "From the time a car rolls on the ferry until you reach the other side of the river it requires only three minutes." Roan Hutcheson was the ferryman during this time, and when the Piney Bluff Bridge was completed, he was appointed "bridgekeeper," responsible for turning the hand crank that pivoted the bridge, allowing steamboats to pass. The original Piney Bluff Bridge was replaced in 1948 and then rebuilt again in 1969. In 2018, the current bridge was completed at a cost of $25.9 million. In 1973, the Georgia General Assembly renamed the Piney Bluff Bridge the "Joseph Simmons Alexander Sr. Memorial Bridge" to honor the Toombs County commissioner who donated land for the bridge and, as a timberman, provided lumber used in the construction of the original Piney Bluff Bridge. Among steamboat pilots, Piney Bluff was notable for its hazardous rock ledges. In the early 1880s, the U.S. Army Corps of Engineers blasted a 100-foot-wide and 4-foot-deep channel through ledges below the bluff, removing 1,480 cubic yards of rock—an amount that would fill four rows of 18-foot roll-off dumpsters stretched end-to-end across the river.

MILE 113.8 (31.938325, -82.344331) Edwin I. Hatch Nuclear Plant. On river right here is the water intake for this Georgia Power Company electric generating facility, which supplies more than 8 percent of Georgia's electricity needs. The massive power plant—like so many advancements in this part of the state—owes its existence to the river. Like the first locomotive in Macon (which was shipped upriver from the coast via steamboat) and one of the river's first bridges, between Baxley and Glennville (parts of which were shipped via steamboat), Georgia's first nuclear reactor, a 700-ton behemoth, arrived at this site via river barge—a task that required dredging and snagging the river to remove any navigational hazards. Construction on Plant Hatch commenced in the 1960s and culminated with the completion of the facility's second unit in 1979. Surrounding communities embraced the new industry. Baxley proudly billed itself as "Georgia's Nuclear City," and one shopping center was renamed "Nuclear City Plaza." It didn't hurt that Georgia Power officials escorted local civic leaders to New York to show them how a nuclear facility had transformed a community along the Hudson River. Of course, the infusion of tax revenue also sold locals

EDWIN I. HATCH NUCLEAR POWER PLANT DISCHARGE, APPLING COUNTY

on the massive project, as did the many jobs created during the plant's construction. Even today, the plant is the largest employer in Appling County (850 jobs) and generates upwards of half the county's tax base.

The river sustains nuclear power generation by providing 64 million gallons of water a day for plant operation. Heat generated from the nuclear fission process converts water to steam, which powers the electrical turbines. River water is used to condense the steam back to liquid, for use again in the process, and it also is employed to safely cool and store radioactive used fuel rods. The used fuel rods are first cooled in pools of water and then transferred to large casks that are made of steel, steel-reinforced concrete, and lead and are designed to withstand natural disasters. Stored aboveground, the spent fuel has a radioactive life that extends from 1,000 to 10,000 years. A permanent repository for the nation's nuclear waste has been planned—the Yucca Mountain site in Nevada—but has yet to be utilized. Thus, each of the nation's nuclear power plants stores its waste onsite. And while the federal government sees this storage as temporary, the federal Nuclear Regulatory Commission, which reviews and inspects storage facilities, also considers it safe. Plant Hatch sits on about 2,000 acres, some of which is managed to provide habitat for the federally endangered red-cockaded woodpecker and to aid in the restoration of the longleaf pine ecosystem. Gopher tortoises and eastern indigo snakes also benefit from these efforts. Georgia Power is a longtime partner in the conservation of the robust redhorse, freshwater mussels, and other aquatic species native to the Altamaha River basin.

MILE 112.7 (31.933745, -82.325955) Moody Forest. On river right here is this state wildlife management area jointly managed by the Nature Conservancy. The 4,432-acre tract stretches along the south bank of the river for more than 4 miles. Protected since 2001, the property is home to 300 acres of old-growth longleaf pine, which provides habitat for federally listed species such as red-cockaded woodpeckers and indigo snakes. The tract also preserves this region's history as the "turpentine capital of the world," with several old trees still showing "catfaces," the V-shaped scars indicating where pine sap was bled from the trees so it could be processed into turpentine and rosin.

MILE 111.4 (31.935573, -82.306942) Jack's Suck. A "suck" is a location at which a river "sucks," or robs flow from the old channel, and begins cutting a new shorter course. This is especially common where rivers cut off looping oxbows. In the early 1900s, Jack's Suck began cutting off a two-mile oxbow to the north where Cobb Creek meets the Altamaha. For 14 months in 1915 and 1916, the U.S. Army Corps of Engineers (USACE) waged an ultimately futile battle to stem this suck. During the effort, workers on the USACE's steamers *Sapelo* and *Oconee* quarried more than 6,000 cubic feet of stone from Fall-in-Rock Bluff (just above Deen's Landing) and another 2,500 cubic feet from upstream on the Oconee. Load by load, they hauled the stone to the mouth of Jack's Suck and built a 400-foot-long dam that rose more than 10 feet from the riverbed. But by the 1930s, the river had shrugged off the dam and made the cut, and Jack's Suck became the main channel, leaving the oxbow leading to Cobb Creek isolated. Today, the oxbow lake and the blackwater Cobb Creek are still accessible from the tail end of the former oxbow. Cobb Creek Landing is 1 mile up this slough.

NEAR JACK'S SUCK, TOOMBS COUNTY

41

In the late 1800s and early 1900s, this oxbow was not insignificant, for near the junction of the river and Cobb Creek was the community of Perry's Mill. A stop on the Darien-to-Macon stagecoach in the 1830s, Perry's Mill bore the name of Dr. James Perry, a physician who established a sawmill and hospital here around 1810. Perry's Mill also became well known for its school, Erasmus Hall, which attracted pupils from far and wide. In 1870, much of the land around Perry's Mill was sold to Charles Brink, a German businessman, who then recruited fellow Germans to immigrate to Georgia and operate an extensive lumber operation. During the late 1800s, more than 100 workers labored in what became known as German Mill, and a shortline railroad carried the lumber to a landing on the Altamaha for shipment to Darien. One of the mill's employees, Louis Tiegten, was responsible for delivering pay from a bank in Baxley to the other workers, a job that required Tiegten and his horse to swim the river once a month.

MILE 109.8 (31.942654, -82.290546) Morris Landing. On river right is this concrete boat ramp and parking area sandwiched between a large sandbar and a small riverside neighborhood. The landing and neighborhood are surrounded by the Moody Forest Wildlife Management Area.

MILE 109.3 (31.942980, -82.283941) Sharpe's Landing. Though no landing exists here today, from the early 1800s until well after the turn of the 20th century, this spot on river left was a steamboat landing associated with John Sharpe, a Revolutionary War veteran who moved his family to this area in the 1790s. Sharpe served as sheriff and justice of the peace in the recently formed Tattnall County and was believed to have run a tavern, likely servicing travelers both on the river and on the stagecoach road that ran close by. His descendants continued to be bound to the Altamaha. His son, John Thomas Sharpe, captained a steamboat, and others carried on commerce here. Maps from the late 1800s show Sharpe's Warehouse located here, as well as a "tramway" or small railroad. Thomas Ross Sharpe, an attorney and the great-great-grandson of the Revolutionary War veteran, played an important role in a tragedy that speaks to the insular nature of the rural Jim Crow South in the mid-20th century. The story un-

MORRIS LANDING, APPLING COUNTY

folded in front of Providence Baptist Church about 1 mile north of this landing. On the evening of November 20, 1948, Robert "Duck" Mallard, an African American, and his wife and family were driving back to their riverside home when a group of hooded men confronted them. The men opened fire on the vehicle, killing Robert. The investigation that followed can only be described as a sham. In fact, the local sheriff arrested Robert's wife, Amy, in the killing.

Joseph Goldwasser, a Jewish NAACP member from Cleveland, Ohio, stepped into the fray, traveling to Georgia and conducting his own undercover investigation that identified two of the men who were among the mob that killed Mallard. Goldwasser's investigation led to intense federal and state pressure that ultimately forced the local sheriff to arrest five white men. Thomas Ross Sharpe represented one of the accused in a crowded Toombs County courthouse less than two months after the killing. Despite Amy Mallard's grief-stricken testimony describing "about twenty men, wearing white stuff and all carrying pistols," Sharpe easily won an acquittal for his client, convincing jurors that his client was not at the scene, that Amy Mallard had a "bad reputation," and that the dead man was a "bad Negro." He even summoned two jurors to the witness stand to serve as character witnesses for the accused. After the trial he derided Goldwasser and his investigation: "That roaring lion of Judea is a disgrace to the Jewish race. He wouldn't even make catfish bait in the Altamaha River." Amy Mallard and her family fled Toombs County, relocating to Buffalo, New York, and the Ku Klux Klan allegedly set their former home ablaze. Motives for the killing—and the true killer—remain unknown, but speculation was that the locals resented the relative wealth of Mallard and his wife. He was a successful traveling salesman who drove a fine new car, and Amy was a college-educated teacher. The couple also had dared to vote in the election earlier in the month, and their descendants say that poll workers warned the Mallards of the "consequences" of exercising their constitutional right. Thomas Ross Sharpe later became well known for his history column that appeared regularly in the *Lyons Progress* newspaper during the 1950s and 1960s. His "Tales of the Altamaha" became the inspiration for a folk-life play performed annually in nearby Lyons.

MILE 105.5 (31.915135, -82.247381) Davis Landing. On river right here, hidden by the island sandbar, is this landing and riverside community along Buckhorn Bluff. Though open to the public, the landing is privately maintained, and launch fees are collected.

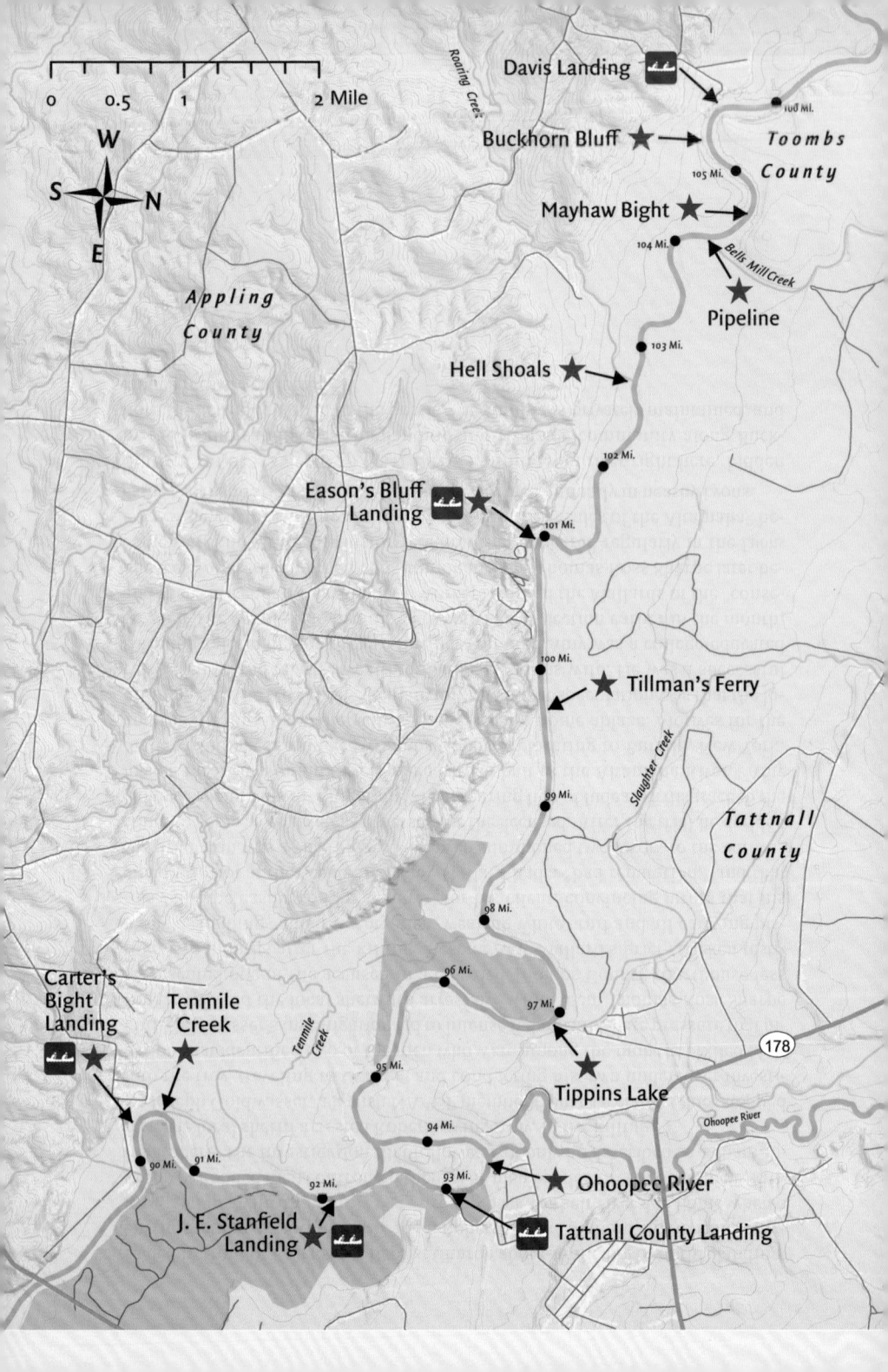

# Ohoopee

**Length**   14 miles (Davis Landing to Carter's Bight Landing)
**Class**   Flatwater/I
**Time**   5–7 hours
**Minimum Level**   Navigable year-round

**River Gauge**   The nearest river gauge is located at U.S. 1, 8 miles upstream from the launch site: https://waterdata.usgs.gov/ga/nwis/uv?site_no=02225000.

**Launch Site**   Davis Landing is located on the south side of the river off Davis Landing Road, with a boat ramp and parking area. This is a privately maintained boat launch open to the public. User fees apply.

DIRECTIONS   From the intersection of U.S. 341 (Golden Isles Pkwy.) and U.S. 1 (Main St.) in Baxley, travel north on North Main Street 0.2 mile and then bear right, continuing on North Main Street for 1 mile. Turn left onto 10 Mile Road and proceed 5.6 miles. Turn left onto Lennox Road and proceed 0.3 mile. Turn right onto Davis Landing Road and proceed 2.5 miles. At the junction with East River Road, turn right onto dirt Davis Landing Road and proceed 1.4 miles to the boat landing on the left.

**Take Out Site**   The take out site is on river right, with a boat ramp, parking area, picnic area, shelter, and restrooms.

NEAR DAVIS LANDING, APPLING COUNTY

DIRECTIONS   From Davis Landing, return 1.4 miles to East River Road. Turn left and proceed 2.9 miles. Turn left onto 10 Mile Road and proceed 6.3 miles. Turn left onto Hershel Tillman Road and travel 0.8 mile to a crossroads. Continue straight on Carter Bight Landing Road and proceed 1.5 miles to the parking area and boat ramp.

Alternative Take Out Sites   Trips of 4 or 12 miles can be created by taking out at Eason's Bluff Landing or at Tattnall County Landing on the Ohoopee or J. E. Stanfield Landing on the mainstem of the Altamaha, respectively.

DIRECTIONS   To reach Eason's Bluff Landing from Davis Landing, return 1.4 miles to East River Road. Turn left and proceed 2.9 miles. Turn left onto 10 Mile Road and proceed 2.5 miles. Turn left onto Eason's Bluff Road and proceed 1.1 miles. Turn left onto Eason Bluff Extension and proceed 0.6 mile. Turn right onto Landing Road and proceed 0.2 mile to the landing. To reach J. E. Stanfield Landing from Davis Landing, return 1.4 miles to East River Road. Turn left and proceed 2.9 miles. Turn left onto 10 Mile Road and travel 7.2 miles. Turn left onto Ga. 144 and travel 2.8 miles. Turn left onto Ga. 169 and proceed 1.7 miles, crossing the Altamaha in the process. Turn right onto Big Hammock WMA Road. Travel a short distance and then turn right onto a dirt road leading back toward the highway. Proceed along this road 2.5 miles to the landing. To reach Tattnall County Landing, continue north on Ga. 169 for 3.9 miles beyond Big Hammock WMA Road and then turn left onto Ga. 178. Travel west on Ga. 178 for 1.6 miles. Turn left onto Oak Grove Road and proceed 2.1 miles. Turn left onto County Road 296 and travel 0.4 mile. Turn left onto Tattnall County Landing Road and proceed 1 mile to the landing.

Outfitters   Three Rivers Outdoors offers canoe and kayak rentals and shuttle service.

   Three Rivers Outdoors, 612 McNatt Falls Rd., Uvalda, Ga. 30473, 912-594-8379, www.explorethreerivers.com

Description   Typical of the Altamaha's other reaches, this 14-mile run is characterized by cut banks, high bluffs, and expansive sandbars, but off-the-main-channel exploration is at its best where the Ohoopee River meets the Altamaha. At high water, the labyrinth-like mouth of the Ohoopee provides nearly endless opportunities to explore the enchanting, flooded bottomland swamp forest surrounding both the Ohoopee and the Altamaha. Likewise, Tippins Lake and Tenmile Creek provide similar options for venturing from the river's wide-open vistas to the more intimate floodplain forests.

## Points of Interest

MILE 105.4 (31.914032, -82.243715) Buckhorn Bluff. Along this bluff on river right is a series of riverfront homes, but in the spring of 1898, Buckhorn Bluff was a stop in the travels of the eccentric self-made archaeologist Clarence Bloomfield Moore. Moore chugged up the Altamaha in his appropriately named steamboat *Gopher*, and with his assistants, he dug in prehistoric mounds from Darien to the Forks. The scion of a Philadelphia paper baron, he eschewed life in the family business and instead invested his inherited fortunes in a life of travel and adventure, exploring on the *Gopher* nearly every navigable river in the Southeast in search of antiquities. In doing so, he became one of the most important archaeologists of his era—though because of his crude techniques, with which he destroyed numerous archaeological sites, some considered him nothing more than a "pot hunter." On the Altamaha, he dug thirty-nine mounds in close proximity to the river, including one located "about 500 yards west of the landing" at Buckhorn Bluff. The mound was nearly four feet high, with a base measuring 38 feet in diameter. Within it, he found multiple skeletons and artifacts, recording his discoveries in his 1898 book *Certain Aboriginal Mounds of the Coast of South Carolina*: "Three feet from the center, on the base, was a flexed skeleton badly decayed. Near the cranium lay a well-made hatchet of polished rock about 8 inches long." Between this site and Carter's Bight Landing, Moore excavated portions of six other mounds. He spent some 30 years digging in the dirt of the Southeast; many of the pieces he unearthed now dwell at the National Museum of the American Indian. He died at age 84 in 1936.

MILE 104.6 (31.920693, -82.234268) Mayhaw Bight. A bight is simply a curve in a river. This bight, noted in an 1890 U.S. Army Corps of Engineers survey map, bears the name of the highly sought-after fruit produced by a native hawthorn tree (*Crataegus opaca*) that thrives in wetlands and river bottoms. In February and March, the tree puts out showy pink-to-white flowers, and the fruit, a yellow-to-red berry born on the limbs of the 20-to-30-foot-tall trees, comes ripe in April and May. Traditionally, the fruits were harvested from boats, using nets to scoop up the floating fruit. In recent years, the mayhaw has become a commercial crop in South Georgia, with the trees being planted in orchards. The fruits are tart, but when boiled and the juice harvested, they make a delectable jelly. The Southwest Georgia city of Colquitt celebrates the native fruit each April with its National Mayhaw Festival.

MILE 104.3 (31.915750, -82.230940) Pipeline.

MILE 102.7 (31.908934, -82.211999) Hell Shoals. Though today you aren't apt to see any shoals here except in extreme low water, an 1881 U.S. Army Corps of Engineers (USACE) survey identified this location as wrought with "dangerous sandstone reefs . . . and isolated rocks so situated as to render it almost impossible to avoid them." Assistant Engineer W. G. Williamson concluded, "Some of these should be blown out." And thus for the next three decades, the USACE's engineers tried to tame these shoals that bedeviled riverboat pilots and raftsmen. In 1910 alone, the Corps removed 728 cubic yards of rock from this shoal. Writing in the *Baxley News-Banner* in 1952 (as documented in Carlton Morrison's *Running the River*), R. S. Wolfe gave a firsthand account of the USACE's work: "Twice I have been witness to blasting the rocks of the channel near Hell Shoals and it seemed to me the whole river had risen in the air." Hell Shoals is not the only devilish name given to the river's most dangerous features. Further downstream, there's Little Hell, Devil's Whirl, and Old Hell Bight. Historian John Goff

BOAT AT EASON'S BLUFF LANDING, APPLING COUNTY

explained in 1955 that the tradition of attaching "hellish" descriptors to "some peculiar, dangerous, or awesome natural formation or site" is borrowed from the English.

MILE 100.9 (31.899884, -82.191957) Eason's Bluff Landing. On river right is this boat ramp and parking area with picnic pavilion. Built in 2007, this site owes its existence to the Federal Aid in Sport Fish Restoration Fund—a fund that has its origins in a federal excise tax first adopted in 1937. That year Congress passed the Pittman-Robertson Act, which placed an excise tax on hunting equipment that was then used to restore game species like deer and wild turkey. This measure was so successful that legislators introduced a bill creating a similar tax on fishing gear that would support sport fish restoration. Unfortunately (for sport fish), the bill hit Congress just as World War II broke out. The excise tax was adopted, but instead of being funneled to the nation's fisheries, the funds it generated went directly to the war effort. Finally, in 1950, Congress adopted the Dingell-Johnson Act, setting aside a 10 percent excise tax, collected from manufacturers, to fund sport fish restoration and water recreation projects. The list of taxable items has since been expanded to include motorboat fuel and certain boat motors and fish finders. States receive a share of these federal collections based on the number of hunting and fishing licenses they sell. For Georgia, that means about $20 million annually. Eason's Bluff was known in the late 1800s as Old Timber Landing; Tillman's Ferry was located about 1.5 miles downstream from this landing.

MILE 99.7 (31.903734, -82.169052) Tillman's Ferry. Though no evidence of it exists today, throughout the 1800s this location was an important river crossing between Tattnall and Appling Counties.

MILE 96.9 (31.908177, -82.132395) Tippins Lake. On river left here is an inlet to this oxbow lake, which lies beyond Ohoopee White Bluff, the sandy bluff on river left, and is surrounded by a small riverfront neighborhood. In the early 1940s, the lake became a flash point over who "owns" water and the critters swimming within that water—the state on behalf of the general public, or individual landowners? Members of the Tippins family had constructed a fish trap between two parts of the oxbow lake, which state game and fish officers deemed illegal. The Tippinses countered that the state prohibition of using fish traps on public streams did not apply here because the family owned the property surrounding the lake and because no stream regularly flowed through the property, it being instead a backwater oxbow filled by the nearby river. The Georgia Supreme Court ultimately ruled in favor of the Tippinses. They kept their fish trap, and what was then known as Trout and Round Lakes is now commonly referred to as Tippins Lake. To the victor go the spoils. Today, however, the oxbow lake is not private, and boaters may explore it. During the river's steamboat and log rafting heyday, Ohoopee White Bluff was a busy landing with an adjacent warehouse. As river commerce slowed, steamboat operators looked to other means of paying the bills, including hosting social outings. In 1916, hundreds of residents of Tattnall and Toombs Counties gathered at the bluff for a round-trip ride on the steamer *Altamaha* to Gray's Landing. The *Tattnall Journal* reported: "Refreshments of various kinds were served aboard the steamer and barbecue of the

RIVERFRONT DEVELOPMENT, APPLING COUNTY

most palatable kind was to be had in abundance. Dancing, too, was one of the features of the occasion."

MILE 93.5 (31.889710, -82.113771) Ohoopee River. On river left, blackwater from this major tributary provides a stark contrast to the sediment-filled Altamaha, which carries dirt from as far away as the Eastern Continental Divide in Northeast Georgia. The Ohoopee, on the other hand, is a true backwater river that has its origins in Georgia's Coastal Plain. Flowing through wetlands, lowland forests, and swamps, it picks up tannins from decaying vegetation that lend the river a transparent burgundy-to-black color.

The junction of the Ohoopee and Altamaha Rivers has long played into schemes to engineer and replumb Georgia's rivers to the benefit of man. Until the mid-1980s there existed a plan to transform the Altamaha into a highway for barge traffic and create inland ports along the Ocmulgee and Oconee Rivers through a series of dams, locks, and canals. As log raft and steamboat traffic all but disappeared from the river by the 1940s, communities along the Altamaha began lobbying congressional leaders to revive this historic and culturally important part of the region's economy. Since the late 1800s, federal "river improvement" funds had been dependable pork with which Georgia leaders could endear themselves to voters, and they were eager to keep the bacon flowing—regardless of the feasibility. Rivers elsewhere had been transformed; the shallow, shoaly Altamaha could surely be next. In 1947, a private engineering firm commissioned by locals to study the feasibility of developing the Altamaha concluded that the economic benefits to navigation, hydropower, agriculture, wildlife, recreation, and flood control would justify a federal expenditure of $500,000,000. In 2020 dollars, that's $6.3 billion. In 1959, the powerful Georgia senator Richard B. Russell predicted a "golden future of progress and prosperity" for Georgia in which cities of Middle and North Georgia—including Macon and Atlanta—would soon become inland ports. Russell secured funding for the U.S. Army Corps of Engineers to study the river; consequently, plans for the river's full development persisted into the 1970s, outlining multiple dams, including one at the mouth of the Ohoopee. But by the mid-1970s, the unintended consequences of dammed rivers became more fully understood, and budget hawks began questioning the multimillion-dollar pork project. In 1987, Representative Lindsay Thomas from Georgia's 1st District finally put the 40-year-old plans to bed, publicly opposing river development while commenting that the Altamaha "is one of the most beautiful freshwater rivers in our nation, not to mention a rare haven for hunters and fishermen. We ought to be promoting it for boating, hiking, hunting, and fishing, not contemplating a plan that would sterilize it."

The 20th-century proposal to replumb the Altamaha was not the first of its kind. In 1824, Georgia's General Assembly incorporated a company whose purpose was to dig a canal connecting the Savannah River to the Altamaha. That canal reached only to the Ogeechee, and even that portion ceased operation by the 1890s. Then in the late 1800s, the U.S. Army Corps of Engineers commissioned a survey to consider a route of rivers and canals connecting the Mississippi

River system with the Atlantic. One route studied was the Tennessee River to the Altamaha via a series of canals connecting first to the Coosa River system in Northwest Georgia, thence to the Chattahoochee, and finally to the Ocmulgee-Altamaha system. Perhaps Altamaha River communities could have saved time and money had they taken to heart the advice given in 1914 by the editors of the *Effingham County News*: "Waterway improvement is good, but we are not in favor of trying to make a river out of a ditch."

MILE 92.1 (31.885481, -82.107452) J. E. Stanfield Landing. This boat ramp on river left bears the name of a Glennville native and former Tattnall County commissioner who was an avid hunter and angler. The landing sits on the northern end of the Big Hammock Wildlife Management Area (WMA), which spans more than 7,000 acres and forms the north bank of the river for the next 10 miles, to the mouth of Watermelon Creek. The Big Hammock WMA is notable as the home of one of Georgia's eleven National Natural Landmarks—a broadleaf evergreen forest, or hammock, that covers a sandy ridge above the river's bottomland forest. Within the canopy of this hammock is the rare and imperiled Georgia plume (*Elliottia racemosa*). Georgia plume, a small tree that is a relative of rhododendrons and azaleas, sports foot-long stalks with clusters of narrow, showy white flowers between June and July. Famed Cumberland Island biologist Carol Ruckdeschel played a role in securing protection of this property in the 1970s.

MILE 90.5 (31.866317, -82.116273) Tenmile Creek. On river right is this tributary, so named because it was approximately 10 miles northwest of Fort James, a frontier fort built along the river in the late 1790s that continued operation for some 20 years. The fort, along with the Georgia militia who manned it, protected settlers from hostile Native Americans and served as a diplomatic outpost for Georgia in dealings with local Creek Indian leaders.

MILE 90.3 (31.862319, -82.114995) Carter's Bight Landing. This curve, or bight, in the Altamaha, with a public boat ramp, parking area, picnic area, and restrooms on river right, is also home to a small riverfront neighborhood, and to Get-A-Way Campground, a private campground that has RV and tent camping sites (912-256-4114). Carter's Bight likely draws its name from the Carter family that settled in Appling County near Tenmile Creek before 1820. George Carter Sr., a Revolutionary War veteran from South Carolina, served as Appling County's first sheriff. For riverfront communities like this, flooding is a routine part of life, so much so that many of the stilt-elevated homes include drain holes in their floors. And when the floodwaters come, the critters of the bottomlands, like us, seek out high ground . . . often in these riverfront dwellings. As recounted in the *Florida Times-Union* newspaper, one resident, James Williamson, found an unwanted guest during an April 2009 flood. After boating up to his front steps amid the floodwater, he stepped into his screened porch and was immediately attacked by a wild hog. He dispensed of the hog with his rifle but wound up in the local emergency room, where he received four stitches and a tetanus shot.

51

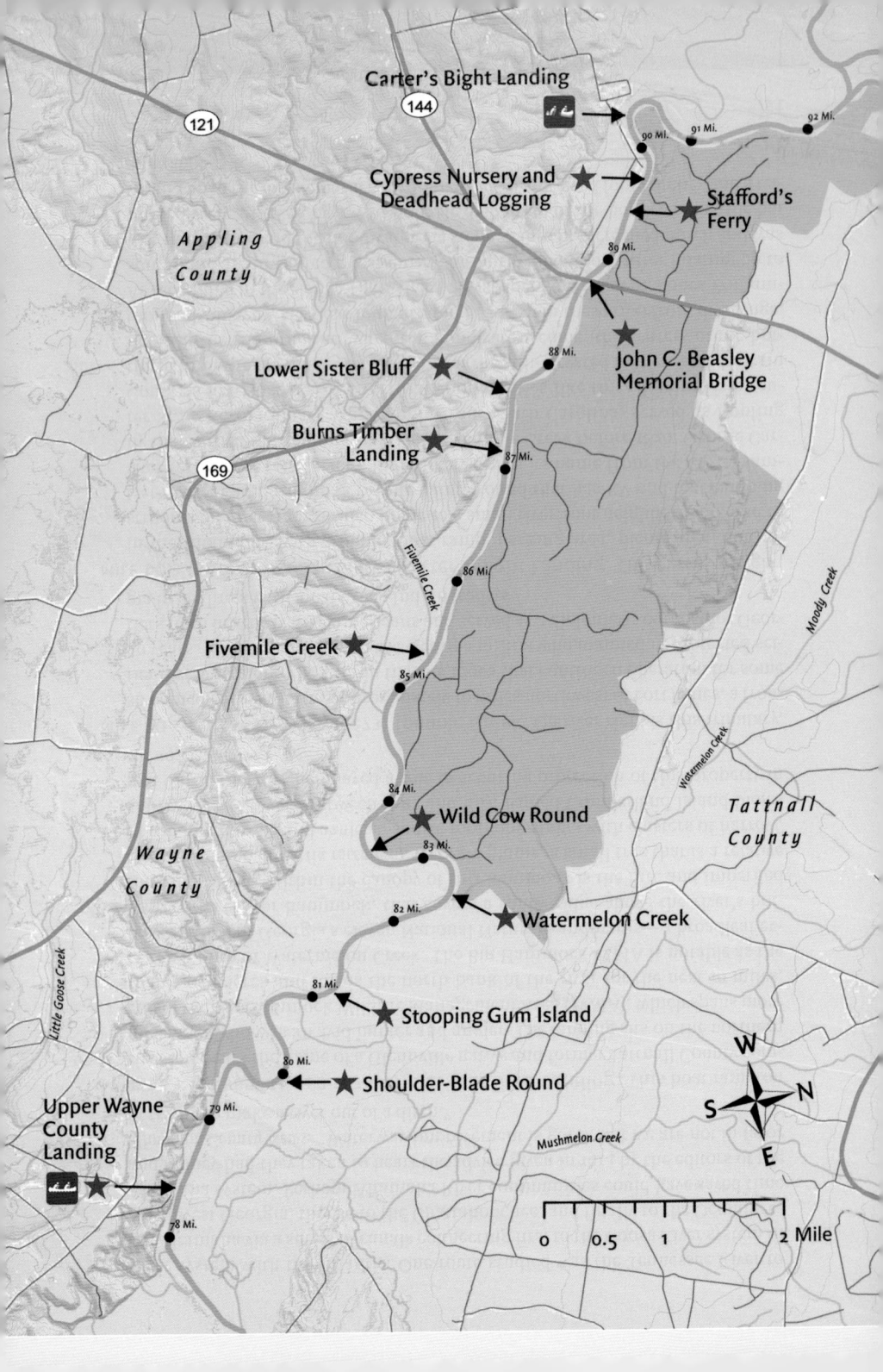

Carter's Bight Landing

121

144

90 Mi.  91 Mi.  92 Mi.

Cypress Nursery and
Deadhead Logging

Stafford's
Ferry

*Appling
County*

89 Mi.

John C. Beasley
Memorial Bridge

88 Mi.

Lower Sister Bluff

Burns Timber
Landing

87 Mi.

169

*Fivemile Creek*

86 Mi

*Moody Creek*

Fivemile Creek

85 Mi.

*Watermelon Creek*

84 Mi.

Wild Cow Round

*Tattnall
County*

83 Mi.

*Wayne
County*

82 Mi.

Watermelon Creek

*Little Goose Creek*

81 Mi.

Stooping Gum Island

80 Mi.

Shoulder-Blade Round

Upper Wayne
County
Landing

79 Mi.

*Mushmelon Creek*

W

N

S

E

78 Mi.

0    0.5    1    2 Mile

# Big Hammock

**Length**   12 miles (Carter's Bight Landing to Upper Wayne County Landing)
**Class**   Flatwater/I
**Time**   5–7 hours
**Minimum Level**   Navigable year-round

---

**River Gauge**   The nearest river gauge is located at U.S. 1, 22 miles upstream from the launch site: https://waterdata.usgs.gov/ga/nwis/uv?site_no=02225000.

**Launch Site**   Carter's Bight Landing is located on the south side of the river, off Carter Bight Landing Road, with a boat ramp, parking area, picnic area, and restrooms.

DIRECTIONS   From the intersection of Main Street and U.S. 341 (Golden Isles Pkwy.) in Baxley, travel north on Main Street 0.2 mile and then bear right, remaining on Main Street for one mile. At the fork, continue right on Lanes Bridge Road (Ga. 144) for 11.7 miles. Turn left onto 10 Mile Road and proceed 0.9 mile. Turn right onto Hershel Tillman Road and proceed 0.7 mile to James Stanfield Road, and then continue straight on Carter Bight Landing Road for 1.5 miles to the parking area at the landing.

**Take Out Site**   The take out site is on river right, with a boat ramp, parking area, picnic shelter, and potable water.

HOME AT CARTER'S BIGHT LANDING, APPLING COUNTY

DIRECTIONS    From Carter's Bight Landing, return 1.5 miles on Carter Bight Landing Road. Turn left onto James Stanfield Road and proceed 0.8 mile. Turn left onto Ga. 144 and proceed 1.8 miles. Turn right onto Ga. 169 (Lanes Bridge Rd.) and travel 0.1 mile before bearing left to continue on Ga. 169 for 7.2 miles. Turn left onto New Hope Road and proceed 1.2 miles. Turn left onto Old River Road and travel 0.4 mile before bearing hard to the right and continuing on Old River Road for another 1.3 miles. Turn left onto Arnold River Road and proceed 0.6 mile to the parking area at the boat ramp.

Outfitters    Three Rivers Outdoors offers canoe and kayak rentals and shuttle service.

Three Rivers Outdoors, 612 McNatt Falls Rd., Uvalda, Ga. 30473, 912-594-8379, www.explorethreerivers.com

Description    Between Carter's Bight Landing and Upper Wayne County Landing, the river alternates between long straightaways and winding oxbows. Cut banks and expansive sandbars are numerous on this 12-mile run. The river's north bank from the Ohoopee River to Watermelon Creek is occupied by the state-owned Big Hammock Wildlife Management Area. This section is also bisected by Ga. 121, carried over the river by the John C. Beasley Memorial Bridge.

## Points of Interest

MILE 89.7 (31.864229, -82.105982) Cypress Nursery and Deadhead Logging. Maps from the late 1800s refer to this crook in the river as Cypress Nursery, perhaps a nod to young cypress trees that once grew here, or to sunken cypress logs that might have been lodged here, the detritus of wrecked log rafts. During the heyday of the Altamaha's log rafting days in the late 1800s and early 1900s, as much as 116 million board feet of timber left the port of Darien annually. An untold number of cypress and pine logs felled and floated in that era never reached the coast, and some have remained preserved in the silt of the river bottom for a century. Today, that wood is highly prized for its fine grain and beautiful color, but the recovery of these prized logs has been controversial. River advocates and Georgia's Department of Natural Resources contend that the logs provide important habitat for fish and other aquatic wildlife and fear that disturbing the river bottom could release toxins and contaminants that might best be left undisturbed. Prohibited in 1998, deadhead logging was revived in 2005 when the state adopted a permitting process that would allow the recovery of sunken logs . . . but at a high price. Loggers deemed the cost too high and didn't apply for the permits. In 2010, a Cairo-based logging company successfully challenged in court the state's claim of "ownership" of the logs buried in river bottoms. Deadhead logging still takes place on Georgia rivers, including the Altamaha. Logs taken from the Altamaha's bottom bear the marks of their origins, including holes where the logs were augered and pegged to keep them together within the massive rafts.

MILE 89.4 (31.860670, -82.101514) Stafford's Ferry. In 1854, the Georgia General Assembly gave Elijah E. Stafford the right to operate a ferry on his property at the Altamaha here, apparently replacing Carter's Ferry. Stafford was the son of Ezekiel and Mary Easterwood Stafford, who, as early settlers of Tattnall County, were instrumental in establishing nearby Hopewell United Methodist Church in 1817. Stafford's Ferry would operate until the 1920s, when the construction of Lane's Bridge less than a mile downstream rendered the ferry obsolete. By the late 1930s, a *Baxley News-Banner* correspondent reported of "four-inch gums (trees)" growing in the road that once led to the ferry. Elijah's descendants now operate Watermelon Creek Vineyards near Glennville, a farm that produces muscadine jellies and wines, including regionally titled vintages such as Stafford's Ferry White, Altamaha River Red, and Ohoopee Whoopee.

MILE 88.8 (31.854340, -82.093830) John C. Beasley Memorial Bridge. Though the present-day bridge is named for a longtime Tattnall County politician of statewide note, when the original bridge was built here in 1920, it bore the name of one of Georgia's best-known business leaders: Mills Lane Sr., who in 1906 founded Citizens and Southern Bank, which would grow to become the South's largest by the 1970s. In 1920, Lane was interested in connecting Savannah with farm products and markets in Southwest Georgia, and bridging the Altamaha was essential. He and his bank put up $2,000 toward construction of the privately funded bridge, and his leadership proved critical to ensuring its timely completion, though he was far from the only investor. The 2,500 residents of Glennville pledged a total of $100,000 for the bridge. Ultimately, Lane's Bridge was completed in 1920 at a cost of $165,000, and the toll bridge proved a wise investment. Within two years of opening, it was raking in $1,000 a week in tolls ($1 per vehicle, plus 25 cents per person); its known success precipitated a brutal robbery of the bridge's toll taker in 1926. Ultimately, the original investors sold the bridge to the state in 1932 for $35,000, ending its run as a toll bridge, but to this day, Ga. 144 in Appling County is still known as Lanes Bridge Road.

The state intended to rebuild the bridge, but those plans became embroiled in a longtime battle between the Talmadge family and the federal government. In the 1930s, Governor Eugene Talmadge engaged in a war of words with the federal government that resulted in federal road funds being withheld, a consequence that occurred twice more during the administration of Eugene's son, Governor Herman Talmadge. By 1943 Lane's Bridge was in such disrepair that it was closed; by 1950, only portions of the new span were completed. The unfinished bridge resulted in the death of a pulpwood truck driver who crashed off the end of the incomplete span. It wasn't until the late 1950s that the bridge was finally completed and named for John C. Beasley, a former mayor of Glennville, Tattnall County commissioner, state representative, and state senator who eventually became director of the state highway department. The existing bridge was completed in 1985, still making use of the high bank on the Appling County side of the river known as Upper Sister Bluff.

LOWER SISTER BLUFF, APPLING COUNTY

MILE 87.6 (31.842497, -82.080549) Lower Sister Bluff. Lower Sister Bluff is typical of the Altamaha's numerous bluffs, sporting the evergreen leaves and (in the spring and early summer) the showy, fragrant blooms of the southern magnolia—a tree native to the southern Coastal Plain from Virginia to Texas. The magnolia is one of the lasting symbols of the romanticized South and one that is closely associated with southern women (see, for example, the movie *Steel Magnolias*). The *Encyclopedia of Southern Culture* opines that the trees have become symbolic of southerners' "unrealistic attitude toward life, of a people blinded by beauty." Viewing the blooms and catching their perfume as you drift beneath these bluffs, you can understand how southerners have become enamored. Both Louisiana and Mississippi claim the magnolia as their state flower. In Mississippi, the decision was based on a vote by schoolchildren in 1900; the magnolia won the contest with 12,745 votes. In second place? The cotton blossom, with just 4,171 votes. Cotton's poor showing in the vote can be explained in part by the fact that magnolias lack the spiny, prickly bolls from which cotton must be dexterously picked.

MILE 87.2 (31.840279, -82.073272) Burns Timber Landing. An 1890 survey of the river notes the low bluff on river right as the site of this landing that was likely one of many places where log rafts were constructed and began their journey downriver to sawmills in Darien and Brunswick. Of course, those rafts depended on adequate river levels (usually during winter and spring). A November 19, 1925, item in the *Baxley News-Banner* reports on a freshet that freed the log rafts yet also makes note of the looming end to the river's log rafting era: "Millions of feet of logs and sawn timber, accumulated along the banks of the upper Altamaha river during the prolonged drought which was recently broken, are coming down stream in an almost endless procession. . . . The decrease in river transportation by boats is becoming particularly noticeable. . . . The inevitable march of progress is seen in this fact as shippers in increasing numbers now haul by trucks to railroads instead of relying on the slower movement of water transportation."

MILE 85.4 (31.826881, -82.048280) Fivemile Creek. On river right is this tributary, so named because it was approximately 5 miles northwest of Fort James, a frontier fort built along the river in the late 1790s that continued operation for some 20 years. The fort, along with the Georgia militia who manned it, protected settlers from hostile Native Americans and served as a diplomatic outpost for Georgia in dealings with local Creek Indian leaders. This creek marks the boundary between Appling and Wayne Counties. Established on a vast expanse of former Creek Indian lands stretching south from the Altamaha to the St. Marys River, Appling County ultimately gave birth to 12 other counties in Southeast Georgia. Notably, it is the one-time home of Georgia's first Pulitzer Prize winner, Caroline Miller, who received the award in 1934 for her novel *Lamb in His Bosom*. The book tells the fictionalized story of a family of early settlers of South Georgia's wiregrass region. To gather material for her writing, Miller traveled the backroads of Appling County and talked with the descendants of settlers to understand the hardships they endured and document their culture and colloquialisms. Those accounts—including stories of timber rafting on the Altamaha—found their way into the book. The mother of three sons (Billy, her oldest, and twins nicknamed Nip and Tuck), Miller often found herself overwhelmed by her duties as mother and wife but said she drew inspiration from the stories of the pioneer women: "They had something, something very real, very tangible, yet almost indefinable, that anchored them and gave them faith and courage, and I needed that something so much." The Pulitzer Prize winner never went to college. Shortly after graduating from high school in Waycross, she married her English teacher, Will D. Miller, whom she credited as "my college."

MILE 84.5 (31.814593, -82.023395) Wild Cow Round. On river left here—at normal-to-low water—is a large sandbar that fronts this curiously named bend in the river. From colonial times through the 1800s, property owners in Georgia bore the responsibility of fencing their crops to prevent damage from livestock. It wasn't until the late 1800s that state laws were flipped to require that livestock be contained within fences. Thus, in early Georgia, cattle ranged freely, and massive stands of river cane found along river bottoms were their preferred forage. In 1776, as many as 10,000 cattle roamed freely in the land between the Savannah and Ogeechee Rivers. Even with backcountry cow pens established, rounding up these creatures proved difficult. Thus many of the creatures remained "wild."

MILE 82.5 (31.824735, -82.015120) Watermelon Creek. In the 1800s, this creek on river left was known as Matlock Water Road, bearing the name of Stephen Matlock Sr., who, prior to the Civil War, operated a plantation of some 3,000 acres worked by 50 enslaved people. The creek provided an avenue to float logs

57

WATERMELON CREEK, TATTNALL COUNTY

and farm products from the plantation's uplands to the Altamaha. Matlock improved this natural course by digging canals. In 1898, the intrepid self-made archaeologist Clarence Bloomfield Moore ventured up the creek to excavate two Native American burial mounds. He described the waterway as a "sort of canal joining Bluff Lake with the river, used for floating out lumber. The length of the 'road' is about 1 mile. . . . At the end of the lake, not far from its union with the canal, is a lumber tramway." Moore found his mounds near the junction of the tramway and Bluff Lake, uncovering "parts of seven skulls" and a "number of shell beads." The Matlock family cemetery lies about 2 miles northwest of the mouth of the creek. The creek marks the downstream extent of the Big Hammock Wildlife Management Area.

MILE 81.2 (31.807319, -82.005942) Stooping Gum Island. On river left is this "island," or rather a remnant island that existed here in the 1800s and early 1900s. In 1880 at this location, the U.S. Army Corps of Engineers (USACE) identified Stooping Gum Cut, which had begun stealing the flow from the old river channel—a nearly 2-mile-long oxbow to the northeast. The USACE recommended the old river be "partially closed in order to divert a greater volume through the cut." Stooping Gum Cut, however, like many new cuts, was full of wood and needed attention as well. In 1889, the USACE expended 15 pounds of explosives in the cut to aid in removing 11 large snags from the course. Thus, by lending Mother Nature a helping hand, the USACE successfully robbed the old river of its flow. Today, nothing remains of the original channel.

MILE 79.9 (31.798623, -81.995656) Shoulder-Blade Round. On river right at normal-to-low flows is a large sandbar associated with this bend, the name of which is anatomically inspired. Make up your own story as to its origin.

MILE 78.3 (31.785148, -81.984342) Upper Wayne County Landing. On river right here is this boat ramp and parking area that sits atop Fort James Bluff. Though its exact location is unknown, Fort James was established 1 mile upstream of Beard's Bluff in the mid-1790s, when land south and west of the Altamaha was considered the property of Creek Indians. For some 20 years, the fort was a hub of activity on what was then the American frontier. Travelers stopped at the fort when passing between Georgia and Creek territory; a Spaniard by the name of John Comas operated a store here; and on occasion, fugitives from slavery who were captured by Creek Indians were returned to Georgia at the fort. The fort proved pivotal in the successful pole boat journey of Philip Cook and his crew, who traveled from mid-January through April on a course from near Milledgeville on the Oconee to St. Simons Island and back. Cook's journal, reprinted in an 1887 edition of the *Atlanta Constitution*, paints a vivid picture of the hardships of these early river journeys: "15 January . . . got as far as about seven miles, after getting on logs and sand five times. . . . [On] the 19th . . . we discovered a raft of old logs and canoes entirely across the river, where we employed ourselves that evening and till 10 o'clock the next day . . . before [we] could get by. . . . On the 23rd . . . got fast on a tree, where I fell overboard." And that was just the first nine days of the adventure. To feed themselves, the crew members purchased provisions where they could (including a barrel of beef and flour at Fort James and venison from Native Americans) and lived off the land, feasting on turkeys and geese shot during the voyage.

CYPRESS AND SPANISH MOSS, WAYNE COUNTY

59

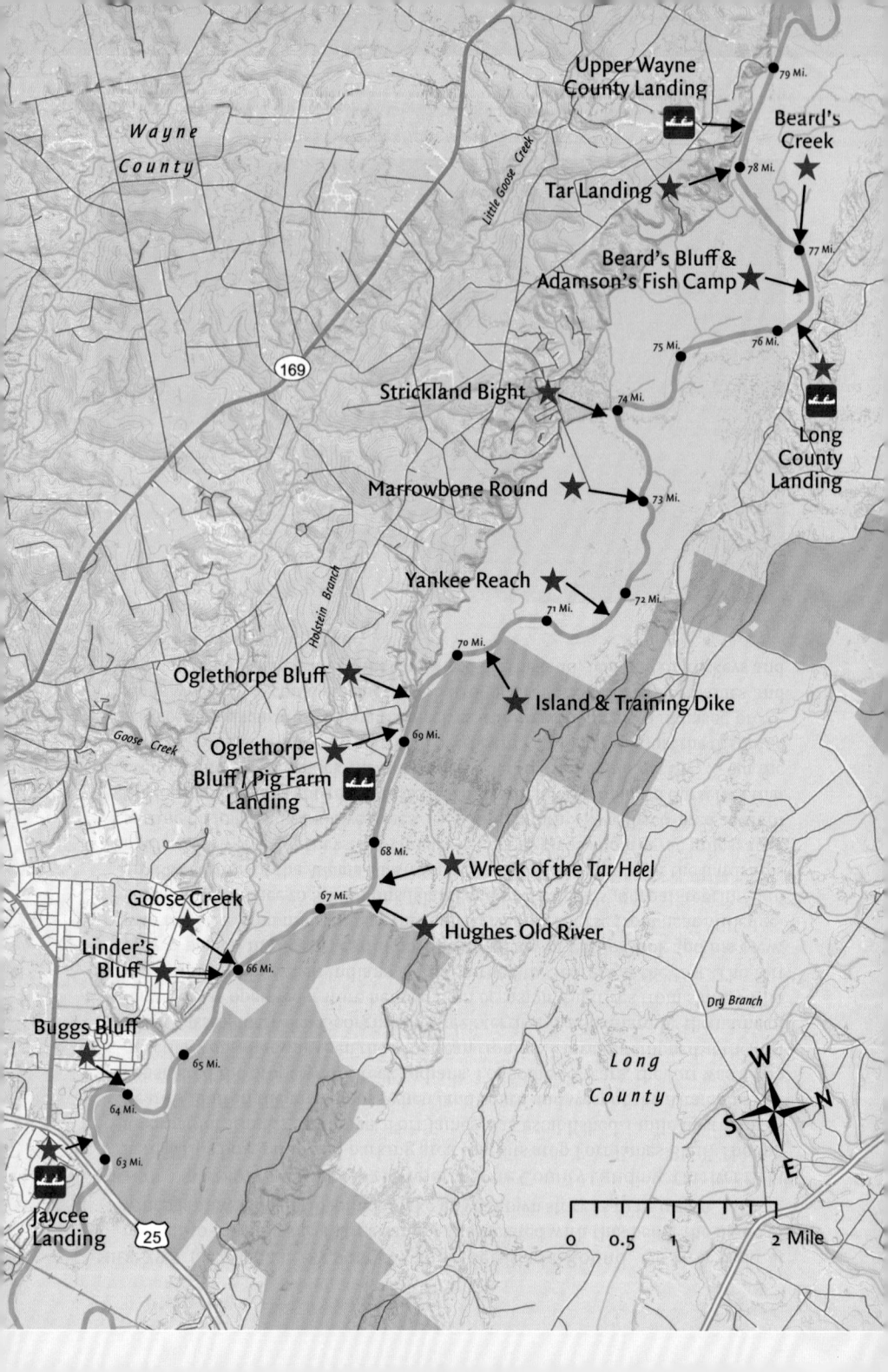

Upper Wayne
County Landing

79 Mi.

Beard's
Creek

Tar Landing
78 Mi.

Beard's Bluff &
Adamson's Fish Camp
77 Mi.

76 Mi.

75 Mi.

Long
County
Landing

Strickland Bight
74 Mi.

Marrowbone Round
73 Mi.

Yankee Reach
71 Mi.    72 Mi.

70 Mi.

Oglethorpe Bluff

Island & Training Dike

Oglethorpe
Bluff | Pig Farm
Landing
69 Mi.

68 Mi.

Wreck of the Tar Heel

Goose Creek
67 Mi.

Hughes Old River

Linder's
Bluff
66 Mi.

Buggs Bluff

65 Mi.

Dry Branch

Long
County

64 Mi.

63 Mi.

Jaycee
Landing
25

Wayne
County

169

Little Goose Creek

Holstein Branch

Goose Creek

W
N
S
E

0    0.5    1    2 Mile

# Beard's Bluff

**Length**  15 miles (Upper Wayne County Landing to Jaycee Landing)
**Class**  Flatwater/I
**Time**  7–9 hours
**Minimum Level**  Navigable year-round

**River Gauge**  The nearest river gauge is located at the Doctortown railroad trestle, 17 miles downstream from the launch site: https://waterdata.usgs.gov/ga/nwis/uv?02226000.

**Launch Site**  Upper Wayne County Landing is located on the south side of the river off Arnold River Road, with a boat ramp, parking area, picnic shelter, and water.

**DIRECTIONS**  From the intersection of U.S. 341 (Golden Isles Pkwy.) and Ga. 169 (Lanes Bridge Rd.) west of Jesup, travel northwest on Ga. 169 11.8 miles. Turn right onto New Hope Road and proceed 1.5 miles. Turn right onto Bonham Road and travel 1 mile. Turn right onto Old River Road and proceed 0.2 mile. Turn left onto Arnold River Road and proceed 0.6 mile to the parking area at the boat ramp.

**Take Out Site**  The take out site is on river right, with a floating dock, boat ramps, a parking area, a picnic shelter, restrooms, potable water, a bait shop, boat gas, and RV camping.

OGLETHORPE BLUFF LANDING, WAYNE COUNTY

DIRECTIONS   From Upper Wayne County Landing, return to Old River Road via Arnold River Road. Turn right and proceed 0.2 mile. Turn left onto Bonham Road and proceed 1 mile. Turn left onto New Hope Road and proceed 1.5 miles. Turn left onto Ga. 169 and travel 8.6 miles. Turn left onto Rayonier Road and travel 4 miles. Turn left onto U.S. 301, travel 0.2 mile, and then turn left onto Jaycee Landing Road. Proceed 0.3 mile to the parking area and boat ramp.

Alternative Take Out Sites   Trips of 2 miles and 9 miles can be created by taking out at Long County Landing and Oglethorpe Bluff Landing, respectively.

DIRECTIONS   To reach Oglethorpe Bluff Landing, return to Old River Road via Arnold River Road. Turn left and proceed 3.9 miles. Turn right onto Talmadge Flowers Road and travel 0.2 mile. Turn left onto Oglethorpe Road and travel 2.3 miles. Turn left onto Osteen Branch Road and proceed 2.3 miles to the parking area and boat ramp. The route to Long County Landing requires a circuitous 35-mile course to the north side of the river, making the 2-mile trip not worth the lengthy shuttle.

Outfitters   Three Rivers Outdoors offers canoe and kayak rentals and shuttle service.

   Three Rivers Outdoors, 612 McNatt Falls Rd., Uvalda, Ga. 30473, 912-594-8379, www.explorethreerivers.com

Description   This 15-mile route is characterized by high bluffs and, during low to normal water levels, expansive sandbars. Beard's, Oglethorpe, Linder's, and Buggs Bluffs all rise majestically from the water, usually opposite wide sandbars. Off-the-main-channel exploration is also possible, especially at high water, at places like Beard's Creek, Marrowbone Round, and Hughes Old River. The trip is also a passage through some 300 years of history. Along the route, travelers will pass the sites of 18th-century frontier forts, 19th-century naval store landings, Civil War–era steamboat shenanigans, and noteworthy points from 20th-century transportation—from navigational dikes built for steamboats to the site of a fatal and senseless airplane crash. The journey ends at Jaycee Landing in Jesup, where there are multiple amenities for river users.

## Points of Interest

MILE 78.0 (31.782559, -81.977560) Tar Landing. According to *Wayne County, Georgia: Its History and Its People*, beginning in 1858, this site on river right became one of the first turpentine mills in the area after the McDuffies, a pair of brothers from North Carolina, ventured south to tap Georgia's seemingly endless stands of longleaf pine. At that time, more than 96 percent of the nation's naval stores (rosin and turpentine) came from North Carolina, but as the forests of North Carolina played out, the industry moved south. (Originally the gum from pines was of value in waterproofing and sealing wooden ships; thus the turpentine industry came to be known as the naval stores industry.) By the late 1800s, Georgia was the country's leading naval stores producer, and through the 1940s, Brunswick and Savannah remained the world's leading ports for the shipment of naval stores. The American Turpentine Farmers Association (ATFA) was established in Georgia in 1936, and for the next 40 years it helped develop new uses for pine gum and popularized spirits of turpentine as a household cleaner. The ATFA even sponsored a yearly beauty pageant, crowning a Miss Gum Spirits of Turpentine at its annual meeting for more than three decades. By the 1960s, naval stores production in Georgia began to wane, and by 2001, the last bucket of commercial turpentine was drawn. Recently, small operations have once again taken to tapping the state's pines to produce turpentine and rosin.

MILE 77.0 (31.789161, -81.963694) Beard's Creek. In the 1880s, river currents at this location, where the Altamaha widens at the mouth of Beard's Creek, created a sandbar and navigational hazard for steamboats and timber rafts. In 1884–1885, the U.S. Army Corps of Engineers attempted to eliminate this sandbar by constructing a 1,700-foot jetty or training wall that extended from the mouth of the creek downstream toward Beard's Bluff. The wood and rock wall employed more than 1,200 cubic yards of stone and gravel and more than 3,500 cubic yards of wooden fascines. An additional 500 feet of shore protection was built along the bluff downstream. At favorable water levels, the channel and sloughs associated with Beard's Creek can be accessed.

MILE 76.7 (31.790285, -81.955755) Beard's Bluff & Adamson's Fish Camp. On river left along this bluff is the boat ramp of Adamson's Fish Camp, a campground established in 1941 by Dewey Adamson. The camp provides cabins, RV/tent sites, and a bathhouse and is privately operated; user fees apply for boat launching and camping (912-654-3632). In 1962, famed outdoor writer Charlie Elliott—who was the model for Ed Dodd's comic strip character Mark Trail—called Adamson's place "one of the most interesting hunting spots in the state." The cultural history associated with the bluff is long and entertaining. In 1742, General James Oglethorpe ordered a stockade built to guard the river crossing at the bluff, and during the Revolutionary War, Georgia militia built a small fort there as well. Following American independence, Fort Telfair, built on Beard's Bluff around 1790, played an important role in relations between the Creek Nation and Georgia citizens; and during the Civil War,

ADAMSON'S FISH CAMP, LONG COUNTY

Confederate soldiers set up post on the bluff to thwart Union incursions up the Altamaha from the coast. By the late 1800s, the bluff had become notable as the birthplace of the steamboat *Altamaha*. F. E. Breen built the 346-ton, 120-foot-long, 29-foot-wide sternwheeler using lumber cut from the surrounding woods. Built to float over the shallow shoals and sandbars of the Altamaha, Oconee, and Ocmulgee Rivers, the ship reportedly drew only 15 inches. That design likely helped keep the boat plying the Altamaha for more than 30 years, making it one of the river's longest-serving vessels. From the early 1800s until the early 1900s, a ferry operated here as well. In 1907, the operation provided a clue to a string of horse

BEARD'S BLUFF, LONG COUNTY

thefts in nearby Jesup, as reported by the *Atlanta Constitution*: "It is alleged that the man suspected has crossed . . . at Beard's Bluff ferry several times, and each time with a different horse." The bluff and creek bear the name of Matthew Beard, who received a land grant alongside the creek in 1774.

MILE 76.2 (31.788382, -81.950496) Long County Landing. The boat ramp and parking area on river left here is owned by Long County, a jurisdiction that occupies the river's north bank for the next 38 miles. Long County was carved out of neighboring Liberty County by the Georgia General Assembly in August 1920, and Georgia voters approved the new county (and four others) at the ballot that November. Georgia has more counties than any other state, excepting Texas (which is nearly five times as large as Georgia). Georgia's profusion of counties is due in part to the state's county unit voting system that developed in the late 1800s and persisted until the 1960s, when it was ruled unconstitutional. In the county unit system, the candidate who received the most votes within a county unit was declared the winner of that county unit's votes; statewide primary winners were determined not by popular vote but by the number of counties each candidate carried. The system concentrated political power in rural Georgia, diluted the power of urban voters, and gave rise to rural populist—and staunchly segregationist—leaders during the first half of the 20th century.

MILE 73.9 (31.758559, -81.942598) Strickland Bight. This sharp oxbow with a sandbar on river left and bluff-top homes on river right is known by this name. The property on river left is owned by Rayonier Forest Resources; the parcel encompasses nearly 6 miles of river frontage and more than 6,000 acres, beginning just downstream of Long County Landing. The forest products company manages some 635,000 acres in Georgia.

MILE 73.0 (31.760196, -81.928842) Marrowbone Round. On river right here is this oxbow lake accessible in high water. The 1.5-mile oxbow was once the river's main channel, but over the last century, the river has carved a new, more direct path, isolating the round. In the late 1890s, Marrowbone Bar, a sandbar that had formed where the river was beginning to create a cut-through, drew the attention of the U.S. Army Corps of Engineers (USACE). In 1896, the USACE built 79 feet of bank protection, presumably to stop the cut-through and keep the river flowing around the round. In this, the engineers were no match for the river.

MILE 71.7 (31.752787, -81.910506) Yankee Reach. The name of this straight stretch of river is seemingly out of place in the Deep South, but the Union army was in fact very active on the Georgia coast and the Altamaha during the Civil War. The saga of the *Gov. Troup*, a steamboat built in Savannah in 1859, is a testament to the vigor with which the Union army pursued its duties. During the war, the Confederate government purchased the *Gov. Troup* for $20,000 and employed the vessel in collecting tithes from farmers along the Altamaha River system. This duty likely did not endear the steamboat to the river's citizenry, for the government demanded 10 percent of everything it raised. In the closing stages of the war, the command of Union major general Quincy Adams Gillmore enlisted two Unionist citizens—Jacob Moody, a prominent resident of Appling County, and Robert T. Williams—in an effort to capture the *Gov. Troup*. During the night of May 1, a group of 41 deserters led by Moody and Williams seized the craft on the Ocmulgee 7 miles upstream from its confluence with the Oconee and proceeded downriver to Darien and then toward Savannah, where they expected to turn the steamboat over to the Union army. Much to the frustration of the river pirates *and* General Gillmore, a Union navy vessel intercepted the *Gov. Troup* and took it as a prize of the navy. The deserters failed to collect the $1,500 they were promised, and the army lost its prize to the navy. Only after a series of tersely worded letters to the navy was General Gillmore able to retrieve his prize and employ it in communications on the Altamaha River system for a brief time. Moody and Williams and their accomplices hired an attorney to press their case with the army, and finally in early 1867, the U.S. government approved payment of $1,500 apiece to Moody and Williams and $100 each to ten of their fellow riverboat pirates. As for the *Gov. Troup*, less than a month after its capture, the ill-fated steamer caught fire and sank on the Savannah River while in the employ of the federal government. Forty people perished in the disaster.

MILE 70.3 (31.735000, -81.909940) Island & Training Dike. Here the river spreads around an island, and during low water, a series of posts extending from the river bottom are visible at the tail of the island. Dating to 1903, this training dike once extended some 500 feet. Between the 334 posts, the U.S. Army Corps of Engineers (USACE) placed "4,296 bundles of brush" and "218 cubic yards of stone" in an attempt to deepen the channel here for steamboats and timber rafts. In 1912, the USACE repaired the dike, driving 15 new piles and adding nearly 1,000 cubic yards of brush and stone between the piles. Timber rafting peaked on the Altamaha in 1900, and in 1902, the USACE reported 102 million board feet of timber, with a value of $1.3 million, passing down the river. By 1914, timber shipments from Darien had fallen to half their peak, and they continued to decline into the 1930s as the vast forests of pine upriver were depleted.

MILE 69.4 (31.723806, -81.903988) Oglethorpe Bluff. Though it is not known whether Georgia's founder, James Oglethorpe, ever ventured this far up the Altamaha, the general did travel extensively along the Georgia coast, and in one instance he made a two-month trip all the way across modern-day Georgia to meet with Native Americans at the Chattahoochee River. An account of that journey provides interesting details of the land in 1739. Along the way, Oglethorpe's entourage killed deer and buffalo, and on more than one occasion they saw herds of 60 or more buffalo. One of Oglethorpe's rangers recorded their encounters with the ruminants more closely associated with the American West: "there is great Plenty and they are very good Eating. Though they are a very heavy Beast they will out Run a Horse and Quite Tire him." In 1850, the Georgia General Assembly authorized the establishment of a ferry at Oglethorpe Bluff, to be operated by James and William Brewer, and as interest in bridging the Altamaha grew in the late 1800s and early 1900s, this site was considered. The bluff was also the home to a problematic shoal for timber raftsmen and steamboat pilots, one at which, in 1881, surveyors with the USACE found the steamer *Adell Moore* wrecked. Over the next 60 years, the USACE would attempt to remedy this shoal, and even as late as 1940, it spent $9,000 building wooden dikes to "improve" the shoal, though by that time river travel, whether via steamboat or timber raft, was almost nonexistent. The straightaway fronted by the bluff is known as Oglethorpe Reach.

MILE 69.1 (31.721191, -81.899383) Oglethorpe Bluff / Pig Farm Landing. Located on river right, this Altamaha River Water Trail access point features a boat ramp, dock, parking area, and restrooms. On June 26, 1987, divers searched the river here to recover the bodies of four men who were killed when their plane collided with trees and crashed into the river. It was a tragic end to a joyride in which the pilot of the single-engine Piper buzzed the Rayonier pulp mill (where he once worked) and then dived beneath the U.S. 301 bridge over the river. Toxicology tests later showed that he was legally drunk.

MILE 67.6 (31.712416, -81.875498) Wreck of the *Tar Heel*. Here, on March 22, 1888, as the captain of the steamer *Tar Heel* tried to navigate around a midriver island that formed a narrow channel known as Oswell's Cut, his ship hit a snag and within 10 minutes sank to its upper decks in 15 feet of water. The wreck stayed here until 1894, when the U.S. Army Corps of Engineers removed the vessel because its boilers had rolled into the navigational channel, creating a hazard. A month prior to the wreck, the captain of the *Tar Heel*, John Swain McBurrows, drew the attention of the *Macon Telegraph*, in part because of the color of his skin, but perhaps mostly because his story played into a convenient narrative of white supremacist ideology in the Reconstruction-era South: that formerly enslaved people had it better in the South than they might elsewhere, including their native land of Africa. Under the headline "Didn't Like Liberia. Its Mechanic Arts Too Primitive and its People's Attire Likewise," the *Telegraph* reported: "Several years ago John [McBurrows] . . . with about 150 more colored people, set out for Liberia, Africa, then pictured as the colored man's haven of rest." Upon arrival in Liberia, McBurrows became homesick and was soon sailing back across the Atlantic. Wrote the *Telegraph*: "He says the costumes of that country didn't suit him. The climate was too hot and the natives wore too little clothing for a man who had any respect for decency."

MILE 67.4 (31.711274, -81.873860) Hughes Old River. Here, on river left, this oxbow lake extends nearly two miles from the river's main channel. The "old river" bears the name of one of Liberty County's leading families of the 19th century. Captain Joseph William Hughes Jr., a Confederate Civil War veteran, represented the county in the Georgia General Assembly and served as county surveyor, but his son, Joseph William Hughes III, left his name on this place when he developed the oxbow into a naval store landing in the late 1800s. By 1898, a tramway moved goods overland to the landing for shipment to Darien. The landing later became a popular hunting and fishing club, and it is in that capacity

ENTRANCE TO HUGHES OLD RIVER, LONG COUNTY

that this locale became a flash point in the legal battle over the rights of boaters to use Georgia's rivers and streams. In the late 1980s, club members took umbrage at non–club members traveling into the Old River to fish and sued to keep the water off-limits to the public. The case ultimately came before the Georgia Supreme Court, where the justices affirmed the club's right to restrict who took fish from the Old River, since the club owned land on both sides of the oxbow slough. But the justices refused to bar boaters from traveling on the water body, citing uncertainty about whether Hughes Old River could be defined as a "navigable" body of water based on Georgia's circa-1863 law defining navigable streams. That law states that water bodies are navigable if they are "capable of transporting boats loaded with freight in the regular course of trade either for the whole or part of the year. The mere rafting of timber or the transporting of wood in small boats shall not make a stream navigable." Much to the chagrin of paddling enthusiasts, the state's dated navigability law, enacted long before widespread recreational use of the state's waterways, has been used to deny the right of passage to boaters on small streams where a landowner holds property on both sides of the stream. Until the General Assembly makes a change or a new legal precedent is set, the 1863 law may continue to be used to deny boaters passage on Georgia's rivers. Griffin Ridge Wildlife Management Area, encompassing 5,600 acres, stretches from the mouth of Hughes Old River downstream to U.S. 25.

MILE 66.0 (31.691645, -81.868554) Goose Creek. This tributary's watershed, encompassing large portions of northern Wayne County, is home to the now-closed Goose Creek Municipal Solid Waste Landfill. The landfill is one of more

FLOATHOUSE ON GOOSE CREEK, WAYNE COUNTY

than 500 sites in Georgia that are included on the state's Hazardous Sites Inventory, a list that identifies locations where pollutants considered a threat to human health have been released into groundwater or soil in quantities that could be dangerous. At this former Wayne County landfill, corrective action has been undertaken to stem the release of vinyl chloride and other pollutants.

MILE 65.8 (31.690286, -81.866957) Linder's Bluff. This has also been referred to as Linden Bluff on some historic maps. In contrast to the river's lowland forests, bluffs provided dry ground on which communities flourished, while the river connected these communities to markets up- and downstream. Given its location on the Altamaha steamboat route, Linder's Bluff was already serving as a postal stop by the mid-1800s. In January 1836, the landing at the bluff was the scene of a tragic boiler explosion aboard the steamboat *Pioneer* that left at least ten men dead and destroyed the boat and the two barges it was towing. By the 1870s, the bluff was home to H. W. Whaley's sawmill. Whaley would serve as mayor of Jesup in the late 1800s, and his family would have its hands in all manner of businesses—from a dry goods store to a local bank. In August 1892, tragedy again struck at the bluff when a ferry sank. The *Savannah Morning News* reported on the peculiar cause of the incident: "One of the mules kicked a plank off the flat, which caused it to sink." Seven men drowned, the paper reported, while noting the miraculous survival of Hiram Bennett: "Mr. Bennett is a one-legged man, having lost his leg during the war, and it was with much difficulty that he swam to the shore." During that same time, Linder's Bluff figured in the lore of the Altamaha's raft hands. Tradition held that rookie rafters were challenged to toss their pocketknives to the top of the 60-foot-high bluff here. If they

WILLOW NEAR LINDER'S BLUFF, WAYNE COUNTY

were successful, they were told, they would be rewarded with a brand new one. Needless to say, many a naïve raft hand was duped into throwing away his knife. Today, Linder's Bluff is topped by one of Jesup's suburban neighborhoods.

MILE 64.0 (31.673243, -81.852686) Buggs Bluff. On river right in the river slough below this high bluff, you'll find numerous floating docks with house-like structures atop them. These and similar "floathouses" on Penholoway Creek (some 25 miles downstream) are all that's left of the Altamaha's once-significant shantyboat communities. Throughout the 20th century, and in particular during the years of the Great Depression, many destitute families turned to the nation's rivers for subsistence or simply for independence and freedom, building floating homes along the banks. In the latter half of the 1900s, floathouses became popular on the Altamaha as weekend getaways, and in many cases as permanent homes. By the early 1990s, in one 4-mile stretch of the river, there were an estimated 200 floathouses, which Georgia Department of Natural Resource regulators said made the river look like "the Shanghai waterfront." While many dwellings were elaborately designed and finely appointed—with some even powered by solar panels—the floating homes were, for the most part, a ramshackle lot, and their heads discharged raw sewage directly into the river. In 1992, in an effort to prevent pollution and keep navigable waterways free of man-made impediments, the state adopted rules outlawing nonmotorized houseboats on navigable streams and gave owners until 1997 to remove their dwellings. They didn't go quietly. Legal appeals kept the fate of many floathouses in limbo until 1999, when the Georgia Supreme Court determined the new rules were constitutional. Since then, the houses on the mainstem of the Altamaha have been removed,

BUGGS BLUFF, WAYNE COUNTY

but a handful still exist on small streams deemed unnavigable, such as Goose and Penholoway Creeks—though these dwellings are required to have proper marine-grade sewage systems.

MILE 63.2 (31.667060, -81.845283) Jaycee Landing. On river right is a dock and large boat ramp that marks this river access that was originally developed by the Jesup Jaycees. It is now operated by Wayne County. Amenities include a convenience/bait store, a pavilion with picnic tables, restrooms, RV and tent sites, and showers. In 2017, community leaders in Wayne County adopted a plan to transform the landing into a regional "anchor for recreation, environmental education, and ecotourism." If the vision is realized, the 50-acre park will be improved to include walking trails, new camping facilities and cabin rentals, bird watching platforms, and an environmental education/interpretive center. The landing hosts numerous community events, including canoe/kayak trips, fishing tournaments, and wild hog and raccoon hunting competitions. Overlooking the landing is a granite marker commemorating the U.S.S. *Altamaha*, an aircraft carrier commissioned in 1942 and named in honor of the river that saw duty during World War II and was decommissioned and scrapped in 1961.

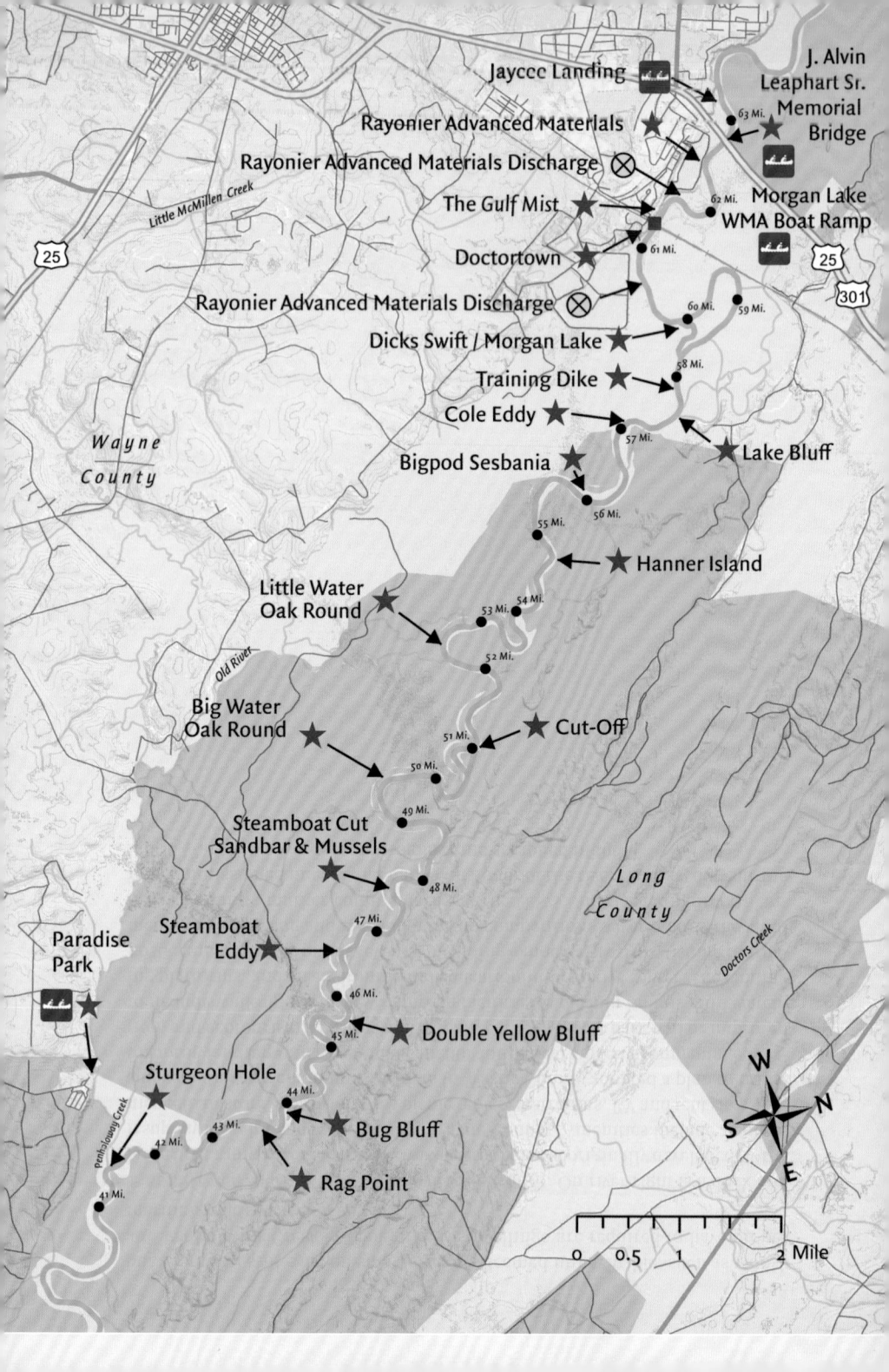

# Penholoway

**Length**   23 miles (Jaycee Landing to Paradise Park; 21.5 miles on the Altamaha and 1.1 miles on Penholoway Creek)

**Class**   Flatwater/I

**Time**   10–12 hours

**Minimum Level**   Navigable year-round

---

**River Gauge**   The nearest river gauge is located at the Doctortown railroad trestle, 2 miles downstream from the launch site: https://waterdata.usgs.gov/ga/nwis/uv?02226000.

**Launch Site**   Jaycee Landing is located on the south side of the river upstream from the U.S. 301 bridge at the end of Jaycee Landing Road, with a boat ramp, parking area, dock, picnic shelter, restrooms, potable water, bait shop, boat gas, and RV and tent camping.

DIRECTIONS   From the intersection of U.S. 84 (North 1st St.) and U.S. 341 (Golden Isles Pkwy.) in Jesup, travel north on U.S. 84 1.4 miles before merging with U.S. 301 and continuing for another 3 miles. Turn left onto Jaycee Landing Road and proceed 0.2 mile to the parking area.

**Take Out Site**   The take out site is located 1.1 miles upstream from the mouth of Penholoway Creek. To reach Paradise Park, travel 0.5 mile upstream from the mouth of the creek and then bear left, continuing up Penholoway Creek 0.6 mile past floathouses to the boat ramp. This is a private boat ramp with parking area; user fees apply.

DIRECTIONS   From Jaycee Landing, return to U.S. 301. Turn right and proceed 3 miles. At the fork, bear left onto U.S. 301 and proceed 2.4 miles. Turn left onto U.S. 341 (Golden Isles Pkwy.) and proceed 5.9 miles. Turn left onto Morning Glory Circle in Gardi, cross the railroad tracks, and then turn right onto River Road. Travel on River Road for 5 miles. Turn left onto Paradise Park Road and proceed 1.5 miles to the boat ramp.

**Alternative Launch/Take Out Sites**   Half a mile downstream of Jaycee Landing is Johnston Station, a boat ramp and parking

WILLOW AND STORM CLOUDS, WAYNE COUNTY

area located immediately downstream from the U.S. 301 bridge on the north side of the river. Additionally, the Morgan Lake Wildlife Management Area (WMA) boat ramp can be used as a launch site for this section to create a 20-mile trip to Paradise Park, or as a take out site to create a 5-mile trip from Jaycee Landing to Morgan Lake.

DIRECTIONS   To reach Johnston Station, return to U.S. 301 via Jaycee Landing Road. Turn left onto U.S. 301 and proceed 0.9 mile to the entrance to the boat ramp on the right. The Morgan Lake WMA boat ramp can be reached by continuing on U.S. 301 for another 1.2 miles. Turn right onto Fishing Road and proceed 0.5 mile. Turn right before crossing the railroad tracks and follow the dirt road 0.3 mile to the boat ramp.

Outfitters   Three Rivers Outdoors offers canoe and kayak rentals and shuttle service.

Three Rivers Outdoors, 612 McNatt Falls Rd., Uvalda, Ga. 30473, 912-594-8379, www.explorethreerivers.com

Description   Though this 23-mile run begins on the outskirts of Jesup and wraps around the Rayonier Advanced Materials pulp mill for its first 2 miles, it soon becomes one of the Altamaha's wildest and most remote sections. The floodplain spreads to nearly 3 miles in width, with the labyrinth-like Penholoway Swamp Wildlife Management Area bordering the river on the south and the Morgan Lake and Townsend Wildlife Management Areas occupying the north bank. At high water, off-the-main-channel exploration can lead to places rarely seen by other humans. The river itself winds around looping oxbows between mostly low banks, with Lake, Double Yellow, and Bug Bluffs being notable exceptions. Sandbars suitable for camping are less numerous in this section. The history is rich through this corridor, as explorers will see shipwrecks and navigational structures dating to the early 1900s amid the wilderness of this run.

## Points of Interest

MILE 62.8 (31.667110, -81.838039) J. Alvin Leaphart Sr. Memorial Bridge. A bridge has spanned the river here since 1931, after an ambitious plan to build a paved cross-state "Oglethorpe Highway" from Savannah to Bainbridge was initiated in the 1920s. The original 1,600-foot-long wood-planked, steel truss bridge was named in honor of Frank M. Oliver, a resident of Savannah who served as president of the Oglethorpe Highway Association. Built with a draw to allow the passage of boats below, the bridge was manned by a bridge tender who lived in a home adjacent to the bridge and who was charged with opening and closing the span and stopping traffic on the highway. In 1964, the original bridge was replaced and renamed the J. Alvin Leaphart Sr. Memorial Bridge in honor of a Jesup physician who served on the city council and as mayor. The current bridge was completed in 1994. Immediately downstream of the bridge on river left is a Georgia Department of Natural Resources boat ramp that serves as an alternative launch site for this section.

MILE 62.5 (31.663433, -81.835541) Rayonier Advanced Materials. On river right is the Rayonier Advanced Materials cellulose specialties plant, a fixture here since 1954. Behind the bulkhead fronting the river is part of the facility's wastewater treatment system. The plant converts the pines and hardwoods of the region's forests into material that finds its way into a variety of consumer products. The cellulose produced at the plant is used in TV, computer, and cell phone screens, sponges, air and oil filters, diapers, run-flat automobile tires, and even sausage casings. The plant occupies more than 3,200 acres and around 4 miles of riverfront, providing some 800 jobs and pumping $1 billion into the local economy. To accomplish this, it relies heavily on the region's water resources, pumping about 60 million gallons of water daily from the Floridan aquifer and releasing a similar volume of treated wastewater into the Altamaha about a mile downstream. The ambient air around the plant has a distinctive odor similar to "rotten eggs" that can sometimes be noticed while on the river.

MILE 61.5 (31.658155, -81.831386) Rayonier Advanced Materials Discharge. On river right is the first of two treated wastewater discharges operated by the cellulose specialties plant. Typically, this discharge releases about 2 million gallons daily.

MILE 61.3 (31.656073, -81.829406) The Gulf Mist. At low water, the rusted remains of the Gulf Mist, the last of the Altamaha's paddlewheelers, can be seen here. The McCann Lumber Company employed the sternwheeler, using it to haul lumber to and from its mill at Doctortown. The boat was abandoned and sunk in 1957, shortly after the sawmill closed. Built in 1931 in Jacksonville, Florida, the 227-ton, 360-horsepower vessel measured 131 feet in length and was 32 feet wide, employing a crew of nine.

WRECK OF THE GULF MIST, WAYNE COUNTY

75

MILE 61.1 (31.654951, -81.827586) Doctortown. The CSX railroad bridge marks the location of Doctortown, a cultural and economic center of the region for centuries. The Native American Alachua Path crossed the river here, and in the late 1700s a Native American named Alleck lived on the bluff at river right. His presence gave rise to the name Doctortown because the Muskogee word *Aleche* translates as "doctor." Conflicts with Native Americans gave rise to the construction of Fort Defense at Doctortown in the 1790s, and by the 1830s steamboats were stopping at the bluff. In 1857, the Savannah, Albany and Gulf Railroad trestle was completed, solidifying Doctortown's importance as a transportation hub with water and rail connections. From the mid-1800s until 1954, when Rayonier began operations, sawmills operated almost continuously on the bluff. At one time, more than 3,000 people lived in the community. Its strategic importance as a transportation hub made it a prime target during the Civil War. When Union forces attacked and destroyed Darien at the mouth of the river in 1863, fears of an attack on the trestle only grew. One evening during the spring of 1864, the crossing was being guarded by young boys when a disturbance on the bridge in the dark of the night stirred the nerves of the inexperienced soldiers. As recounted in a 1917 issue of the *Pearson (Ga.) Tribune*, "It was about eleven o'clock when the watchman and soldiers discovered two shining eyes apparently coming up through the bridge. It was at once in the minds of all that the eyes were those of a Federal spy. The intruder was hailed but no response came . . . [and] after parleying for some minutes, they determined to fire upon the eyes. Twelve carbines were aimed and at the command, fired; the shining eyes disappeared . . . [T]ogether they went into the bridge and found—what do

DOCTORTOWN TRESTLE, WAYNE COUNTY

you suppose?—a great big raccoon pierced with twelve carbine balls. The boys were frightened and a bit nervous, but their aims were true." In December 1864, the real Union army did descend upon the trestle during its march from Atlanta to Savannah but was repulsed by a force of 1,000 Confederate troops, and the Doctortown trestle was saved.

MILE 60.7 (31.651351, -81.818934) Rayonier Advanced Materials Discharge. On river right, Rayonier Advanced Materials discharges about 53 million gallons of treated wastewater daily from its cellulose specialties plant. Since the facility started operations in 1954, this discharge has epitomized the evolution of industrial pollution control in Georgia. When the facility opened, the hundreds of jobs and the tax revenue it brought to the area were hailed as progress. Jesup's leaders honored the plant's opening ceremonies by declaring the day a civic holiday, and more than 1,000 people celebrated with a barbecue feast. But within months, the consequences of unchecked pollution, at a time when no environmental regulations existed, became clear. In September 1954, the Atlanta Constitution reported on massive fish kills in which dead fish lined the riverbanks from the mill to Darien. In 1956, lawyers representing more than 200 commercial fishermen were petitioning state leaders to force changes at the facility.

Similar sagas played out across Georgia, as jobs competed against clean rivers; the consensus at the time was that you couldn't have both. The state adopted its first water pollution statutes in 1956, but these efforts proved ineffective, as pollution abatement measures were encouraged but not mandated. During the 1960s, the state became more forceful in mandating cleanups, and by 1966 the Jesup mill had installed a primary wastewater treatment system. Secondary treatment was completed in the early 1970s, but still the pollution persisted. Into that decade, shad fisherman still complained of a crude slime that coated their nets and made them useless. Passage of the Clean Water Act in 1972 led to more stringent industrial wastewater treatment requirements. By 1976, Rayonier leadership touted its $250 million investment in environmental controls at its many facilities, while questioning whether the new federal rules could realistically be implemented.

As the 20th century wound down, however, nonprofit citizen-based river protection groups began organizing in Georgia to hold polluters and environmental regulators accountable. The rise of these organizations would play into the mill's saga, as they claimed that the permitted discharges continued to impact the river. Anglers complained of inedible fish that smelled of the pulp mill, and aerial photographs showed a dark black plume of wastewater discoloring the river for miles below the discharge into the 2010s. In 2008, Rayonier Advanced Materials agreed to a consent order with Georgia's Environmental Protection Division to spend more than $70 million to reduce the color of its discharge, but change was slow in coming, and in 2015, Altamaha Riverkeeper challenged the state-issued water pollution control permit, arguing that the limits established by the state did not adequately address the color and odor associated with the discharge. The advocacy organization contended that while the discharge might

77

not unduly impact the biological or chemical health of the river, it still violated what are known as "narrative water quality standards" by interfering with legitimate uses of the river like boating, swimming, and fishing. Between 2010 and 2020, Rayonier Advanced Materials reduced the amount of color in its discharge by more than 80 percent and reduced the total amount of pollutants discharged to the river by 70 percent. That said, conflicts between competing river users remain, and the question of how much pollutant removal is enough is still up for debate. Nevertheless, over the course of nearly seven decades, the jobs-versus-fishes debate so prevalent when Rayonier opened its Jesup facility in 1954 has been relegated to one for the previous century, thanks to federal environmental laws, local advocacy groups, and corporate attention to environmental stewardship.

MILE 60.1 (31.657842, -81.810448) Dicks Swift / Morgan Lake. Here the river narrows through this cut-off. Just downstream on river left is the old channel— an oxbow lake created by the cut-off sometime in the 1900s that extends away from the river for more than a mile. The oxbow, which encircles Knee Buckle Island, connects via a narrow channel to Morgan Lake, an even older remnant oxbow lake. Morgan Lake is the centerpiece of the Morgan Lake Wildlife Management Area that encompasses 1,117 acres and more than 2 miles of Altamaha riverfront, extending from the CSX railroad bridge to Lake Bluff. The Nature Conservancy was instrumental in securing this property in 2014, and it is now part of more than 165,000 acres of protected land stretching along the length of the Altamaha. A boat ramp is located on Morgan Lake 1.1 miles from the Altamaha's main channel, adjacent to the railroad trestle, and the private Morgan Lake Wilderness Campground and RV Park is located 0.2 mile from the boat ramp. 300 Boat Landing Road, Ludowici, Ga. 31316, 912-545-9026, www.morgan lakecampground.com.

MILE 57.9 (31.653358, -81.801679) Training Dike. At the head of the island here is a series of wooden posts embedded in the river bottom. These are the remains of a navigational weir or training dike likely constructed in the early 1900s by the U.S. Army Corps of Engineers (USACE). Commissioned by Congress to maintain a navigable channel three feet deep from Darien to the confluence of the Ocmulgee and Oconee Rivers, the USACE was earnest in its efforts from the 1890s through the early 1940s, despite its own misgivings about the wisdom of these efforts. As river boat commerce dwindled in the 1930s and 1940s, the USACE concluded that "due to the physical characteristics of the [rivers] the cost of providing a dependable channel suitable for the movement of any considerable volume of commerce cannot be economically justified." The decline in shipping on the river supported the USACE's recommendations. Through the 1910 and 1920s, the annual value of goods shipped or rafted down the Altamaha averaged about $2.5 million, but by 1932, only $299,000 worth of goods were shipped on the channel. Still, the appropriations continued, and in 1939 the USACE informed Congress it would "improve" the shoal here at Dicks Swift with "dikes and dredging." By 1940, more than $1.6 million had been spent trying to make the Altamaha navigable.

LAKE BLUFF, LONG COUNTY

MILE 57.5 (31.653250, -81.796368) Lake Bluff. On river left here is an oxbow slough that leads to this high sandy bluff on the east side of the slough. This location played a strategic role in the defense of the Savannah, Albany and Gulf Railroad bridge during the Civil War. In November 1862, Confederate general G. T. Beauregard put some 300 enslaved people to work obstructing the river near here to prevent Union forces operating on the coast from steaming upriver and attacking the important railroad bridge located just upstream. On the high ground at Lake Bluff overlooking the river, he placed a battery of cannons to further protect the bridge. In the last decades of the 1800s, Clarke's Mill, a lumber mill, operated atop the bluff.

MILE 57.1 (31.645683, -81.797893) Cole Eddy. A narrow passage on river right leads to this calm backwater slough. On Georgia's fast-moving rivers of the Blue Ridge and Piedmont, the term "eddy" typically refers to the slack water that pools behind a rock or other obstruction in an area of otherwise swift-moving water. On Georgia's slower-moving Coastal Plain rivers, eddies often form on the tail end of a sandbar or inside a sharp bend. Such is the case here and a half mile downstream at a slough on river left known as Doe Eddy.

MILE 56.0 (31.636792, -81.788090) Bigpod Sesbania. On river right during the growing season (and at many other locations), you may encounter this conspicuous native plant (Sesbania herbacea). It grows in large, dense colonies along sandbars to heights of up to nine feet, sporting leaves that are up to 12 inches long and composed of as many as 70 narrow leaflets on opposing sides of the main stem. In the late summer, it produces large yellow flowers. The fruit that follows

79

is a 4-to-8-inch seed pod that can contain up to 40 seeds, which some studies have suggested are toxic. Many species within the *Sesbania* genus are used as a substitute for hemp and have been used to produce paper, fishing nets and fishing line, leading to another common name: river hemp.

MILE 54.7 (31.631917, -81.779087) Hanner Island. On river left here is Hanner Island. An island in name only now—except perhaps at extreme high water—it was once distinguished by a cut-through to the north, now a remnant oxbow known as Johnson Lake. This may be the Hannah's Island of raftsmen's folklore, which held that the island was haunted by the ghost of a young woman named Hannah who was brutally raped and murdered by a gang of raft hands. To this day, it is

BIGPOD SESBANIA AND WILLOW, WAYNE COUNTY

said, Hannah's ghost haunts the island, and many a man has met dreadful misfortune in the vicinity. There are no historical records of this rape and murder, and no historical maps show a Hannah's Island in the area.

MILE 52.6 (31.614261, -81.768399) Little Water Oak Round. This mile-long oxbow that loops to the south borrows its name from *Quercus nigra*, the native oak tree that is partial to stream banks in the Coastal Plain. It is easily identified by its 2-to-4-inch leaf that is narrow at the stem and widest at the tip, where it typically sports three nondistinct lobes. At the southern tip of this round, in high water, a "suck" known as Old River siphons off a portion of the Altamaha's flow into Penholoway Swamp, the vast river bottom swamp forest between here and Penholoway Creek. Protected as a state wildlife management area, this 10,000-acre tract is a maze of remnant oxbow lakes, islands, and narrow channels that are accessible during high water and offer limitless opportunities for exploration (and getting lost). These bottomland forests are also rich in wildlife, providing a critical stopover for millions of migratory birds. Prothonotary warblers, bright yellow songbirds with gray wings, and Swainson's warblers, with olive-gray backs and pale yellow-to-white bellies, are among the birds that call these river bottoms home.

MILE 51.0 (31.615443, -81.750653) Cut-Off. Here, the river cuts off an oxbow to the southwest, carving a narrow channel through the tongue of land creating the oxbow. Over time, it's likely that this cut-through will become the main channel, creating from the original channel an isolated oxbow lake.

MILE 47.7 (31.600321, -81.731262) Steamboat Cut Sandbar & Mussels. At low water a sandbar appears here—and with it, on occasion (as with all of the river's sandbars), freshwater mussel shells. Opened shells are commonly seen washed up on sandbars, but careful examination of the river bottom along the river's shallow banks or in shallow sloughs behind sandbars will reveal "mussel tracks" in the silt, sand, and mud. The tracks look as if someone has dragged a stick along the river bottom, leaving a small, irregular line. Follow these lines and you can find the live mussels mostly buried in the silt, filtering the water through their siphon that looks like a small dark eye. Indeed, mussels are the river's "kidneys," filtering nutrients from the water to help keep the river healthy. They are also food for a variety of critters—from shell-busting fish to otters and raccoons. The Altamaha River basin is home to 20 species of freshwater mussels. Among the more common are the Altamaha spike, easily identified by its long, thin black shell shaped like a lance; the Altamaha pocketbook, with a thick, round yellow-to-brown shell that is occasionally streaked with dark bands; and the Altamaha slabshell, with its heavy, oval-shaped black-to-brown shell. Among the river's rarer mussels are the state-threatened Altamaha arcmussel, with a delicate, inflated shell that in adults is brown to yellow with dark rays, and the federally endangered Altamaha spinymussel, easily identified by the spike-like spines that grow on the shell; only three species of mussels in North America produce spines.

MILE 46.6 (31.591341, -81.722699) Steamboat Eddy. On river right is this narrow slough, near the mouth of which is a small floathouse. Immediately downstream of the eddy is the approximate location of the wreck of the steamboat *Louise*. The wreck was noted in a river survey conducted by the U.S. Army Corps of Engineers in 1888 and is believed to have been removed by the Corps in subsequent years because it impeded navigation. The wreck is also noted on U.S. Geological Survey maps dating to the 1940s.

MILE 45.7 (31.591041, -81.711392) Double Yellow Bluff. On river left here is this appropriately named bluff that rises up to some of the rare uplands in this lowlying swampy stretch of river. This high and dry land now known as Joyner Island has long attracted humans and was occupied at some point by Native Americans. Clarence Bloomfield Moore, an amateur archaeologist who explored the Altamaha River in 1899, found two mounds on Joyner Island, one of which contained cremated human bones. One of the mounds that Moore examined here was 68 feet in diameter at its base and rose 7 feet above the surrounding land.

MILE 44.1 (31.582759, -81.701294) Bug Bluff. On river left here is this low sandy bluff. Bugs, in the context of the lives of the raft hands and steamboat crews that likely named this bluff, are worrisome creatures that sting and bite (there are lots of those in the Altamaha's swamps), but in the context of the river's bottomland swamps, bugs are keystone species. That's because they convert the plants they eat into food (themselves) for other fauna. Virtually all of North America's terrestrial birds depend on insects to feed and raise their young, including swamp dwellers like prothonotary and Swainson's warblers as well as hooded

SPATTERDOCK NEAR RAG POINT, LONG COUNTY

warblers and flycatchers. The late, renowned ecologist E. O. Wilson (who never guided a timber raft down the Altamaha River) felt differently than raft hands about bugs, calling them "the little things that run the world." Indeed, without their efforts at converting plants to food for omnivores, the natural web of life would disintegrate.

MILE 43.5 (31.576230, -81.697704) Rag Point. You'll not find them there now, but during the Altamaha's rafting era, the vegetation on river left here would likely have been decorated with pieces of fabric. Tradition held that when the current pushed the rafts to this point, first-time raft hands were supposed to tie a piece of clothing or a strip of cloth to the nearby trees. Failure to make this sacrifice to the river was considered bad luck.

MILE 41.5 (31.553495, -81.696999) Sturgeon Hole. The mouth of Penholoway Creek is known by this name, suggesting that historically this water body may have served as a thermal refuge for Atlantic and shortnose sturgeon during their annual spawning runs. Once abundant along the Eastern Seaboard and prized for their meat and roe, these species live in coastal estuaries and the Atlantic Ocean but travel up rivers in the late winter and early spring to spawn, seeking out rock cobble and gravel river bottoms near the fall line. Largely due to overfishing and dams that prevent them from reaching traditional spawning grounds, the populations of these species declined steadily throughout the 20th century. In 1889, some 206,000 pounds of sturgeon were caught in Georgia, but by the 1940s, sturgeon harvests were down more than 75 percent from pre-1900s catches. The shortnose sturgeon was among the first animals placed on the endangered species list in 1973; the Atlantic sturgeon joined the list in 2012. The Altamaha supports one of the largest populations of these species in the Southeast. Known for their long, pointed snout and mouth surrounded by whisker-like barbels, these prehistoric-looking fish are long-lived and large. Shortnose typically grow to about 3 feet in length; Atlantic can surpass 8 feet and weigh up to 200 pounds. Their size, coupled with their ability to leap fully out of the water, has proven a hazard for boaters. In neighboring Florida, gulf sturgeon have been responsible for the deaths of boaters; on the Altamaha and its tributaries, leaping sturgeon can sometimes be seen. Locals caught sturgeon until 1997, when the state banned their harvest to protect the dwindling populations. Howell Boone of Darien was among those still netting sturgeon when the ban went into place. For a time in the late 1980s and early 1990s, his Georgia sturgeon roe was a hot commodity, selling to upscale restaurants in Los Angeles and New York. According to a 1993 *Washington Post* feature on "Georgia's Sturgeon General," Boone counted Jane Fonda, Ted Turner, and Jackie Onassis among his past customers. In listing the Altamaha's sturgeon as endangered, the U.S. Fish and Wildlife Service hopes to restore the species to sustainable populations, but that is likely to take time. It can take female Atlantic sturgeon up to 20 years to reach sexual maturity.

MILE 41.5 (31.553998, -81.711453) Paradise Park. Located 1 mile up Penholoway Creek, Paradise Park is a privately owned landing and creekside community and one of only two public accesses to the river in the 26 miles between Jesup and Williamsburg Landing. Person-powered vessels may find the journey up Penholoway to the boat ramp arduous, especially at high flows. Upon nearing the boat ramp at the park, you'll see on the south side of the creek a number of floathouses; these are among the last holdouts of an Altamaha River subculture that was lost when Georgia enacted laws in 1992 prohibiting nonmotorized houseboats on Georgia's navigable rivers. In response to the ban, some floathouse owners towed their floathouses to Penholoway Creek and took the state to court, arguing that since the structures were no longer on a navigable stream, they could remain. Georgia's Supreme Court agreed. Among those who migrated to Penholoway was one of Jesup's most famous native sons, Len Hauss. An All-American fullback on Jesup High's 1959 state championship football team, the hometown hero went on to play center at the University of Georgia and then played 14 years with the Washington Redskins, with whom he was a five-time Pro Bowler. He notably introduced himself during televised games this way: "I'm Len Hauss from Jesup, Georgia, and I catch more redbreasts than anyone in the NFL." After his playing career ended, he returned to Jesup and to fishing on his beloved Altamaha. After his death in 2021, the Wayne County Commission moved to name a section of the Altamaha River in his honor. According to historian John Goff, the name "Penholoway" is derived from the Creek Indian words *fina*, meaning "foot log," and *halwa*, meaning "high"—high foot log. Goff argues that the name described a crossing of the creek along the Native American Alachua Path and offers as evidence an account from one of General Andrew Jackson's officers, who referred to the stream as "Slippery Log Creek."

83

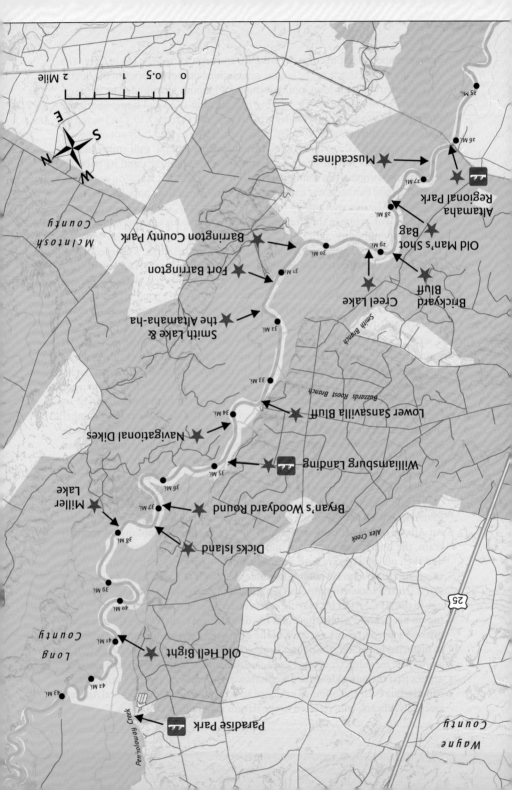

# Sansavilla

**Length**   16 miles (Paradise Park to Altamaha Regional Park; 1.1 miles on Penholoway Creek and 15 miles on the Altamaha)

**Class**   Flatwater/I

**Time**   6–8 hours

**Minimum Level**   Navigable year-round

---

**River Gauge**   The nearest river gauge is located at Altamaha Regional Park, the take out site for this section: https://waterdata.usgs.gov/ga/nwis/uv?02226160.

**Launch Site**   The launch site is located on Penholoway Creek at Paradise Park, 1.1 miles west of the creek's confluence with the river. The site is a private boat ramp with parking area; user fees apply.

DIRECTIONS   From the intersection of U.S. 301 and U.S. 341 (Golden Isles Pkwy.) in Jesup, travel southeast on U.S. 341 5.9 miles. Turn left onto Morning Glory Road, cross the railroad tracks, and take an immediate right onto River Road. Proceed on River Road for 5 miles. Turn left onto Paradise Park Road and proceed 1.5 miles to the boat ramp.

**Take Out Site**   The take out site is located on river right at Altamaha Regional Park, immediately upstream of an abandoned railroad trestle, with a boat ramp, dock, parking area, campground, camp store, restrooms with showers, and cabin rentals.

DIRECTIONS   From Paradise Park, return to River Road. Turn left and proceed 2.9 miles. Turn right onto Akin Road and proceed 3.7 miles. Turn left onto U.S. 341 (Golden Isles Pkwy.) and proceed 5.7 miles. Turn left onto Altamaha Park Road and proceed 3.4 miles to Altamaha Regional Park.

**Outfitters**   Three Rivers Outdoors offers canoe and kayak rentals and shuttle service.

   Three Rivers Outdoors, 612 McNatt Falls Rd., Uvalda, Ga. 30473, 912-594-8379, www.explorethreerivers.com

**Description**   This 16-mile route beginning on Penholoway Creek takes in more of the Altamaha's wild and remote corridor, with virtually the entire route sandwiched between the protected lands of the Sansavilla, Townsend, and Altamaha Wildlife Management Areas. Cut banks and bluffs, sandbars, and off-river oxbow sloughs are numerous. Miller Lake, with its impressive stands of tupelo and cypress trees, is of particular note. Smith, Barrington, Harper, and Gamecock Lakes are also worthy of exploration. As always, the river flows through a land rich in cultural history, and near Sansavilla Bluff at low water, the remnants of wooden navigational dikes built in the early 1900s stand as testament to a bygone era.

## Points of Interest

MILE 40.9 (31.550175, -81.688326) Old Hell Bight. This bend earned its name in the early days of boating on the Altamaha. Just downstream on river left is a slough known as Old Hell Lake. As noted by famous Georgia place-name historian John Goff, there is no lack of hellish names assigned to river features in Georgia. From Hell's Gate on the Satilla to Hell's Gate Shoals on the Flint, the term "Hell" was used by early boatmen to distinguish dangerous locations.

MILE 37.9 (31.539380, -81.661881) Miller Lake. On river left is a slough that ascends 0.3 mile through open water before narrowing into a maze of cypress and tupelo forest. Accessible well upstream in high water, this slough provides access to some scenic river swamp and some of the largest bald cypress and tupelo trees in the state. The largest of the bald cypresses on the state-owned property (part of the 20,000-acre-plus Townsend Wildlife Management Area) measure 45 feet in circumference and up to 15 feet in diameter at breast height. The knees are 8 to 12 feet tall. These ancient cypresses are particularly important to Rafinesque's big-eared bats, which roost in the hollow insides of both cypress and tupelo trees. Considered a rare species in Georgia, these mammals are appropriately named, as their big ears (about one and a quarter inches long) make up a full quarter of their total length.

MILE 37.4 (31.531722, -81.666287) Dicks Island. On river right is an oxbow that in high water extends 0.7 mile upstream and reconnects with the main channel opposite Miller Lake, creating this 40-acre island. In 2011, the Georgia Supreme

CYPRESS AT MILLER LAKE, LONG COUNTY

Court ruled that the state of Georgia, not local residents who had paid property taxes on the island in McIntosh County since 1972, owned the island. Georgia law states that islands in navigable rivers that were not deeded to an individual by a crown grant (from the king of England prior to the Revolutionary War) or through a grant from the state are considered property of the state. After the ruling, Adam S. Poppell III, the attorney representing the Rozier family, which contested the state's claim to the island, told news outlets: "The state jerked the property out from under these people without any effort at all to offer them any kind of compensation. . . . This is another case of the government not being responsive to, or respectful of, the people." Today, Dicks Island—or, if you prefer, Rozier Island—is part of the larger Townsend Wildlife Management Area.

MILE 36.9 (31.527848, -81.660649) Bryan's Woodyard Round. An 1890 U.S. Army Corps of Engineers map notes this bend, the name of which may trace its origins back to Jonathan Bryan, one of early Georgia's largest landholders. In 1760 Bryan laid claim to 2,100 acres on the Altamaha River "just above Fort Barrington." Originally from South Carolina, Bryan accompanied James Oglethorpe on his first visit to Yamacraw Bluff in 1733, and he would later use his political connections to land a post on the Georgia colony's Executive Council, which made important decisions about the distribution of public land. That post enabled him to acquire prized lands from Savannah to the Altamaha, which he used to spread the rice plantation culture of his native South Carolina into Georgia—a culture that demanded enslaved labor and eventually brought an end to colonial Georgia's prohibition on slavery. Bryan also played a role in bringing a notorious invasive plant to the colony. Noted as an expert on native plants and for his success in cultivating gardens, Bryan received seeds of the Chinese tallow tree from Benjamin Franklin in the early 1770s. Bryan (and many others) dutifully planted the seeds, and Chinese tallow is now arguably one of the most damaging invasive tree species in the Southeast. Today Bryan is celebrated for his role in the Revolutionary War. A patriot, he was captured in 1779 and held for two years on British prison ships. Bryan County and a city street in Savannah are named in his honor.

MILE 34.8 (31.508603, -81.658892) Williamsburg Landing. On river right is Williamsburg Landing, with a boat ramp and parking area along Upper Sansavilla Bluff, where, based on archaeological records, it appears European occupation dates to the early 1600s, some 130 years before the founding of the Georgia colony. The bluff, which stretches a mile and a half downstream to Lower Sansavilla Bluff, is thought to have been the location of a Spanish mission—perhaps Santa Ysavela—between 1615 and 1650. The place-name is believed to be a derivation of that original Spanish name, and shards of majolica pottery found during an archaeological dig are believed to be of Spanish origin and to date from that period. In 1741, the Georgia colony established Fort Mount Venture on the bluff, at the same location where Mary Musgrove, the famed translator for General James Oglethorpe, and her second husband, Jacob Matthews, operated a trading post. In November 1742, Mount Venture was attacked by Spanish-allied Yamasee Indi-

87

WILLIAMSBURG LANDING, WAYNE COUNTY

ans, who captured or killed five soldiers and reportedly murdered the wife and child of the commander of the fort. Following the Revolutionary War, Sansavilla Bluff became the site of one of the first white settlements in Wayne County: Williamsburg, which was incorporated in 1792. Today, the property is part of the 19,500-acre Sansavilla Wildlife Management Area that stretches along the river's south bank to Altamaha Regional Park. It was permanently protected in 2017 when the Georgia Department of Natural Resources completed its purchase of the parcel with assistance from the Conservation Fund and the Nature Conservancy. The total cost was $36 million. The slough that ascends upriver from the landing is the outlet of Alex Creek, a name that is connected to Doctortown upstream. It is believed that the Native American named Alleck who settled at Doctortown previously lived here. The Muskogee word *Aleche* translates as "doctor."

MILE 34.1 (31.502042, -81.649404) Navigational Dikes. As early as 1881, river surveys noted this location as a problem for steamboat and timber raft pilots, and for the next 60 years, the U.S. Army Corps of Engineers (USACE) did its best to float boats over this shoal, even after most navigation on the river had ceased. In 1911, a USACE dredge boat pumped more than 8,000 cubic yards of sand here, and as late as 1940, the USACE installed "pile dikes" in an effort to narrow and deepen the channel. The rows of posts that are visible here during low water are likely those driven in the summer of 1940.

MILE 33.4 (31.494768, -81.647715) Lower Sansavilla Bluff. Where the powerlines cross the river here marks the lower extent of Sansavilla Bluff on river right.

MILE 31.8 (31.485671, -81.624433) Smith Lake & the Altamaha-ha. On river left here, opposite a sharp point on river right known as Knee Buckle Point, this large slough ascends nearly a half mile northward, parallel to the river, before running up against chains across the waterway holding NO TRESPASSING signs. The properties surrounding the lake are owned by the Fort Barrington Club, a private hunting club that controls close to 1,800 acres along the river. It is common practice for private landowners along the Altamaha to restrict access to oxbow lakes like this despite their direct connection to the navigable river. Georgia law, in fact, allows people to restrict fishing on an oxbow lake if they own the property surrounding it. It was on this lake in 1981 that two fishermen, Larry Gwin and Steve Wilson of Brunswick, claim they saw the legendary river monster the Altamaha-ha. Their account was recorded in the *Weekly World News* in March of that year: "All of a sudden a large wave—like one made by a large boat—almost tipped our boat. I looked around and saw these two humps about five feet apart like what would be on a serpent. They were as thick around as a man's body." This was not the first (or last) reported sighting of what has been described as a snakelike monster, some 15 to 20 feet long, with slick, greenish-brown skin, a pushed-in face, and large eyes. Reports of such a creature in and around the Altamaha have surfaced periodically since the 1830s. In fact, drawings by sixteenth-century artist Jacques le Moyne, who accompanied French expeditions to the Southeast (and possibly to the Altamaha River in 1564), depict a similar monster. In 2017, the "body" of a strange Altamaha-ha-like sea creature was found washed ashore on a beach near Darien and created quite a stir. That turned out to be a hoax perpetrated by New York–based artist Zardulu. The sea creature was part taxidermied shark, part papier-mâché; as Zardulu later ex-

plained to the online magazine *Vice*, "Darien is the home of a great American legend of the Altamaha-ha, I wanted to breathe some new life into and incorporate it into my larger narrative." The piece had a special place in the artist's 2018 exhibit at a New York City gallery space; no sightings of the Altamaha-ha have been reported since, but . . .

MILE 31.2 (31.481415, -81.618100) Fort Barrington. On river left is a floating dock and boat ramp that marks the location of this colonial fort. This site has been privately owned since 1910, when a group of outdoor enthusiasts from the Atlanta area purchased the property and established the Fort Barrington Club, a private hunting preserve. The fort that gives the club its name was built in 1761 as a defense for the Georgia colony against the Spanish and allied Native Americans. It was named for Josiah Barrington, a close associate of General James Oglethorpe. The 75-foot-square structure sat on the banks of the river, with walls built of split logs and bastions at each corner. In 1762, 25 rangers occupied the fort, living in barracks within the fortified walls. The site was chosen because of its location along the Augustine Trail, a Native American path that ran from present-day Savannah to St. Augustine. For more than a century after its founding, the site served as a major river crossing because it avoided the multiple braided channels of the Altamaha closer to the coast. Just three years after the establishment of the fort, newspapers reported the construction of an improved road for carriages running from St. Augustine to the fort. Yet despite these signs of progress, duty at the frontier outpost must have been trying, for in August 1766 three soldiers stationed there deserted. Their treachery was noted in a September edition of the *Georgia Gazette*, which reported that the men "stole a canoe and a box with some clothes. . . . Forty shillings reward will be given for each of the above deserters."

During the Revolutionary War, the fort was alternately occupied by patriot and British forces, with the patriots renaming it Fort Howe, in honor of their general in command of troops in Georgia. In 1808, the General Assembly passed a measure to establish a ferry across the river at the fort, and that ferry operated into the 20th century . . . but not without some controversy. By 1823, a McIntosh County grand jury was calling on state legislators to bring local citizens relief from exorbitant ferriage fees for Jersey wagons, which, they claimed, were "oppressive to the poor." The ferry would remain important until the first bridges were built across the river in the 1920s. At the onset of the Civil War, citizens from Darien recovered from Fort Barrington what newspaper accounts described as an "old Continental cannon," which had been exposed on the riverbank after a severe flood in 1840. Wrote a correspondent to the *Savannah Morning News* in March 1861: "We are justly proud of our rusty, time-honored relic of Oglethorpe. . . . It was brought to Darien on a raft of timber and is now planted on the wharf, our only defense, should the invader come."

Into the early 1900s, Fort Barrington remained a gathering place of consequence. A 1902 edition of the *Savannah Morning News* reported on a heated gubernatorial campaign rally there at which "there were more than one hundred

THE SWEATBOX, McINTOSH COUNTY

of the juicy brass back shad that swim in the waters of this historical old stream, caught, fried, and devoured." In 1972, the property was placed on the National Register of Historic Places. At that time, according to the application, evidence of "sand breastworks and two bastions" were still visible. In 2008, the Fort Barrington Club permanently protected a large portion of the property from future development through a conservation easement.

MILE 30.4 (31.471991, -81.610608) Barrington County Park. This eight-acre park in McIntosh County features a boat ramp and dock located 0.2 mile up the slough known as Harper Lake on river left. Park amenities include campsites, picnic tables, and restrooms with showers; user fees apply (912-437-6657). The narrow slough leading off of Harper Lake adjacent to the campground goes by the oppressive name of the Sweatbox.

MILE 29.2 (31.455990, -81.621466) Creel Lake. This narrow slough, a remnant of one of the Altamaha's former channels, extends more than a mile into the river bottom forest on river right.

MILE 28.8 (31.450694, -81.625589) Brickyard Bluff. The low bluff on river right is given this name on 1890 U.S. Army Corps of Engineers survey maps. The slough on river right is the mouth of Smith Branch, which also marks the boundary between Wayne County (upstream) and Glynn County. For the river's remaining miles to the Atlantic Ocean, it will be flanked by McIntosh County on the north and Glynn County on the south. Glynn was one of Georgia's eight original counties that were created in 1777 when the state adopted its first constitution. McIntosh was carved from Liberty County (another of the original eight) in 1793.

91

WILLOW AND CYPRESS, LONG COUNTY

MILE 27.9 (31.445810, -81.611814) Old Man's Shot Bag. On 1890 U.S. Army Corps of Engineers survey maps, this point on river right is designated by this name. Today, a powerline spans the river here. Having been navigated by pole boaters, timber raftsmen, and steamboat pilots from the late 1700s to the early 1900s, the Altamaha is home to some colorfully named features. Research by Dr. Delma E. Presley—recounted in Carlton Morrison's *Running the River*, a history of navigation in the Altamaha River basin—tells the story of Old Man's Shot Bag. Wrote Dr. Presley: "Several raftsmen we have interviewed chuckled when they referred to Old Woman's Pocket (an oxbow located 3 miles downstream from this spot) and Devil's Shot Bag (also Old Man's Shot Bag). The first name originated when an old woman was asked how deep the river was where she crossed it. 'It came up to my pocket,' she replied. After an old devil (old man) crossed, he answered that the river came up to his 'shot bag.' These place-names were the subject of a conversation we had with a former raftsman and his wife. When 'Devil's Shot Bag' was mentioned, the wife shook her head, saying 'Tsk, tsk!' But the husband laughed and winked at us, knowing perhaps we would catch the double entendre." Gamecock Lake, opposite Old Man's Shot Bag, extends 0.3 mile off the river. It is home to significant colonies of floating spatterdock and stately cypress and swamp tupelo trees.

MILE 26.7 (31.432269, -81.607300) Muscadines. On river right here, and at many other locations, look for this wild grape vine. The dark green, spade-like leaves with deeply serrated margins are not terribly conspicuous, but in the late summer and early fall, the sweet aroma of the ripening fruits gives this plant away. Look for the round, purple grapes in clusters beneath the leaves. Often these vines climb several stories into riverside trees, making the fruit inaccessible, but it is possible to grab a low-hanging vine and shake it to release the ripe grapes above. Strategically placed boats (preferably canoes or johnboats) can catch the falling "dines," but those that hit the water sink rapidly. The skins are tough and chewy, but the fruits are like eating a sweet candied oyster. The naturalist William Bartram, who traveled through Georgia in the 1700s, noted that Native Americans dried the grapes as raisins over fires and stored them for the winter. They make excellent jams and a very sweet wine and in recent years have garnered the attention of scientists, who have found that the seeds and skins contain exceptionally high levels of antioxidants, known to bolster our immune system.

MILE 26.1 (31.427184, -81.606147) Altamaha Regional Park. Altamaha Regional Park boasts bathhouses, a camp store stocked with cold drinks and ice cream, a coin laundry, a playground, and a quarter-mile nature trail. The park is leased from Glynn County and operated by the Altamaha Park Association of Glynn County. In addition to a campground catering to tent campers and RVs, the park also includes a "vacation village" occupied by year-round residents. Bisecting the park is the Seaboard Coast Line Railroad bridge, which was abandoned in the 1980s. In the heyday of passenger rail, the tracks carried the famous "Orange Blossom Special," which capitalized on the rapid growth and development in Florida during the mid-1900s. Of course, the train also inspired the equally famous bluegrass tune of the same name.

93

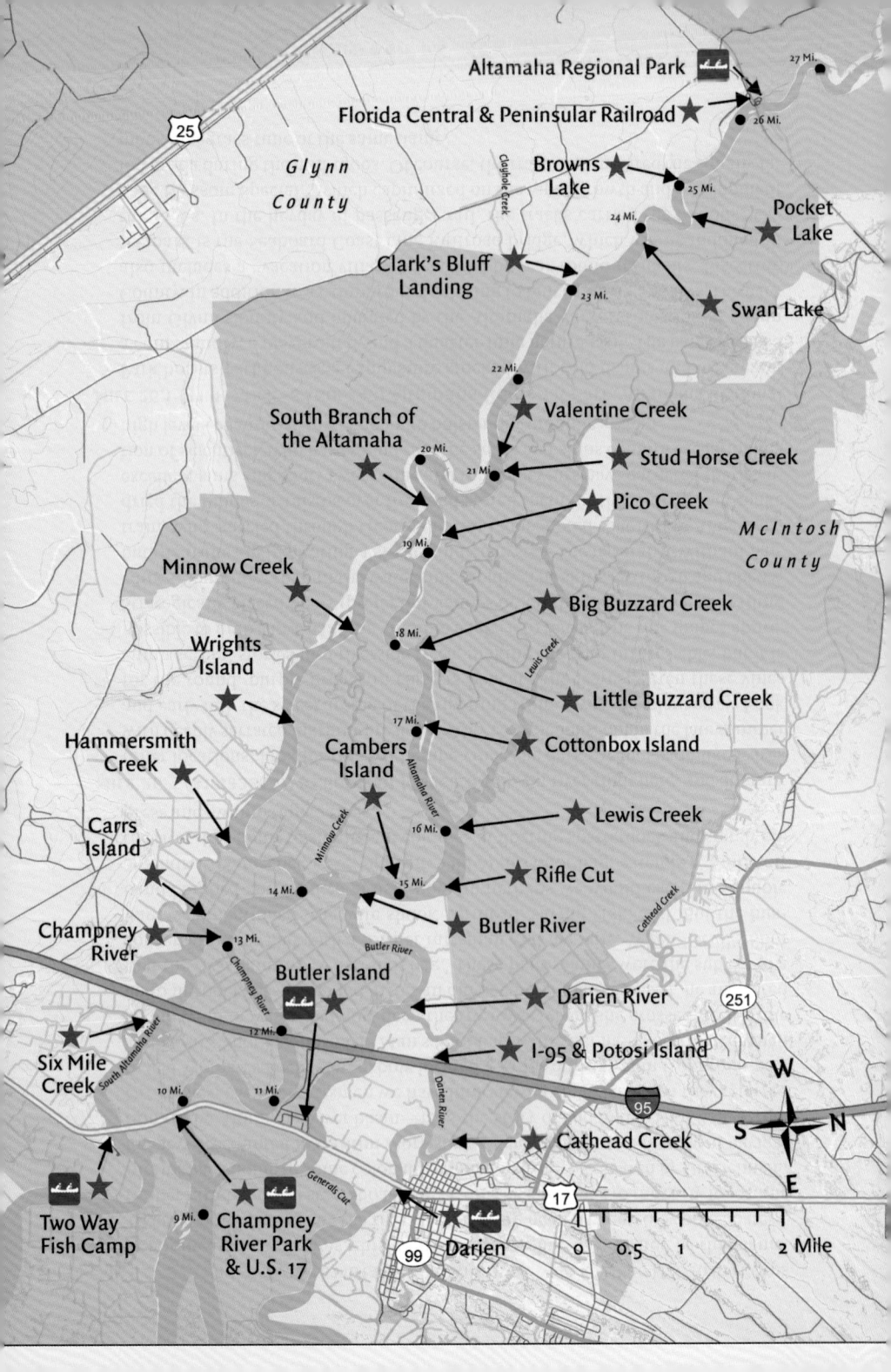

# Clayhole Swamp

Length    15 miles Altamaha Regional Park to Darien via Butler and Darien Rivers;
14.5 miles to Butler Island via Butler River; 15.5 miles to Champney River Park via
South Altamaha and Champney Rivers; 16 miles to Two Way Fish Camp via South
Altamaha River

Class    Flatwater/I

Time    6–9 hours

Minimum Level    Navigable year-round

River Gauge    The nearest river gauge is located at Altamaha Regional Park, the
launch site for this section: https://waterdata.usgs.gov/ga/nwis/uv?02226160.

Tidal Gauge    The river is tidally influenced downstream (and a short distance upstream) from Altamaha Regional Park. Before embarking on journeys downstream
from this location, consult tidal charts, including:

Darien: https://tidesandcurrents.noaa.gov/noaatidepredictions.html?id
=8675779

Champney Island: https://tidesandcurrents.noaa.gov/noaatidepredictions
.html?id=8676012

High and low tides at Altamaha Regional Park run about six hours behind high and
low tides at Darien and Champney Island. If high tide is at noon at Darien, you can
expect an incoming tide, or flood current, at Altamaha Regional Park until about

RIVERSIDE CABIN, GLYNN COUNTY

6 p.m. If low tide is at noon at Darien, you can expect an outgoing tide, or ebb current, at Altamaha Regional Park until about 6 p.m. As you near the coast, the influence of the tides increases, as does the importance of timing downriver excursions to maximize the ebb tide.

**Launch Site**   The launch site is located on the south side of the river at the abandoned Seaboard Coast Line Railroad trestle, at the end of Altamaha Park Road. Amenities include a boat ramp and dock, parking, camp store, campsites, restrooms with showers, coin laundry, playground, and nature trail.

DIRECTIONS   From the intersection of U.S. 341 and Altamaha Park Road in Everett, travel north on Altamaha Park Road for 3.4 miles to the park and boat ramp.

**Take Out Site**   The most commonly used take out for this section is located on river left on the Darien River immediately upstream of the U.S. 17 bridge in Darien, adjacent to Skippers' Fish Camp Oyster Bar and Grill. Amenities include a boat ramp, parking area, and nearby riverfront park.

DIRECTIONS   From Altamaha Regional Park, return to U.S. 341 via Altamaha Park Road. Turn left onto U.S. 341 and proceed 9.6 miles. Turn left onto Ga. 99 and proceed 7 miles. Turn left onto U.S. 17 and proceed 4.7 miles to Darien. Turn left onto Broad Street and travel one block. Turn left onto Screven Street and proceed one block to the parking area and boat ramp at Skippers' Fish Camp.

**Alternative Take Out Sites**   River access is also located at river right on the Butler River at Butler Island, 0.2 miles upstream of the U.S. 17 bridge; on the Champney River at Champney Island, immediately downstream of the U.S. 17 bridge; and at river right at Two Way Fish Camp on the South Altamaha River. The take out at Two Way Fish Camp is boat dock only (no boat ramp).

DIRECTIONS   From Altamaha Regional Park, return to U.S. 341 via Altamaha Park Road. Turn left onto U.S. 341 and proceed 9.6 miles. Turn left onto Ga. 99 and proceed 7 miles. Turn left onto U.S. 17 and proceed 1.4 miles to the entrance to Two Way Fish Camp on the right. To reach Champney Island and James Allen Williamson Champney River Park, continue on U.S. 17 for another 0.8 mile to the entrance to the boat ramp and parking area on the right. To reach Butler Island and the Butler Island Public Dock, continue on U.S. 17 1.3 mile beyond the entrance to Champney River Park, turn left into Butler Island and travel 0.2 mile to the boat dock.

**Outfitters**   Three Rivers Outdoors provides canoe and kayak rentals and shuttle service on the Altamaha, as well as on portions of the Ocmulgee and Oconee Rivers.

Three Rivers Outdoors, 612 McNatt Falls Rd., Uvalda, Ga. 30473, 912-594-8379, www.explorethreerivers.com

Southeast Adventure Outfitters provides kayak tours, shuttle service, and boat charters, working primarily between Altamaha Regional Park and the coast.

Southeast Adventure Outfitters, 313 Mallery St., St. Simons Island, Ga. 31522, 912-638-6732, www.southeastadventure.com

Altamaha Coastal Tours provides guided kayak trips as well as boat rentals and shuttle service, working primarily between Altamaha Regional Park and the coast.

Altamaha Coastal Tours, 85 Screven St., Darien, Ga. 31305, 912-437-6010, www.altamaha.com

Description  In this 15-mile run to the coast, the river changes character as it spreads into a river delta that stretches to more than 4 miles wide at Darien. Multiple oxbow sloughs, islands, and narrow channels offer almost limitless exploration options. About 6 miles downstream from Altamaha Regional Park, the main channel splits around Cambers and Wrights Islands, forming the north and south branches of the Altamaha and providing four routes to river access points at Darien, Butler Island, Champney Island, and Two Way Fish Camp. The routes are rich in cultural and natural history, passing by numerous "rice islands" where extensive rice plantations were developed during the colonial and antebellum periods. Today it's possible to paddle up canals that were dug by enslaved people and used to flood the islands' rice fields. At Lewis Island, a hike inland will take you to a stand of virgin cypress trees. As the river reaches I-95 and U.S. 17, marsh grass becomes the predominant riverside vegetation. Virtually the entire route—on both the north and south banks of the river—is protected as part of the state-owned Altamaha and Clayhole Swamp Wildlife Management Areas.

## Points of Interest

MILE 26.0 (31.426761, -81.605599) Florida Central & Peninsular Railroad. Adjacent to Altamaha Regional Park is this abandoned trestle, with a swing section now permanently swung to allow the passage of vessels. A railroad has spanned the river here since 1894, when the Florida Central and Peninsular Railroad Company opened its 138-mile track running between Savannah and Jacksonville.

FLORIDA CENTRAL AND PENINSULAR RAILROAD TRESTLE, GLYNN COUNTY

97

Completion of the road created a stir, for the swampy lands of Georgia's coastal counties were generally thought impassable. In the railroad wars of the day, the route gave the Florida Central and Peninsular the upper hand in the competition to connect Florida with population and trade centers along the Atlantic Coast, setting off a bitter 70-year-long rivalry between railroads that would become the Seaboard Air Line Railroad and the Atlantic Coast Line. In 1967, the competitors finally merged, becoming the Seaboard Coast Line Railroad, but in 1985, the line was abandoned. In its heyday, the route carried the famed Orange Blossom Special, a luxury passenger train that ran from 1926 to 1953, coinciding with land development and tourism booms in Florida. That train, in turn, inspired in 1938 one of bluegrass music's most beloved tunes, "Orange Blossom Special," a raucous, fast-moving romp that imitates the train that rushed passengers some 1,400 miles from New York City to Miami. For years, the difficulty of playing this tune has been the measure of virtuoso bluegrass fiddlers.

MILE 25.1 (31.415513, -81.594348) Browns Lake. On river right is the entrance to this oxbow slough that extends more than half a mile into the 8,555-acre Clayhole Swamp Wildlife Management Area. Previously owned by the timber companies Plum Creek and International Paper, this parcel and an additional 3,500 acres in Penholoway Swamp were purchased in 2005 by the state of Georgia using $5.2 million in state funds, $6.1 million in federal grants, and $3.8 million from the Nature Conservancy. Occupying some 7 miles of riverfront from here to Cambers Island, the property harbors many rare species. Among them are the federally threatened eastern indigo snake, a thick-bodied black snake that reaches lengths beyond 8 feet and is considered the longest snake in North America; and the state-threatened floodplain tickseed, a showy yellow wildflower often forming large colonies along blackwater streams. Upon entering Browns Lake, the slough almost immediately connects on river left to another off-channel slough known as Alligator Congress. Alligator Congress reconnects with the main channel about 0.8 mile downstream. The trip through Browns Lake and Alligator Congress is about a third of a mile shorter than following the main channel.

ALLIGATOR CONGRESS, GLYNN COUNTY

MILE 24.7 (31.415195, -81.586912) Pocket Lake. Opposite the point on river right known as Old Woman's Pocket is Pocket Lake, which extends off the main channel more than a half mile. This area immediately downstream from Altamaha Regional Park sits at the heart of the Altamaha's American and hickory shad fishery. American and hickory are two of the state's anadromous shad species, which spend most of their life in saltwater but return to the coastal rivers in which they hatched in the winter and early spring to spawn. Historically, shad were a staple of Native American diets, and early settlers also depended heavily on the spring runs of this fish. Into the 1900s, the Atlantic coast shad fishery was one of the most important commercial fisheries in the country, as shad were considered one of the tastiest native fish; American shad's Latin species name, *sapidissima*, means "most savory," and famed 20th-century chef and writer James Beard described a meal of shad as "pure eating joy." In 1950, the country's commercial shad anglers landed more than 11 million pounds of fish, but by 2017, the annual catch had dwindled to about 350,000 pounds. In Georgia, the catch has not exceeded 60,000 pounds since the 1990s. Fisheries biologists blame dams, habitat degradation, and overfishing for shad's demise and have estimated that 40 percent of the fishes' historic spawning habitat has been blocked by dams. Today in Georgia, commercial shad fishing is permitted only in the Altamaha and Savannah Rivers. Shad in the undammed Altamaha range as far upstream as Juliette Dam on the Ocmulgee River and Sinclair Dam on the Oconee River. During Georgia's commercial shad fishing season, which runs from January to March, anglers use drift nets floating downstream in the water and set nets anchored to the riverbank to entangle their quarry. Georgia's Department of Natural Resources has for the past 40 years tagged hundreds of shad annually to gauge populations; these studies suggest that populations are stable.

MILE 23.9 (31.410345, -81.584488) Swan Lake. On river left here is the mouth of Swan Lake, a narrow slough that extends more than a mile into the 19,000-acre state-owned Altamaha Wildlife Management Area (WMA). This WMA occupies the north bank of the river for the next 8 miles, to Rifle Cut. The bulk of the riverfront was among the first lands protected along the Altamaha corridor. In the early 1970s, the Nature Conservancy began courting state leaders to protect the property and found a sympathetic ear in Governor Jimmy Carter. After he became president, Carter, an avid birder, would write in the Nature Conservancy's magazine, "Although the Altamaha River means many things to many people, I'll always remember it as the place where I added the Lesser Yellowlegs [a bird] to my list." In 1972, after leasing the property for more than a decade, Georgia finally purchased a 6,900-acre tract centered around Lewis Island from the paper products giant Georgia-Pacific. Within the protected area is a virgin stand of cypress trees believed to be centuries old. Since the 1972 acquisition, the Nature Conservancy has had a hand in conserving almost 100,000 acres in the Altamaha River corridor, and today, land on both sides of the river, from near Jesup to the Atlantic Ocean—a stretch of 42 miles—is permanently protected.

99

MILE 23.2 (31.401209, -81.580317)
Clark's Bluff Landing. A
boat ramp and the remains of
a wooden dock mark this location, which throughout the
1800s was an important and
well-known landing. In 1814,
William Cooke, who owned a
residence and plantation here,
advertised it for lease in the *Savannah Advertiser* newspaper,
no doubt placing the property
in the best possible light: "The
plantation (has) upwards of 200
acres of land, opened, that can
be made fit for cultivation with
little additional labor; its soil is
equal to any on the Altamaha
River, its situation is pleasant, as
any in the Southern country; and

NEAR CLARK'S BLUFF, GLYNN COUNTY

a ten years' experience, proves to be healthy. The situation is peculiarly favorable to raising of stock; and what may be a consideration to a planter, is, that the
best Shad Fishery in the Southern States, can be established, at little expense, at
the bluff." In 1819, proponents of a Brunswick-to-Altamaha canal were propos-
ing the bluff as the starting point of the ambitious project. In 1823, at the dawn
of the Altamaha's steamboat era, the bluff was noted in the *Darien Gazette* as a
wood landing at which vessels could refuel with "dry pine and lightwood . . . 4
feet long and split about six inches square." A year later, grand juries were petitioning for a road to be built from Darien to this bluff to facilitate land travel to
points south and west of the Altamaha and Ocmulgee Rivers. Today the property
is part of the state-owned Clayhole Swamp Wildlife Management Area. Clayhole
Creek, located just downstream on river right, is a blackwater creek worthy of
exploration at high water.

MILE 21.2 (31.388206, -81.550611) Valentine Creek. This narrow, winding 1.7-
mile passage connects the mainstem of the Altamaha with Lewis Creek. Upon
reaching Lewis Creek, it's possible to follow that body more than 4 miles upstream as it narrows and winds further into the Altamaha Wildlife Management
Area; following Lewis Creek east and downstream leads some 4 miles back to
the Altamaha's northern arm at Cambers Island immediately upstream from Rifle Cut, the shortcut to the Darien River.

MILE 21.1 (31.388255, -81.548138) Stud Horse Creek. This passage connects
the mainstem of the Altamaha with Lewis Creek. Upon reaching Lewis Creek,
it's possible to follow that body more than 5 miles upstream as it narrows and
winds further into the Altamaha Wildlife Management Area; following Lewis
Creek east and downstream leads some 3 miles back to the Altamaha's north-

ern arm at Cambers Island immediately upstream from Rifle Cut, the shortcut to the Darien River. For travelers seeking more intimate courses through the river's swamp forest, this is the preferred route to Darien.

MILE 19.5 (31.377856, -81.543373) South Branch of the Altamaha. On river right a channel leads southeast to the south branch of the Altamaha River at the head of Cambers Island. This is the preferred route for travelers planning to disembark at Champney Island and Two Way Fish Camp. The south branch winds below Cambers and Wrights Islands before reconnecting with the mainstem at the tail of these islands. For the guide to this southern route to Champney Island and Two Way Fish Camp, go to page 108.

## Northern Route to Darien via Altamaha, Butler, and Darien Rivers

MILE 19.2 (31.378690, -81.538792) Pico Creek. Yet another passage connecting the mainstem of the Altamaha with Lewis Creek, this narrow creek winds 0.8 mile to Big Buzzard Creek, which connects to Stud Horse Creek and then Lewis Creek.

MILE 17.8 (31.374746, -81.521184) Big Buzzard Creek. Cutting through Lewis Island, this creek winds tortuously for 2.2 miles to Stud Horse Creek, offering another connection to Lewis Creek. Approximately 1 mile up Big Buzzard Creek from the Altamaha, a narrow canal on the east bank of the creek leads into the depths of Lewis Island. From this point, it is possible to hike along the canal to reach a stand of massive virgin cypress trees. Some of the trees are 7 feet in diameter and are estimated to be more than 1,300 years old.

MILE 17.6 (31.376367, -81.519378) Little Buzzard Creek. This 3-mile passage on river left offers still another connection to Lewis Creek.

MILE 17.1 (31.375380, -81.509876) Cottonbox Island. This island splits the Altamaha just downstream from the mouth of Little Buzzard Creek and bears the name of some of the earliest vessels to ply the river. Cottonboxes were large wooden barges that at first were poled downriver and later were pulled or

ALLIGATORS ON LITTLE BUZZARD CREEK, McINTOSH COUNTY

101

pushed by steamboats. In one day in March 1823, four poled cottonboxes arrived at Darien from upriver, delivering nearly 1,000 bales of cotton; one vessel alone carried 293 bales, which at the time amounted to more than 77,000 pounds of cargo. Typically, upon arrival in Darien, the boxes, which were bulky, square, and ill-suited for upstream navigation, were purchased by nearby rice plantation owners, who dismantled them and put the wood to use in their operations.

MILE 16.0 (31.378379, -81.492581) Lewis Creek. On river left, Lewis Creek leads 8 miles upstream into the Altamaha Wildlife Management Area, connecting with Little and Big Buzzard Creeks as well as Pico, Stud Horse, and Valentine Creeks. Lewis Creek's name comes from Samuel Lewis Sr., who arrived in Georgia around 1758 and received a headright grant on property along the creek in 1759. In the fall of 1765, John and William Bartram wandered through the area near Lewis Creek, discovering along their route *Franklinia alatamaha*, a flowering tree that sports showy white camellia-like blooms in the late summer and early fall, when the tree's large leaves turn yellow to scarlet. The father and son botanists were among the last to see the tree in the wild; the last definitive sighting was in 1803, and though there were reports of the tree along the river in the mid-1800s, no modern-day sightings have been recorded. The Bartrams collected seeds from the tree and propagated them, thus saving the species. Today the tree can be seen in domesticated settings, including Bartram Gardens in Philadelphia and the Atlanta History Center grounds in Atlanta, which claims the Georgia state champion. All of today's living *Franklinia* came from seeds or cuttings from the "mother" tree at Bartram Gardens. In recent years, attempts have been made to reestablish the plant in the wild along this stretch of river.

MILE 15.4 (31.376689, -81.482013) Rifle Cut. On river left here is a narrow channel about 70 feet wide that runs straight as an arrow for 1 mile to the Darien River. Taking this route to Darien eliminates 3 miles on the Altamaha, Butler, and Darien Rivers and takes in a unique piece of Altamaha River history. The cut was dug sometime before 1819 and was intended not only to create a shortcut that would avoid a troublesome sandbar on the Butler River but also to divert the Altamaha's flow to Darien. It was believed that the cut would divert enough of the river to eventually establish it as one of the river's main channels. The river had other ideas. By 1819, river commissioners were employing the steamboat *Samuel Howard* to clear logs from the channel, and the *Darien Gazette* enthusiastically editorialized that when the steamboat completed its snagging operation, the river would be open "at all seasons" and would make Darien "what nature intended it to be, the greatest seaport in Georgia." But Rifle Cut proved intractable. In 1827, river commissioners were soliciting enslavers in Savannah newspapers for "25 to 30 prime negro fellows not over 30 years of age" to clear Rifle Cut of snags. That same year, Georgia's state engineer, Hamilton Fulton, inspected the cut and determined that the dense, deeply rooted vegetation, with its web of cypress knees and roots, made it "hopeless" that the river's current would deepen and widen the cut as originally hoped. It remained a channel useful only for small boats. But Darien boosters never gave up, and into the 20th century locals lobbied the U.S.

RIFLE CUT, McINTOSH COUNTY

Army Corps of Engineers (USACE) to improve the cut. Repeatedly the USACE deemed the project unworthy of taxpayer investment. Still, the agency continued maintaining the channel by removing snags until 1950, when most maintenance of the Altamaha River system ceased.

MILE 15.0 (31.369546, -81.483824) Cambers Island. On river right here is the tail of this 1,100-acre island bordered by Minnow Creek to the south. Cambers was among the westernmost Altamaha islands to be cultivated for rice in the 1700s and 1800s. The plantations on these islands utilized the rise and fall of the tidal river and an elaborate system of canals and floodgates to inundate the rice fields. Rice cultivation on these plantations was brutal work in a malaria-infested environment and depended on enslaved labor for success. In the 1840s, the island was owned by Thomas Spalding, a leading antebellum planter and politician who, despite enslaving hundreds at his Sapelo Island plantation, held serious misgivings about the institution, and especially about the use of enslaved persons on these swampy islands. Urged by a son to expand rice cultivation on Cambers, Spalding told him that he would not subject any enslaved people of his to the rigors of the island, saying, "If you cannot get men of their own choice to undertake the danger of sickness and malaria, I will have nothing to do with it." Spalding died in 1851, and ultimately his offspring and others produced rice on the island. In 1854, the *Savannah Daily News* reported a shipment of 282,000 pounds of Cambers Island rice, and in 1859, virtually the entire island was under cultivation at the hands of some 200 enslaved people.

Rarely did plantation owners themselves live year-round on the islands, but the islands did provide their owners with opportunities for entertainment

103

and sport. A May 6, 1851, issue of the *Savannah Daily Republic* gave a glowing account of a boat race pitting rowing vessels of the Spalding family against a boat owned by neighboring plantation owner James Hamilton Couper: "The place of rendezvous was Mr. Charles Spalding's rice plantation—and a beautiful spot it was for the occasion. . . . Most of the gentlemen and ladies of the surrounding country are gathered upon the bluff . . . [and] the boats are arranged for the contest. . . . Now the sable oarsmen extend their sinewy arms, and the boats glide over the quiet water . . . friends shout on shore—ladies join in cheers—and the far off woods echo to the cry. . . . After the races were over, the party partook of a fine collation, which had been prepared by different persons in the neighborhood. Too much cannot be said of the hearty cheer which was afforded. It was but a picnic on a rice plantation, where the owner does not reside; yet there were observable in everything connected with this entertainment that order and graceful arrangement which refined taste and high social habits alone can give." The correspondent also noted that the boats were all crafted from local cypress by plantation carpenters. P. M. Nightingale took ownership of the island in 1855 for the handsome sum of $100,000 (the equivalent of $3.1 million today); it proved an unwise investment, as he would die in 1873 having still not paid off the mortgage. In 1878, the property was advertised for sale in the *Darien Timber Gazette* and was described as including a "good residence, barns, mill, and outhouses for tenants." Today Cambers Island is part of the 19,000-acre state-owned Altamaha Wildlife Management Area. At the right water levels, it is possible to boat into the remnant rice canals that meet the Altamaha along the tail of the island.

MILE 14.7 (31.363189, -81.483207) Butler River. On river left here, the Butler River diverges off the north branch of the Altamaha toward Darien. At the tip of the island are a row of wood pilings, the remains of attempts by the U.S. Army Corps of Engineers to divert the river's flow and deepen the channel to mitigate the impact of Couper's Bar. This troublesome sandbar was the bane of many a raftsman and steamboat captain during the 1800s and early 1900s. Timber rafts would routinely run aground on the bar, with the raft hands forced to wait for the incoming tide so they could complete their journey to the sawmills in Darien. In the early 1880s, surveyors recommended spending $18,000—the largest single expenditure within the USACE's plan for improving the Altamaha—to dredge the channel here and construct dikes to deflect water into the Butler River and deepen the channel. By the mid-1890s, at least 932 linear feet of wood dikes had been constructed, with more than 556 wooden posts being driven into the river bottom. Between these posts were placed brush and rock. Milled timber was also employed. In 1895, the USACE fastened nearly 5,000 feet of timber to the piles here using 631 pounds of iron bolts. While the dikes were effective in the short term, the structures required regular maintenance; the river won in the long run, and today the sandbar appears at low water, just as it did in the 1800s.

MILE 1.2 FROM ALTAMAHA RIVER MILE 14.7 (31.372726, -81.469456) Butler Island. At this sweeping oxbow known as Reaphook Bend, on river right, is 1,600-acre Butler Island, which features a public boat launch and dock 2 miles downstream on the Butler River as well as a rich and tragic history. The isle is notable for being the plantation of Major Pierce Butler, a South Carolinian who was a delegate to the constitutional convention in 1787 and was instrumental in securing for the South the fugitive slave provision and the "three-fifths" clause. The former codified that fugitives from slavery must be returned to their owners; the latter established that each enslaved person would be counted as three-fifths of a person for the purposes of taxation and representation in Congress. Butler's grandson, Pierce Butler, later took control of the plantation, and in December 1838, he brought his wife, Frances Anne "Fanny" Kemble (a famous English actress), and their two young daughters to the island. During that brief stay, Fanny kept a journal recording her life on the island, giving special attention to the oppressive conditions under which the enslaved people on her husband's plantation were forced to live and work. Eventually published in 1863, *Journal of a Residence on a Georgian Plantation in 1838–1839* was applauded by abolitionists for its unvarnished depiction of the institution that had so recently plunged the country into war. Fanny described the island thus: "It would be difficult to define it by either the name of land or water, for 'tis neither liquid nor solid but a kind of mud sponge floating on the bosom of the Altamaha. . . . The product of this delectable spot is rice—oranges, negroes, fleas, mosquitoes, various beautiful evergreens, sundry sort of snakes, alligators, and bull rushes enough to have made cradles not for Moses alone but the whole Israelitish host besides."

Their time in the South only highlighted the differences between Fanny and Pierce, and they would ultimately divorce in 1849. Fanny continued supporting herself through her acting, while Pierce squandered his fortune through gambling and poor investments. To satisfy his debts, much of his property was sold, including 436 enslaved people in a single auction. That 1859 auction is said to be the largest sale of humans in U.S. history and came to be known by the enslaved persons, who saw families separated during the event, as the Weeping Time. The sale netted $303,850 (the equivalent of about $8 million today), keeping Pierce Butler solvent. Following the Civil War, Butler returned to the island in hopes of reviving the plantation but died after contracting malaria in 1867. In 1926, Colonel Tillinghast Huston, part owner of the New York Yankees, purchased the island, improved the dikes around the island, and in short order transformed it into a successful farm that experimented with oranges, lemons, grapefruits, onions, celery, cabbage, and dairy cattle, though it was iceberg lettuce that proved the best cash crop. The island later fell into the hands of the R. J. Reynolds family, and then in the early 1950s, the state began managing the old rice fields as waterfowl impoundments. Today, through state-managed hunts, the island annually draws hundreds of hunters who shoot wood ducks, mallards, black ducks, pintails, and green-winged teals.

**MILE 1.6 FROM ALTAMAHA RIVER MILE 14.7 (31.370147, -81.463761) Darien River.** On river left here, the Darien River runs north and provides the most direct route to the boat ramp in Darien. Alternatively, boaters can continue 1.5 miles on the Butler River to the Butler Island boat landing, or 2 miles to Generals Cut located on river left immediately downstream of the U.S. 17 bridge. Generals Cut, dug in

DARIEN RIVER, McINTOSH COUNTY

1808 as a shortcut between the Darien and Butler Rivers, runs 0.7 mile north to the Darien River, from which it is 0.5 mile upstream to the Darien boat ramp just west of the U.S. 17 bridge. Continuing downstream on the Butler River will bring travelers within sight of the Butler Island Plantation home, a dwelling built by Colonel Tillinghast Huston after he purchased the island in the late 1920s. The home replaced the rough dwelling in which Pierce Butler and his wife, Fanny Kemble, had lived during their brief stay on the island in the winter of 1838–1839. In 1949, *Atlanta Constitution* editor Ralph McGill recounted Huston's demolition of the old Butler-Kemble home: "He tore it down in a great rage at Pierce Butler," wrote McGill, "and ordered all hands to attention when the job was done. He passed out grog to one and all and raised his glass: 'Any man who would bring a fine woman to a house like that was no gentleman. Down with him and the drinks.'" Huston, as part owner of the New York Yankees, hosted many baseball greats at the elegant, circa-1927, three-story clapboard home, including Babe Ruth, Lou Gehrig, and Ty Cobb. Also visible from the river is a brick chimney associated with the steam-powered rice mill that was built in 1832.

MILE 2.6 FROM ALTAMAHA RIVER MILE 14.7 (31.373301, -81.455244) I-95 & Potosi Island. Here the Darien River passes beneath the country's longest and most-used north–south highway. The interstate runs some 1,900 miles from Maine to Miami, serves 40 percent of the nation's population, and, in terms of vehicle miles traveled, ranks as the nation's busiest interstate. On river left, the highway spans Potosi Island, which in 1859 was home to a rice plantation of around 650 acres that was worked by some 120 enslaved persons. Some of the old rice canals dug into the island are still accessible along Cathead Creek. Today the island is part of the 19,000-acre Altamaha Wildlife Management Area.

CATHEAD CREEK, McINTOSH COUNTY

MILE 3.3 FROM ALTAMAHA RIVER MILE 14.7 (31.372146, -81.444490) Cathead Creek. On river left, Cathead Creek meets the Darien River. During the timber rafting days of the late 1800s and early 1900s, public booms stretched from here to Darien, and this confluence represented the last obstacle for raftsmen. As noted in Carlton Morrison's *Running the River*, strong crosscurrents at this confluence caused the rafts to collide with one another at the boom, breaking up the rafts and releasing the logs downstream, much to the dismay of their crews, who'd already managed a harrowing journey of 100 miles or more. At this confluence, the raftsmen could also likely smell or hear what awaited them in town—food, drink, and women. After a long journey downriver, many raftsmen enjoyed the pleasures of civilization to a fault. Local historian Bessie Smith said that some were as "wild as the river itself," and Morrison wrote: "Flush with money from the sale of timber, they heeded advertisements representing Darien whiskey as 'liquid music' and 'bottled poetry.' The result, although frequently musical, was seldom poetic." Being a port city that welcomed seagoing vessels from afar, Darien surely attracted a wild crowd, but most raftsmen were in fact upland farmers who floated timber during the winter to supplement their farm income. Most were anxious to get back home after their river journey. The *Darien Gazette* in 1902 described them as "about as orderly a set of laborers as we ever saw."

MILE 4 FROM ALTAMAHA RIVER MILE 14.7 (31.368118, -81.437008) Darien. The small boat ramp in Darien, located on river left and tucked between Skippers' Fish Camp and the shrimp boat docks, is easy to miss, especially when an outgoing tide is pushing you along briskly. Darien was established in 1736, just three years

107

after the founding of Georgia, and was initially intended as an outpost to defend the Georgia colony against the Spanish to the south. After the American Revolution, Darien became an increasingly important port, shipping out cotton rafted downriver from the uplands and rice cultivated on the Altamaha delta's numerous islands. The Civil War generated one of the town's defining moments when on June 11, 1863, the city was destroyed by Union troops of the 54th Massachusetts and 2nd South Carolina Infantry Regiments, two African American units. The troops arrived from their camps on St. Simons Island via warships and captured the town without conflict. They then proceeded to take everything. A firsthand account from a Union soldier in The Rebellion Record described the scene as follows: "Soon the men began to come in in twos, threes, and dozens. . . . We had sofas, tables, pianos, chairs, mirrors, carpets, beds, bedsteads . . . china sets, tin ware, earthen ware. . . . A private would come along with a slate, yardstick, and brace of chickens in one hand, and in the other hand a rope with a cow attached." The largesse was loaded on the ships and carried back to camp while the town was torched. Descriptions of the incidents by Darien residents were also documented in The Rebellion Record: "Darien is now one plain of ashes and blackened chimneys. The accursed Yankee negro vandals came up yesterday with three gunboats and two transports, and laid the city in ruins." Wrote another: "The wretches shot the mil[k] cows and calves down in the streets, took some of them on board their vessels, and left the rest lying in the streets." Tabby ruins a short distance from the boat ramp attest to this history. Dating to the early 1800s, these warehouses were among the buildings destroyed in the attack. Not surprisingly, the destruction of an undefended town was controversial, in both the South and the North.

After the Civil War, Darien rebounded quickly, buoyed by the timber trade. Logs rafted downriver became the dominant commodity, making the town the leading exporter of timber on the South Atlantic coast. The timber boom, however, was short lived. As the forests along the Altamaha, Ocmulgee, and Oconee Rivers were exhausted, Darien's sawmills began to shut down; the last one closed its doors in 1916. In 1900, Darien's population was 1,739, but by 1930, the town claimed only 937 residents. Today, the town's population has rebounded to timber boom levels, with the city's economy largely dependent on the seafood industry and tourism. Each spring the town celebrates its seafood industry with a Blessing of the Fleet festival.

## Southern Route to Champney Island Park and Two Way Fish Camp via South Altamaha River

MILE 1.4 FROM ALTAMAHA RIVER MILE 19.5 (31.366086, -81.524795) Minnow Creek. On river left here, this narrow passage leaves the south branch of the Altamaha and winds for 3 miles between Cambers and Wrights Islands, reconnecting with the river immediately upstream of Butler Island. It is an intimate alternative to the wider and more open channel of the South Altamaha.

MILE 2.5 FROM ALTAMAHA RIVER MILE 19.5 (31.356313, -81.510997) Wrights Island. On river left is this 800-acre island that is part of the Altamaha Wildlife Management Area and that bears the name of Georgia's last colonial governor, James Wright, who owned extensive lands within the colony and many enslaved people. In the 1800s, the island was acquired by James Hamilton Couper and became part of his extensive Hopeton Plantation, with Couper's residence located 1 mile south of here, overlooking the south branch of the Altamaha. Since 2015, that land has been protected as part of the 3,900-acre Altama Plantation Wildlife Management Area that stretches along the south bank from here to the I-95 bridge. A Renaissance man in the Age of Enlightenment, Couper was noted for his extensive system of irrigation and transportation canals, as well as for the innovative sugar and cottonseed oil mills that he developed at Hopeton. But he also made a name for himself in other fields, such as architecture (he designed Christ Church in Savannah), paleontology (he discovered numerous fossils during construction of the Brunswick–Altamaha Canal and donated them to museums), and biology (he collected the first recorded specimen of the eastern indigo snake on his plantation in 1842, and other scientists later named the snake in his honor: *Drymarchon couperi*). It should be noted that the 400-plus enslaved persons who worked his plantation enabled his many intellectual pursuits. In 1845, Scottish geologist Charles Lyell visited Couper and described his passage on the Altamaha from Darien to Hopeton: "[Couper] came down the river to meet us in a long canoe, hollowed out of the trunk of a single cypress, and rowed by six negroes, who were singing loudly, and keeping time to the stroke of their oars. . . . For many a mile we saw no habitations, and the solitude

109

was profound; but our black oarsmen made the woods echo to their song." Today, this stretch of the Altamaha appears as wild as it did to Lyell more than 170
years ago.

MILE 3.9 FROM ALTAMAHA RIVER MILE 19.5 (31.346794, -81.491779) Hammersmith Creek. On river right, this narrow, winding channel flows 2.5 miles before reconnecting with the south branch of the Altamaha. The route is a half
mile longer than the main channel but provides access to rice canals on Carrs Island, and it passes by historic Hammersmith Landing, which, after the completion of the Macon and Brunswick Railroad in 1870, became an important point
on the route of the Altamaha's upcountry timber raftsmen as they journeyed
back home after delivering their rafts to Darien. They boarded a ferry in Darien
that delivered them to Hammersmith Landing and then walked 7 miles, with
the tools of their trade on their backs, to a rail station west of Brunswick, where
they then boarded a train that could take them as far north as Macon on the Ocmulgee River. The raftsmen were thus described by Brunswick historian Marga-
ret Davis Cate: "The equipment of their river trip was fastened to their bodies.
The iron skillet and pot and tin coffeepot hung on the right side, while the axe
or hatchet was on the left side. The manila rope was wound around the body—
over the right shoulder and under the left arm—so that the man's head and one
shoulder protruded from the coil like a musician playing . . . a Sousaphone. His
rifle was carried over his left shoulder. As these raft hands walked, with pots and
pans rattling against one another, they were heard even before they were seen."

## Middle Route to Champney Island Park
## via Champney River

MILE 13.1 (31.345558, -81.477171) Champney River. On river left, the Champney
River branches off the south branch of the Altamaha and flows 3 miles, passing beneath I-95 and U.S. 17, to the boat ramp and dock at Champney River Park.
Champney Island, flanked by its namesake river on the north and the south
branch of the Altamaha on the south, is managed by the state as part of the Altamaha Waterfowl Management Area, in which a network of water control structures and dikes are used to create habitat for wintering waterfowl on the nearly
1,000-acre island. The state allows a limited number of hunters on the island
from November through January. From the mid-to-late 1700s to the latter half
of the 1800s, Champney Island was another of the many Altamaha islands developed into rice plantations. In 1859, some 600 acres of the island were under cultivation and worked by a force of 175 enslaved persons. That year, some 51 million pounds of rice were produced in Georgia, with 6 million pounds originating
in the McIntosh County portions of the Altamaha delta. Following the Civil War,
rice production steadily declined—a product of global competition, a series of
hurricanes, and the reluctance of free Blacks to toil in the dangerous, mosquito-
infested fields. By 1919, Georgia was producing just 2 million pounds of rice annually. Champney Island is named for James Champney Tunno, who owned the
island in the early 1800s, when it was also known as Tunno's. At the height of

rice production on the island in the 1850s, Jacob Barrett was its owner, and it was known for a time as Barrett's.

MILE 10.0 (31.337866, -81.450253) Champney River Park & U.S. 17. Here the Champney River flows beneath U.S. 17 and, 300 feet downstream from the bridge on river right, meets the boat ramp and dock associated with this park. U.S. 17 exists at this location in large part because of the failure of a railroad. In 1914, the Georgia Coast and Piedmont Railroad (GCPRR) built multiple bridges across the Darien, Butler, Champney, and South Altamaha Rivers to connect the railroad's depot in Darien with Brunswick. Following the completion of this engineering feat, motorists who wanted to travel across the delta could pay $6 to have their vehicles transported on a railcar; for a time, as many as 600 cars a month took advantage of this service. But despite the ferriage revenue, the GCPRR was short lived, and the rails were abandoned by 1919. That's when boosters in Darien and Brunswick took up the cause of raising money to purchase the abandoned spans, ultimately acquiring the nearly four miles of rail for $60,000. They then turned to the state for assistance in converting the railroad to a highway. Between December 1920 and June 1921, Georgia repurposed 4,430 feet of bridges, including two 245-foot metal swing spans over the Darien and South Altamaha Rivers, to create the state's first coastal highway. Its opening on July 2, 1921, marked the first time a highway bridge spanned the Altamaha delta, and it was an occasion for great celebration in Darien and Brunswick. Some 5,000 people attended the dedication ceremonies, at which Governor Thomas Hardwick addressed the crowd.

The river access immediately below the bridge is named in honor of James Allen "Jimmie" Williamson (1920–1975), who served as the mayor of Darien and as a member of the board of the Georgia Department of Natural Resources. As mayor, he was instrumental in establishing Darien's Blessing of the Fleet festival, a celebration of the town's seafood industry. He also has the distinction of having one of the state's barrier islands named in his honor—a 1.6-mile-long island believed to have been formed by erosion from Tybee Island during the 20th century. Williamson Island is located on the southeast end of Little Tybee Island.

## Southern Route to Two Way Fish Camp via South Altamaha River

MILE 13.3 (31.342204, -81.480155) Carrs Island. On river right is an entrance to a 19th-century rice canal that provides access to the interior of Carrs Island and additional rice canals. Carrs Island is bordered on the north by the south branch of the Altamaha and on the south by Hammersmith Creek. Dug by enslaved people during the antebellum period, the island's canals were equipped with tidal gates that regulated flows into the island and were used to flood and drain the rice fields. Now a 345-acre nature preserve owned by the Nature Conservancy, Carrs Island, like the Altamaha's other "rice islands," is rich in history. It bears the name of Mark Carr, the first settler and "founder" of Brunswick, who received land grants from Georgia's colonial government in the mid-1700s. Somewhere around the time of the American Revolution, the island came into the hands of Basil Cowper, a patriot who fought the British and then joined them when it appeared the American cause for independence was lost. Having failed to read the winds of war wisely, Cowper fled the newly independent country, and the Georgia legislature took possession of his properties, including Carrs Island. In 1813, the state advertised the sale of the island in the *Savannah Evening Ledger*; by 1818, the island was again up for sale by the estate of George V. Proctor, and by the 1850s, it was part of James Hamilton Couper's extensive Hopeton Plantation.

RICE CANAL ON CARRS ISLAND, McINTOSH COUNTY

Along the island's marshy borders and its rice canals (as well as at numerous other locations in the Altamaha delta) are found a host of flowering aquatic and semiaquatic plants. Summer flowering plants include lizard tail, sporting conspicuous nodding spikes covered in tiny white flowers; marsh rose gentian, a showy pink flower sporting nine petals surrounding a bright yellow center with a narrow red border; and eastern false dragonhead, with clusters of pink-to-white tubular flowers at the ends of long stalks—the flowers have a nodding tongue that is mottled pink and white. Carrs Island was donated to the Nature Conservancy by the Jones family, owners of the Sea Island Company, which was instrumental in developing St. Simons and Sea Islands into a high-end residential and tourist destination.

MILE 2.1 FROM ALTAMAHA RIVER MILE 13.3 (31.334166, -81.464277) Six Mile Creek. On river right, this Altamaha tributary runs south through the marsh for about a mile before narrowing to the ruins of locks that mark the northern end of the Brunswick–Altamaha Canal, a 12-mile transportation canal built between 1836 and 1854. Though Darien sat at the mouth of Georgia's largest river and enjoyed direct connection to the forests and farms of Georgia's inland, it lacked a deepwater port. Brunswick, on the other hand, lacked the water con-

PICKEREL WEED AND FALSE DRAGONHEAD, McINTOSH COUNTY

nection to Georgia's inland but had an excellent deepwater port. The canal was the answer to this conundrum. It connected the commodities produced along the Altamaha, Ocmulgee, and Oconee Rivers directly to seagoing vessels. Construction on the canal began in 1836, but from the get-go, it was plagued by labor problems, financial shortfalls, and the sheer difficulty of digging a path through the marsh. The canal finally opened in 1854 to much fanfare, but by 1860 it was completely abandoned. The initial work was completed by enslaved laborers, but in 1837 a group of 500 Irish immigrants was hired. During that period, the *Brunswick Advocate* newspaper reported that the Irish "kept the whole country in alarm by their drunken riots and vagrant habits." Interestingly, during the excavation of the canal, James Hamilton Couper of nearby Hopeton Plantation collected a host of mammalian fossils, including ones identified as mastodon, mammoth, giant ground sloth, horse, and whale. Through the years, various efforts have been made to restore the historic path in hopes of preserving the history of the site and increasing tourism, but to date, none of those efforts have been successful. Reportedly, portions of the original lock can still be seen. The ruins, however, are on private property, and the creek becomes too clogged with deadfall to reach them.

MILE 3.4 FROM ALTAMAHA RIVER MILE 13.3 (31.328082, -81.446106) Two Way Fish Camp. Home to Mudcat Charlie's restaurant, this marina is so named because anglers have two options when embarking from the facility—they can go east for saltwater fishing or head west for freshwater fishing. An iconic establishment along the Altamaha, Two Way features a marina store that shows off an ancient dugout canoe recovered from the nearby marsh. The facility caters primarily to motorized vessels, with floating docks, gas, and numerous lifts for transferring vessels to and from the water. There is no boat ramp, but it is possible for canoes and kayaks to access the facility from the floating docks. 250 Ricefield Way, Brunswick, Ga. 31525, 912-265-0410.

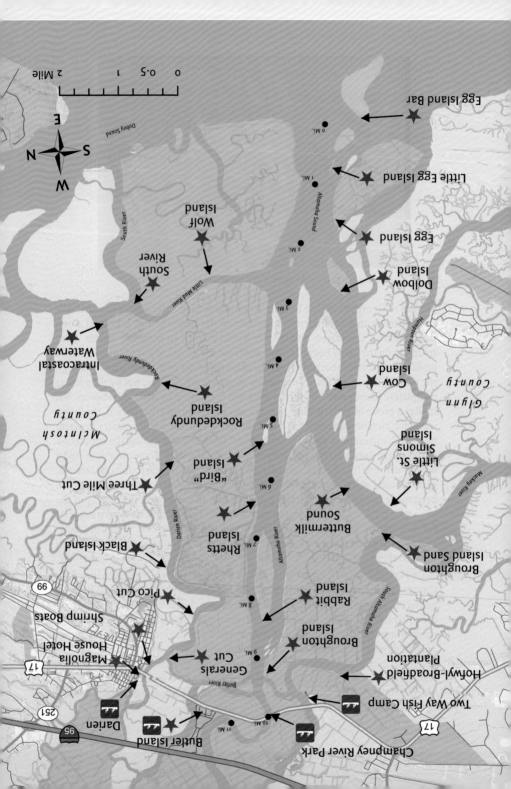

# Altamaha Sound

**Length**  Due to the tidal nature of Altamaha Sound, trips originating from Darien, Champney and Butler Islands, and Two Way Fish Camp are usually out-and-back excursions utilizing the outgoing and incoming tides. Trips will vary in length depending on the desired destination. The Southeast Coast Saltwater Paddling Trail, which generally follows the Intracoastal Waterway, provides opportunities for multiday or long-distance journeys along the Georgia coast originating from the Altamaha River delta.

**Class**  Flatwater/I

**Time**  Trip times vary depending on the destination.

**Minimum Level**  Navigable year-round

---

**River Gauge**  The nearest river gauge is located at Altamaha Regional Park, 14.5–16 miles upstream from the launch sites for this section: https://waterdata.usgs.gov/ga/nwis/uv?02226160.

**Tidal Gauge**  The river is influenced by the tide, and anyone planning a trip originating from Darien, Champney or Butler Island, or Two Way Fish Camp should take into consideration the outgoing and incoming tides. Understanding these tides is especially critical to providing safe navigation for person-powered vessels. Tides on the Georgia coast are semidiurnal, meaning that within each 24-hour period, there are two high and two low tides of equal magnitude. Low and high tides are approxi-

MORNING ON ALTAMAHA SOUND, McINTOSH COUNTY

mately six hours apart. The difference between high and low tides is typically 7 feet, except during spring tides, which occur twice a month, and during which the tidal range expands to 10 feet. Tidal range is the difference between water elevation at low tide and water elevation at high tide.

Darien: https://tidesandcurrents.noaa.gov/noaatidepredictions.
html?id=8675779

Champney Island: https://tidesandcurrents.noaa.gov/noaatidepredictions.
html?id=8676012

Launch Sites   There are four possible launch sites along the primary branches of the Altamaha providing access to Altamaha Sound: Darien, Butler Island, Champney Island, and Two Way Fish Camp.

Darien: This launch site is located on the north side of the Darien River at the end of Screven Street in Darien, immediately upstream of the U.S. 17 bridge. Amenities include a boat ramp, floating dock, parking area, riverfront park and nearby restaurants, convenience stores, and lodging.

DIRECTIONS   From the intersection of U.S. 17 and Broad Street in Darien, travel west on Broad Street one block. Turn left onto Screven Street and proceed one block to the parking area and boat ramp adjacent to Skippers' Fish Camp Oyster Bar and Grill.

Butler Island: This launch site is located on the south side of the Butler River along Butler Road, 0.1 mile upstream from the U.S. 17 bridge. Amenities include a floating dock with kayak launch, parking area, and partially sheltered dock.

HUSTON HOUSE ON BUTLER ISLAND, McINTOSH COUNTY

DIRECTIONS From the intersection of U.S. 17 and Broad Street in Darien, travel south on U.S. 17 1.2 miles. Turn right onto the Butler Island access road (immediately past the rice mill chimney) and proceed 0.1 mile. Turn right at the dead end and proceed 250 feet to the dock.

Champney Island: This launch site is located on the south side of the Champney River immediately downstream of the U.S. 17 bridge. Amenities include a boat ramp, floating dock, parking area, and portable toilet.

DIRECTIONS From the intersection of U.S. 17 and Broad Street in Darien, travel south on U.S. 17 2.5 miles. Upon crossing the Champney River, turn left into the James Allen Williamson Champney River Park.

Two Way Fish Camp: This privately operated launch site is located on the south side of the South Altamaha River at the end of Ricefield Way, immediately downstream of the U.S. 17 bridge. Amenities include floating docks, boat hoists, a marina/bait shop, boat gas, a restaurant, and event rental facilities. This access does not have a boat ramp, but person-powered vessels can use the floating docks. 250 Ricefield Way, Brunswick, Ga. 31525, 912-265-0410.

DIRECTIONS From the intersection of U.S. 17 and Broad Street in Darien, travel south on U.S. 17 3.4 miles. Turn left onto Ricefield Way and proceed 0.3 mile to the parking area at the marina.

Take Out Sites Unless you are planning a multiday or overnight journey, the launch sites for Altamaha Sound will also serve as take out sites for out-and-back journeys utilizing the outgoing and incoming tides.

Outfitters Southeast Adventure Outfitters provides kayak rentals, shuttle service, and guided trips.

Southeast Adventure Outfitters, 313 Mallery St., St. Simons Island, Ga. 31522, 912-638-6732, www.southeast-adventure-outfitters.myshopify.com

Altamaha Coastal Tours provides kayak rentals, shuttle service, and guided trips.

Altamaha Coastal Tours, 85 Screven St., Darien, Ga. 31305, 912-437-6010, www.altamaha.com

Description The Altamaha River delta between Darien and the Atlantic Ocean is a labyrinth of marshes, barrier islands, and sinuous channels. Large portions of the land surrounding Altamaha Sound, including Rockdedundy and Broughton Islands, are protected as part of the Altamaha Wildlife Management Area, while Wolf Island and the Egg Islands, fronting the Atlantic Ocean, are part of the Wolf Island National Wildlife Refuge. On the south side of the sound is the privately owned Little St. Simons Island. The scenery is expansive and beautiful, and the wildlife, particularly the shore and coastal nesting birds, is abundant. Many of the channels are broad and open to the sea, and trips on this section of the river should be undertaken only by experienced paddlers with self-rescue skills. Travelers should make note of tidal and weather conditions before embarking from launch sites.

117

## Points of Interest

### Darien Route

(The following is a description of points of interest along the northernmost route to Altamaha Sound via the Darien, Rockdedundy, and Little Mud Rivers, with the distance from Darien given for each point of interest.)

MILE 0.1 FROM DARIEN (31.367357, -81.435575) Magnolia House Hotel. The spot where the boat dock floats on river left was, from the early 1870s to 1887, the wharf for Darien's Magnolia House, a hotel that rode the boom of the city's timber trade. Editions of the *Darien Timber Gazette* from 1874 advertise the rates of the establishment: $30 per month for meals and lodging, or $2 per day. Ads in 1877 issues of the *Gazette* boast of a billiard saloon with "tables of different styles, with other varied amusements," and a bar with "liquors, wines, and ales, among which Massey's celebrated Philadelphia ale and Schlitz's Milwaukee lager may be mentioned." The wharf on the river was particularly important to the establishment, as it provided guests with convenient access to steamboat lines traveling upriver and along the coast. While an in-town hotel still operates in Darien, the preponderance of the city's overnight lodging is now located along I-95, for convenient access to today's primary transportation artery.

MILE 0.3 FROM DARIEN (31.364950, -81.433326) Shrimp Boats. On river left are docks that hold a portion of Georgia's 200-plus-strong commercial shrimp boat fleet. Georgia is one of the nation's leading harvesters of wild-caught shrimp, with its commercial shrimpers bringing in an average of more than 2 million

SHRIMP BOATS AT DARIEN, McINTOSH COUNTY

pounds annually, a haul valued at more than $11 million. That said, Georgia's shrimp boat fleet is a shell of what it once was. While today the state issues around 200 commercial licenses annually, in the late 1970s it issued more than 1,400 licenses a year. Competition from imported farm-raised shrimp (more than 90 percent of the country's shrimp are imported), an aging workforce, and the rising cost of operating and maintaining trawlers have driven many from the traditional work that is part of Georgia's coastal culture. Darien is famous not just for its historic shrimp boat fleet but also for being the home port of Sinkey Boone, the fisherman responsible for developing turtle excluder devices (TEDs). In 1968, Boone invented a device he called the Georgia Jumper, a trawling net with an escape hatch that he hoped would keep cannonball jellyfish out of his nets. With assistance from University of Georgia Marine Extension and Georgia Sea Grant, Boone developed his invention into a device that prevented sea turtles from getting caught in the nets. Today all trawlers in the United States, as well as foreign trawlers that sell shrimp in the United States, are required to use TEDs. In 2011, the International Sea Turtle Society posthumously honored Boone, who died in 2010, with its Sea Turtle Champion award. The recognition is particularly noteworthy considering that when federal regulations aimed at protecting sea turtles were implemented in the late 1980s, shrimpers revolted. In one incident, shrimpers formed a blockade of a shipping channel in Texas and rammed Coast Guard boats sent to disperse it. Prior to the TED mandates, as estimated 10,000 sea turtles were killed in shrimp nets annually in the Southeast.

MILE 0.5 FROM DARIEN (31.361722, -81.431905) Generals Cut. On river right is this man-made channel that runs 0.7 mile to the Butler River. The channel was dug in 1808 as a shortcut to the rice plantations situated on islands in the Altamaha River delta. The name of the cut and that of the island that it bisects are associated with Lachlan McIntosh. Lachlan was the son of Scottish settlers who arrived in Georgia in 1736 and, at the request of General James Oglethorpe, established New Inverness (which became Darien) as a bulwark against Spanish invasion of the Georgia colony. Thus Lachlan grew up on the banks of the Altamaha and witnessed firsthand the dangers of the colonial frontier. A brother was killed by an alligator while swimming in the river, and his father, John Mor McIntosh, was captured by the Spanish. As an adult, Lachlan would ultimately take possession of the island, becoming a successful rice planter prior to the Revolutionary War. During the war for American independence, Lachlan ascended to the rank of brigadier general in the Continental army, while being simultaneously engaged in a bitter political feud with Declaration of Independence signer and fellow Georgian Button Gwinnett. That feud boiled over into what became Georgia's most famous duel, at which, on May 16, 1777, McIntosh shot and killed Gwinnett. Generals Cut was primarily used by small craft operating between the Altamaha's rice plantations and Darien, but in the early 1900s, the cut saw barges carrying automobiles across the Altamaha delta. In 1914, the U.S. Army Corps of Engineers reported to Congress that in 1912, "130 automobiles were reported to have been carried through the (cut)" while en route between Jacksonville and Savannah.

119

GENERALS ISLAND, McINTOSH COUNTY

MILE 1.5 FROM DARIEN (31.353938, -81.420286) Pico Cut. This man-made cut, developed in the antebellum period, was an effort to divert the river and shorten the passage to Darien for seagoing vessels. The cut was said to have been dug by "50 able-bodied men," but their toil resulted in only a small channel that failed to redirect the river's main flow, and soon the cut closed. Following the Civil War, extensive dredging was conducted at Pico Cut, and slowly the river claimed the man-made channel as its own. In 1881, the U.S. Army Corps of Engineers reported that Pico Cut "is gradually widening and the old bend of the river is shoaling." The cut bears the name of Charles Pierre César Picot de Boisfeuillet, a Frenchman who owned a Sapelo Island plantation in the 1700s. The channel on river left (the former channel of the river) leads 0.7 mile to the Fort King George State Historic Site, a restored British colonial fort occupied from 1721 to 1736. The fort features a reconstructed blockhouse, barracks, guardhouse, moat, and palisades. The bluff on which the fort sits was, from 1819 until the early 1900s, the site of the Lower Bluff sawmill, which during that era milled much of the lumber floated down the Altamaha. Seagoing vessels were loaded at this bluff.

MILE 3.2 FROM DARIEN (31.360129, -81.406957) Black Island. On river left is a dock and boardwalk leading to Black Island, a 250-acre hardwood hammock surrounded by marsh and sitting less than 10 feet above sea level. In the early 1800s, the island was part of Thomas Spalding's vast plantation centered on Sapelo Island, on which he grew cotton, rice, and sugarcane. In 1807, he advertised in local newspapers that the island and its 100 enslaved occupants were for sale, but accounts of a devastating hurricane in 1824 show that Spalding was still owner of the island, having lost all his crops and buildings on the island during the tempest. In the 20th century, Black Island was owned for a time by tobacco heir R. J. Reynolds Jr., who used it as a hunting preserve. Today the island is a gated community managed by the Black Island Homeowners Association. Residents of the low-lying barrier island are, like many who live in coastal areas, faced with the uncertainty of a changing climate and the weather it will bring. Sea levels along the Georgia coast have risen a foot since the 1930s, and scientists predict that within the next century, sea level rise caused by climate change will result in the loss of between 14 and 34 percent of the state's 400,000 acres of coastal marshes, like those that surround Black Island.

MILE 5 FROM DARIEN (31.357555, -81.376397) Three Mile Cut. Dating to before 1807, this man-made passage between the Darien and Altamaha Rivers was a major thoroughfare throughout the 1800s and into the early 1900s for small steamers plying between Darien and Brunswick, but the currents and shifting sands of Altamaha Sound proved problematic. The cut was constantly filling with sand and logs, resulting in dangerous conditions for larger vessels. In 1856 the steamer *Welaka* lost its rudder in the cut; the *Hessie* gave up its propeller there in 1892; and in 1899 the *Angie and Nellie* sank after striking a log in the cut. The U.S. Army Corps of Engineers was enlisted in dredging the channel in the early 1900s, but Darien's diminishing importance as a seaport led to the abandonment of maintenance of the cut by the 1930s. Today the cut is filled and is passable no more. In its heyday, however, the cut was notable for its population of alligators. A May 1839 edition of the *Darien Herald* included the following report about a pleasure excursion from Darien to Brunswick: "In passing through three mile cut—or more appropriate perhaps, Alligator Creek—the juvenile portion of the party amused themselves in shooting at alligators, which by the bye, were very numerous."

MILE 7 FROM DARIEN (31.360463, -81.353240) Rockdedundy Island. On river right is this island that spreads over more than 3,700 acres and is part of the Altamaha Wildlife Management Area. Largely a salt marsh, Rockdedundy is one of a labyrinth of coastal barrier islands along Georgia's 100-mile coast. The island's marshes are dominated by smooth cordgrass, a large, coarse grass that can reach a height of up to 8 feet. It is a keystone species of the Georgia coast, serving as food for everything from manatees to periwinkle snails and providing habitat for myriad other animals, including ribbed mussels, mud fiddler crabs, and diamondback terrapins.

MILE 8.6 FROM DARIEN (31.373075, -81.337321) Intracoastal Waterway. At this location, the Rockdedundy River splits, with the Little Mud River flowing south and the Rockdedundy River flowing north. This is part of the Intracoastal Waterway, a designated boating channel maintained by the U.S. Army Corps of Engineers that runs from a few dozen miles north of Boston to the southern tip of Florida and then continues along the Gulf Coast to Brownsville, Texas. The waterway utilizes natural inlets, rivers, bays, and sounds to provide a navigable route along the country's coast that avoids the hazards of travel on the open sea. The Intracoastal Waterway follows the Little Mud River south to Altamaha

121

NEAR WOLF ISLAND, McINTOSH COUNTY

Sound. From this location, it's 3 miles to Altamaha Sound via the Little Mud River, and then another 2.5 miles east along Altamaha Sound to the southeastern tip of Wolf Island, where the Altamaha River meets the Atlantic Ocean.

MILE 9.2 FROM DARIEN (31.365934, -81.333421) South River. On river left, the South River flows some 3 miles to Doboy Sound opposite the southern end of Sapelo Island.

MILE 10.8 FROM DARIEN (31.346524, -81.327686) Wolf Island. On river left is this barrier island that contains more than 4,000 acres of salt marsh, tidal creeks, and oceanfront beach and sand dunes. Portions of the island were originally preserved in 1930 as a sanctuary for migratory birds; then in 1969, the Nature Conservancy raised over $80,000 to purchase the entire island and protect it in perpetuity. Finally, in 1975 Congress designated Wolf Island a wilderness area. While the island is now managed by the U.S. Fish and Wildlife Service as a national wildlife refuge and is off-limits to human visitors, in the past it was frequented by bipeds. In the late 1700s, it served as a quarantine area for sailors infected with yellow fever, and in the early 1800s, owners Samuel and David Hamilton published ads in local papers warning against trespassers on the island. By 1822, it was home to two lighthouses, both of which were destroyed by the Confederacy during the Civil War to prevent their use by the Union navy. In 1869, the Wolf Island beacons were rebuilt, along with a home for the lightkeeper, but those too were destroyed in 1898 by a hurricane that killed 129 people along the Georgia coast, including the Wolf Island lightkeeper and his family. In an account instructive of the population of Georgia's barrier islands at the time, the *Atlanta Constitution* reported that of the fatalities, "nine-tenths" were "colored"—largely formerly enslaved persons or their offspring still living on the barrier islands and Altamaha Sound's rice islands. Today Wolf Island is reserved for wildlife, especially wintering birds like scaups, scoters, mergansers, and buffleheads, as well as the federally threatened piping plover. It is also used by many marsh nesting birds such as clapper rails and seaside sparrows, and during the fall and spring, it can play host to large flocks of long-billed curlews, red knots, and American oystercatchers.

## Champney Island and Butler Island Routes

(The following is a description of points of interest along the central route to Altamaha Sound via the Butler, Champney, and Altamaha Rivers, with distances given for the main river channel and the distance from the Champney Island boat ramp.)

LOCATED ON THE BUTLER RIVER 1.3 MILES UPSTREAM FROM THE CONFLUENCE OF THE CHAMPNEY AND BUTLER RIVERS (31.355608, -81.447383) Butler Island. After passing beneath the U.S. 17 bridge, the Butler River flows due south to rejoin the Champney. Together the two form the main channel of the Altamaha through Altamaha Sound. On river right, Georgia's Department of Natural Resources manages the portion of Butler Island east of U.S. 17 as a wildlife viewing area in which bird hunting is prohibited and in which three wildlife observation towers are maintained. Among the birds that might be seen here are snipes. For generations, many a child has been sent on the fool's errand of a "snipe hunt" during campouts, leading many to believe the snipe is a mythical creature. In truth, snipes do exist, and though they are among the most widespread shorebirds in North America, they are very difficult to spot because of their cryptic brown and buff coloration and their elusive habits (they sleep most of the day and feed at dawn and dusk). Wilson's snipes winter along Georgia's coast, and the mud flats of Butler Island, where the birds use their long bills to probe for prey, are a favorite habitat. Snipe hunting season (with rifles, not nets!) on other portions of Butler Island runs from late January to the end of February.

MILE 9.2 (0.7 MILE FROM CHAMPNEY ISLAND) (31.338842, -81.438232) Broughton Island. On river right is a half-mile channel connecting to the South Altamaha River that separates Champney Island to the west from Broughton Island to the east. The forest on Broughton visible to the right represents virtually the only high ground on this island of nearly 3,000 acres. As occurred on the neighboring islands, Broughton's marshes were converted to rice fields as early as 1767, when Henry Laurens set enslaved workers to shovel and began diking and ditching the island. A founding father who served as president of the Continental Congress, Laurens was also a partner in the largest slave-trading business in the colonies. After Laurens's death in 1792, William Brailsford took ownership of the island; his foray into rice planting resulted in tragedy when a hurricane blew onshore in 1804, killing 85 of his enslaved laborers.

By the 1830s, the property had come into the hands of Thomas Bryan Forman, the son-in-law of Georgia governor George M. Troup. While Forman re-

123

NEAR BROUGHTON ISLAND, McINTOSH COUNTY

portedly developed Broughton into one of the region's most productive rice plan-tations, visitors to his plantation home, once located on the island's western high ground, were unimpressed. In her book *Journal of a Residence on a Georgian Plantation in 1838–1839*, Fanny Kemble, who visited Forman in 1839, described the house as "ruinous [and] tumble-down," concluding that the "smallest Yankee farmer has a tidier estate, a tidier house, and a tidier wife than this member of the proud Southern chivalry." A generation later, another visitor, Nathaniel H. Bishop, landed on the island in 1875 during his 2,500-mile journey from Quebec to the Gulf of Mexico in a 50-pound canoe. His account, recorded in *Voyage of the Paper Canoe* (published in 1878), suggests that little had changed for the island's now free workforce. The guest of Captain Richard A. Akin, the plantation's "pro-prietor," Bishop found himself "a rather willing captive for several days," during which time he witnessed the workings of the plantation and the "freedmen" who now worked the rice fields for wages, noting that Akin was a "thorough discipli-narian" and that "the negroes . . . stuck to him with greater tenacity than they did to those planters who allowed them to do as they pleased." Rice cultivation on the island continued into the early 1900s. Today, the vast majority of the island is pub-lic land—part of the Altamaha Wildlife Management Area.

MILE 8.4 (1.5 MILES FROM CHAMPNEY ISLAND) (31.337630, -81.423123) Rabbit Island. This 200-acre tidal marsh island in the middle of the Altamaha's main channel is presumptively owned by the state and considered part of the Altamaha Wildlife Management Area. The island's name may be derived from the marsh rab-bits (*Sylvilagus palustris*) that inhabit Georgia's Coastal Plain, being partial to wet bottomlands, swamps, and hammocks. They are the smallest of Georgia's native rabbits and are well adapted to their coastal habitat, being good swimmers. While marsh rabbits may roam the island, hunters more commonly seek out the hogs and ducks that inhabit it. A mile and a half downstream of the tail of Rabbit Island, the main channel of the Altamaha divides around long, narrow Tama Island.

MILE 6.3 (3.6 MILES FROM CHAMPNEY ISLAND) (31.337473, -81.389212) Rhetts Island. On river left is a dock connected to the state-owned Rhetts Island, an 1,800-acre isle that is part of the Altamaha Wildlife Management Area. The public land is accessible, and primitive camping is permitted on the small hammock adjacent to the dock, making this the only place in Altamaha Sound where travelers can legally camp on public land. Like the Altamaha's other islands, Rhetts was once intensively cultivated for rice production. Today, the hydrology of the island is still intensively managed, but for birds. Since the 1990s, Ducks Unlimited has partnered with Georgia's Department of Natural Resources to maintain flood control devices on the island to create three wetland impoundments and provide habitat for waterfowl, shorebirds, and migratory species. Hunting is permitted on Rhetts Island on Wednesdays, Saturdays, Sundays, and state holidays until noon during the state's migratory bird season, which includes specified dates from September through February. Teals, wood ducks, shovelers, ring-necked ducks, and black-bellied whistling ducks are among the common species spotted on Rhetts.

MILE 5.4 (4.5 MILES FROM CHAMPNEY ISLAND) (31.335011, -81.371403) "Bird" Island. In the summer, this unnamed three-acre island traditionally hosts thousands of wading birds. White and glossy ibises, egrets, and little blue, tricolored, and night herons can often be found here in abundance.

SUNSET AT RHETTS ISLAND, McINTOSH COUNTY

125

MILE 1.0 (8.5 MILES FROM CHAMPNEY ISLAND) (31.318155, -81.309359) Egg Island. On river right is the head of this 685-acre island, the last of Altamaha Sound's islands before the river empties into the Atlantic. Egg Island is best known as the birthplace of efforts to protect Georgia's barrier islands. In 1969, the Nature Conservancy spent more than $1 million purchasing Egg, Wassaw, and Wolf Islands to prevent them from being developed like neighboring isles. The leader in that movement was Atlanta's Jane Yarn, who worked to raise the money needed to purchase Egg and Wolf Islands. An unlikely advocate in that era, she was heralded by the *Atlanta Constitution* as the "housewife" who saved an island. She went on to serve on the board of the Nature Conservancy and was instrumental in activating the Garden Club of Georgia for conservation efforts, which the club continues to be involved in today. Her husband, Dr. Charles Yarn, told the *Constitution* in 1969: "I remember she said garden clubs in the state had so much talent which seemed to be wasted on little parks and flower shows. She felt they could do so much and had so much potential." Yarn created the state's first full-time environmental lobbying organization, helped secure passage of the state's Coastal Marshlands Protection Act in 1970, and served in President Jimmy Carter's administration as a member of the White House Council for Environmental Quality. Today, the education center at Tallulah Falls State Park is named in her honor.

Despite Egg Island's location at the very edge of Georgia, where islands are dominated by tidal marshes, about 34 percent of the island is uplands. This characteristic attracted previous generations to inhabit the island—often with tragic consequences. In October 1898, Egg Island resident James Stockley lost his wife during a hurricane. His harrowing tale was recorded in local papers: "A wave came and tore his wife's body from his hands and sent Stockley into a nearby tree. His wife's body floated by him to sea. . . . He spent a night of horror in the tree, and when the water subsided, built a raft and drifted to St. Simons, being several days without food." Undeterred by this tragedy, W. A. Wilcox, a saloon and storekeeper from Darien, began raising horses and cattle on the island in 1899, while also working to harvest oysters from beds surrounding the isle. "Oyster thieves" frustrated the latter effort, and by 1901 he'd tired of the island ranching business, offering the entire island—including a "watchman's house" and "fine flowing artesian well"—and its livestock for sale. Today, the island is part of the Wolf Island National Wildlife Refuge and is off-limits to human visitors. As their names suggest, Egg Island and the associated landmasses of Little Egg Island and Egg Island Bar have historically been an important breeding ground for a host of shore birds, including black skimmers, gull-billed terns, and brown pelicans. Federally threatened red knots and piping plovers are migratory visitors to the island.

MILE 0.8 (9.1 MILES FROM CHAMPNEY ISLAND) (31.315712, -81.300228) Little Egg Island. Some 9,000 breeding pairs of royal terns once nested on this small island that is located due north of Egg Island (and is also part of the Wolf Island National Wildlife Refuge). But over the last several decades, erosion and sea level rise have forced the beach-nesting terns to Egg Island Bar to the east, and then

ROYAL TERNS, McINTOSH COUNTY

still further away, to dredge spoil islands near Savannah and Brunswick. The terns, like other shore birds, need nesting sites above high tides and free of predators (like raccoons). Rising tides associated with sea level rise—and shifting sands caused by major weather events—have thus greatly reduced the number of shorebirds that nest in Altamaha Sound. Today, during high tides, Little Egg Island is completely inundated, with only the tops of the tallest grasses exposed. The dynamic nature of Altamaha Sound is nothing new. In the late 1800s and early 1900s, the shifting sandbars in the sound created a ship graveyard. In 1898, the Portuguese ship *Isabel* was lost here; likewise, in 1907 and 1911 the American barks *Rose Innes* and *Sunbeam* wrecked near here.

MILE 0.0 (10 MILES FROM CHAMPNEY ISLAND) (31.311144, -81.285436) Egg Island Bar. This landmass of about 120 acres offers a lesson in the ever-changing nature of the Georgia coast. Formed in the late 1980s and early 1990s, this bar has, in its short life, proven to be critical habitat for nesting shorebirds and migratory birds. When erosion and sea level rise made Little Egg Island to the west inhospitable for royal terns, the birds shifted to this bar. As recently as 1996, some 9,000 pairs of royal terns and 4,000 pairs of brown pelicans nested here, but even this newly formed bar soon fell victim to the dynamic nature of the Atlantic coast. Since the turn of the century, the island's sandbars have migrated westward toward Egg Island, making it easier for raccoons on that island to access the bar and the shorebird nests it hosts. The result has been an abandonment of Egg Island Bar by colonial nesting birds like royal terns and brown pelicans. Colonial nesters are particularly susceptible to predation because raccoons can easily find and devour the eggs of an entire colony. Though a small colony of brown pelicans was still nesting on the island in 2021, solitary nesters have found better success there (their nests are harder for predators to locate and ravage). Nesting season on the bar peaks from mid-April through July, during which time you'll find oystercatchers and Wilson's plovers tending their young. By state law, only scientific researchers are allowed access to Egg Island Bar.

Off the northwest shore of Egg Island Bar is a small, uninhabited 30-acre island, which the presumptive owners have dubbed "Pelican Brief Island," a nod to the popular 1992 John Grisham novel turned motion picture. McIntosh County native Erik Kauffman assumed "ownership" of the island as a novelty when he began paying property taxes on the land in the early 2000s. While McIntosh County tax records show him as the rightful owner, his claim would not likely stand up in court. Georgia law conveys to the state any island in a navigable river unless a citizen can trace ownership of the island to an original grant from the state or to a king's grant dating from before the Revolutionary War.

## South Altamaha Route

(The following is a description of points of interest along the southernmost route to Altamaha Sound via the South Altamaha River and Buttermilk Sound, with distances given from Two Way Fish Camp.)

MILE 1.5 FROM TWO WAY FISH CAMP (31.319736, -81.439128) Hofwyl-Broadfield Plantation. On river right, Dents Creek, also called New Hope Creek, ascends into this 1,200-acre state historic site, which preserves a circa-1850s plantation home and property. Along the creek and the river itself are numerous canals, the last vestiges of the rice fields that were flooded using an elaborate system of hand-built canals, dikes, and floodgates. Rice was cultivated here for nearly a century beginning in the early 1800s. At the plantation's height in the mid-1800s, more than 370 enslaved persons labored on the property. Originally owned by the Revolutionary War hero General Lachlan McIntosh of Darien, the property was purchased and developed as Broadfield Plantation by William Brailsford in 1806. It remained in the same family until 1973, when the last surviving family member, Ophelia Dent, left the home and property to the Nature Conservancy, which transferred ownership to the state.

Notable stories from the Brailsford-Troup-Dent family include James Dent's decision to screen the porch and windows of the home in 1903, becoming the first local to side with science and acknowledge mosquitoes as the cause of malaria (the link between mosquitoes and malaria wasn't confirmed definitively until the turn of the 20th century). The Dents also were the beneficiaries of their friendship with the wealthy DuPont family, which owned nearby Altama Plantation. In the early 1900s, the DuPonts gifted the sisters Ophelia and Miriam Dent an electric chandelier for their dining room. The sisters graciously accepted it but, preferring candlelight to electric light, never installed it. However, whenever the DuPonts paid a visit, the Dents would reportedly hire an electrician to hook up the chandelier. Hofwyl (pronounced HOF-will) was the name given to the home built by George and Ophelia Troup Dent in the 1850s. It was named after a school in Switzerland that Dent attended as a child. Though it is not accessible from the water, the state historic site, located on U.S. 17 two miles south of the South Altamaha River, is open Tuesday through Sunday. 5556 U.S. 17, Brunswick, Ga. 31525, 912-264-7333.

MILE 4.4 FROM TWO WAY FISH CAMP (31.306931, -81.400304) Broughton Island Sand. On river left on the southernmost tip of Broughton Island is a rare (for Altamaha Sound) sandy shore . . . and it's wholly unnatural. The sand was deposited here during dredging of the Intracoastal Waterway. The spoil spreads over nearly 15 acres of this tip of Broughton Island, which is part of the state-owned Altamaha Wildlife Management Area.

MILE 4.8 FROM TWO WAY FISH CAMP (31.307262, -81.392502) Little St. Simons Island. On river right is the westernmost portion of this barrier island, which is bordered on the south by the Hampton River and St. Simons Island and on the north by Buttermilk and Altamaha Sounds. Little St. Simons spans over 11,000 acres and is home to the Lodge on Little St. Simons Island, a privately operated, upscale eco-lodge accessible only by boat. The island's owners have placed the entire island under a permanent conservation easement with the Nature Conservancy to ensure that the island's wild beauty is preserved. Its protection, like that of Georgia's other coastal barrier islands, is linked to ownership by mostly northern industrialists who sought out the islands as retreats beginning in the late 1800s and early 1900s. The steel baron Carnegies purchased Cumberland Island; department store magnate John Wanamaker took Ossabaw; Life Savers candymaker Edward Noble acquired St. Catherines; and the members of the Jekyll Island Club, which owned Jekyll Island for some sixty years beginning in 1886, included the Vanderbilts, the Rockefellers, and the Morgans. In 1908, the Eagle Pencil Company purchased Little St. Simons Island in hopes of harvesting its trees, but finding the windswept trees too gnarled for pencil production while also falling for the beauty of the isle, company president Philip Berolzheimer purchased the property himself, turning it into a retreat for family and friends. In 1979, in an effort to pay taxes, the Berolzheimer family opened the island to guests, giving birth to the current eco-resort owned by Henry Paulson—a former CEO of Goldman Sachs who served as secretary of the Treasury in President George W. Bush's administration—and his wife, Wendy Paulson. The Paulsons spent nearly $33 million acquiring the property from the Berolzheimers in 2015.

What is now a birder's paradise (more than 280 species have been spotted) was, in the 1800s, far from paradise for those who lived along its marshy fringes. On the northwestern end of the island, near this location in Buttermilk Sound, could be found the slave quarters known as Five Pound Tree, associated with Major Pierce Butler's Hampton Point Plantation on St. Simons Island. Author Malcolm Bell Jr., in his history of the Butler family, *Major Butler's Legacy*, called Five Pound Tree "the Botany Bay of the Butler plantations . . . the home of troublesome, unruly slaves where the scant amenities a slave might expect were scarce indeed."

MILE 5.5 FROM TWO WAY FISH CAMP (31.315480, -81.387132) Buttermilk Sound. In December 1932, a month after Franklin D. Roosevelt had soundly defeated him in the presidential election, President Herbert Hoover embarked on a holiday retreat to the southern coast for fishing, hunting, and relaxation. After a Christmas Day visit to Sapelo Island as the guest of the island's owner, Hudson Motor Company cofounder Howard Coffin (who would be responsible for developing Sea Island into a resort), Hoover spent Christmas night anchored here, in Buttermilk Sound, along what is now part of the Intracoastal Waterway. Prior to the dawn of railroads, Georgia was rarely visited by sitting presidents. Before the Civil War, Georgia hosted only two sitting presidents—George Washington and James Monroe. In the late 1800s and early 1900s, presidential visits became more common, especially on the coast, where the scions of industry and the beauty of the barrier isles attracted the country's most powerful political figures.

SANDBAR IN BUTTERMILK SOUND, McINTOSH COUNTY

MILE 7.2 FROM TWO WAY FISH CAMP (31.318371, -81.359763) Cow Island. This 522-acre island is owned by the state of Georgia, and as the name suggests, cows have been grazed on the island in the past. Raising livestock on Georgia's barrier islands is a practice that goes back to colonial days. The island has also been used as a dredge spoil site by the U.S. Army Corps of Engineers in its maintenance of depths on the Intracoastal Waterway.

MILE 8.8 FROM TWO WAY FISH CAMP (31.314902, -81.333765) Dolbow Island. Immediately southeast of the eastern tip of Cow Island is this 81-acre isle that, along with several smaller islands to the southeast, was owned for years by Joseph Iannicelli, a well-known Jekyll Island resident, businessman, and chemist who, along with several friends, used Dolbow Island as a hunting and fishing getaway. In 2017, Hurricane Irma destroyed the crude bunkhouse on the island's uplands, and within a year of that natural disaster, Iannicelli passed away at the age of 89. A local legend, he held a doctorate in organic chemistry from the Massachusetts Institute of Technology and secured more than 50 U.S. patents while founding the Aquafine Corporation, a company that specializes in water purification systems. In the 1980s, he hatched a plan to revive rice cultivation in the

COW SKULL AND HORSE NETTLE ON COW ISLAND, McINTOSH COUNTY

salt marsh, but his ideas were met with opposition from the Georgia Department of Natural Resources, which denied his applications to ditch and dike his marshland. Undaunted, Iannicelli sought relief from the General Assembly, but there, too, his effort to exempt agricultural projects from the state's marshland protection rules failed to gain traction. At age 80, he famously chose jail time rather than pay court-ordered alimony to a former wife. His then current wife ultimately paid the $68,000 bill to spring him from his self-imposed imprisonment. Dolbow is also known for a herd of goats that mysteriously appeared on the island; it is uncertain how long they will survive in a harsh environment subject to major weather events.

# OHOOPEE

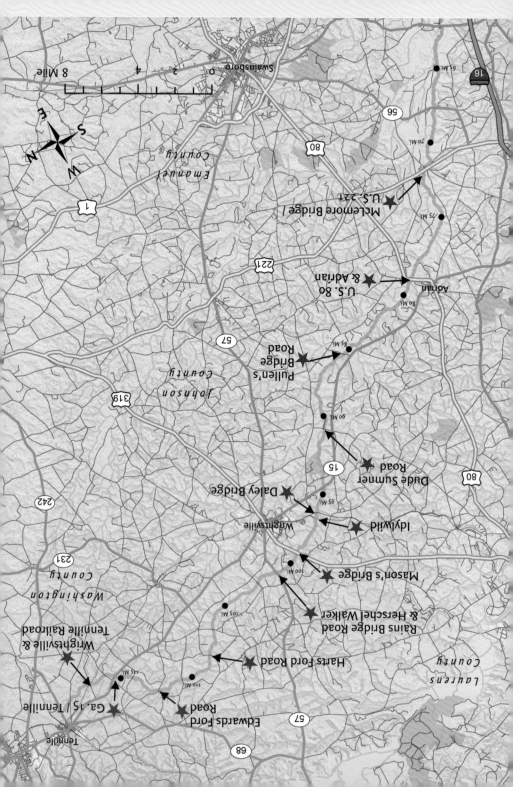

# Headwaters

**Length** 45 miles (Headwaters to Ga. 56)

**Class** Unnavigable (foot, bike, vehicle travel only)

**Time** Not applicable

**Minimum Level** Not applicable

**River Gauge** The nearest river gauge is located at Ga. 297 south of Swainsboro: https://waterdata.usgs.gov/ga/nwis/uv?02225270.

**Trailhead** The upper reaches of the Ohoopee River, from its headwaters east of Tennille to Ga. 297, are unnavigable, and because the full length of this section flows through private land, foot travel is prohibited without permission from landowners. Thus it is best explored from public roads, via bicycle or motorized transportation.

**DIRECTIONS to Headwaters** The Ohoopee first becomes distinguishable as a small stream along Grady Mertz Road, southeast of Tennille. From the intersection of Main Street and South 4th Street (Ga. 15) in Tennille, travel south on Ga. 15 0.4 mile. Turn left onto East 3rd Avenue and proceed 0.1 mile. Stay to the right and continue on East 3rd Avenue for another 1.1 miles (East 3rd Ave. becomes Grady Mertz Rd.). The Ohoopee flows from a clearing on the north side of the road, travels through a culvert beneath the road, and then continues on the south side of the road.

**DIRECTIONS to Ga. 56 (Launch Site for Next Section)** From Exit 78 (U.S. 221) on I-16, travel north on U.S. 221 1.7 miles. Turn right onto Ga. 56 and travel 3.1 miles to the river.

## Points of Interest

**MILE 116.9 (32.906252, -82.781422) Wrightsville & Tennille Railroad.** This railroad, which crosses Stephens Road just west of where the Ohoopee passes beneath the same road, dates to 1886, when the 17-mile track from Tennille to Wrightsville was completed. By 1899, the railroad ran west all the way to Hawkinsville on the Ocmulgee River. In 1932, the 75-mile ride from Tennille to Hawkinsville, with 24 stops, took four hours to complete. The line was known as the "Wiggle and Twist" because of its meandering route.

**MILE 115.3 (32.887097, -82.785796) Ga. 15 / Tennille.** From this Ohoopee River bridge, it's nearly four miles north to the town of Tennille (pronounced ten-NIL) and less than a mile south to the town's famous "UGA Football Barn Sign." Tennille, incorporated in 1875, is a town that grew up around the Central of Georgia Railroad, which was completed in 1843. By the end of the 19th century, two other

UGA FOOTBALL BARN SIGN, WASHINGTON COUNTY

railroads converged on Tennille, and those roads still course through its downtown and remain an important part of the local economy. As a railroad town, Tennille suffered greatly during the Civil War when Union general William Sherman marched his army from Atlanta to Savannah. On November 26, 1864, Union troops set fire to the town's depot, water tank, and other rail facilities while destroying four miles of nearby track. Today, Tennille might be best known as the home of the UGA Football Barn Sign. In 2000, locals Ross Smith and James and Jonathan Hitchcock painted the side of a former general store with a message about their beloved University of Georgia football team. Since then, new messages have appeared regularly on the barn, and over the course of two decades it has become a point of community pride. In 2012, when the roof of the structure collapsed, Georgia football fans contributed funds to rebuild the landmark, and a local building supply store offered discounted supplies. Following the team's national championship victory in January 2022, the friends posted an announcement on social media: "Finally . . . after 21 years and 47 messages . . . ," accompanied by a photograph of the barn emblazoned with the message "2021 National Champions."

MILE 111.9 (32.859471, -82.814222) Edwards Ford Road.

MILE 108.0 (32.811244, -82.806218) Harts Ford Road.

MILE 100.9 (32.736931, -82.764360) Rains Bridge Road & Herschel Walker. Ga. 57 crosses the river here, over what was known as Rains Bridge in the early 1900s, and continues for two miles into Wrightsville, the hometown of Herschel Walker, a Heisman Trophy–winning running back with the University of Georgia who, as a freshman during the 1980–1981 season, led the school's football team to the national championship. As a senior at Johnson County High School in 1979, Walker was among the most sought-after recruits in the nation, and the intense battle to win his services reached its climax on an Ohoopee River bridge just outside of town. By February 1980, the recruiting war had come down to Clemson University and Georgia, but by that time, Walker's father had tired of the persistence of one Clemson booster and told Mike Cavan, Georgia's recruiter, "I'm fixing to shoot the guy from Clemson down on the Ohoopee River Bridge." Cavan followed the elder Walker to the bridge to witness the confrontation and later described the encounter to the *Atlanta Constitution* in 1988: "I noticed that everybody on the bridge had a gun except me and the other coaches. Mr. Walker started yelling at this Clemson booster: 'I don't want you talking to my son. Don't bother him anymore.' The whole time he's . . . walking around this Clemson booster in circles. By this time I'd picked out a spot in the river where I would jump when people started pulling the guns. I figured if I didn't break my neck jumping I'd be all right. At least I wouldn't get shot. Finally, Mr. Walker stopped and looked that guy square in the eye and said, 'Now this is the last time. If you do it again I'll kill you.'" And thus a confrontation over the Ohoopee River led to the state university landing one of its most famous student-athletes.

MILE 99.4 (32.716534, -82.755143) Mason's Bridge. Turner Mason settled in this area in the early 1800s, and into the 20th century, the bridge bore the Mason name. A freshwater spring here is also known as Mason Spring, and for a portion of Johnson County's history it was a popular gathering place and swimming hole. This river crossing has witnessed both humorous and tragic chapters over the years. The current bridge, dating to 1962, carries U.S. 319, which leads two miles northeast to Wrightsville, Johnson County's seat of government. According to local historian Scott Thompson, when local leaders met to determine the site of the county courthouse in 1858, they agreed that whoever donated the most money to the establishment of the local government would have naming rights for the county seat. A man named William P. Hicks offered to donate his property for the courthouse near Mason's Bridge, but John B. Wright chipped in with a $1,000 cash donation. Thus, perhaps to the relief of today's residents, Wrightsville won out over Hicksville. On May 15, 1919, the bridge was the scene of a horrific incident, when a mob of some 150 men blocked the road at the bridge to intercept a sheriff's deputy as he transported Jim Waters, a local Black man accused of assaulting a white girl. The mob asked the deputy to turn over the prisoner and turn his vehicle around. He did so, later telling investigators that he did not know any of the men who abducted Waters. The lynchers tied Waters to a tree outside the nearby African American Aikins Chapel Church and then shot and killed him, riddling his body with bullets. *The Crisis*, the official magazine of the NAACP, published an eyewitness account of the lynching in 1920: "Just about all the white mens in town was out there[,] hardly no clerks in the stores. Automobiles full and after the lynching little white children all over town playing with the empty shells from the pistols that done the lynching."

MILE 96.4 (32.691245, -82.735739) Idylwild. Just north of this spot on the river was the well-known Idylwild resort. Built by the Wrightsville and Tennille Railroad in the 1890s—undoubtedly to encourage riders on their trains—it served for years as a popular gathering place and swimming hole. In addition to taking a dip in the swimming area created by diverting water from the river, visitors could enjoy basketball, baseball, skating, dancing, and even golf. In its heyday, Idylwild hosted everything from Sunday school picnics to Masonic gatherings and even political rallies. In 1908, Thomas Watson, as the Populist Party's candidate for president, spoke at the resort. Idylwild was subsequently purchased by the Mount Vernon Baptist Association and later by Woodmen of the World. The pavilion still stands on the property and is visible from Idylwild Road.

MILE 96.1 (32.689117, -82.731046) Daley Bridge. Early 20th-century maps designate this crossing of the Ohoopee as Daley Bridge, a nod to the prominent Daley family of early Johnson County history. Alexander W. Daley moved to this area in the mid-1800s, but it was his son Alexander F. Daley who most left his mark on the county. A. F. Daley, an attorney, represented the area in the state senate, was elected to a local superior court judgeship, and helped establish the Exchange Bank of Wrightsville (now the Community Bank of Johnson County); however, he is best known for his leadership in building the Wrightsville and Tennille Railroad, which once spanned the river 0.3 mile upstream from this bridge. In 1904, in his duties as superior court judge, Daley was witness to a familiar travesty of justice during that era. After two Black men were lynched in Statesboro, he charged a local grand jury with bringing indictments against those suspected in the lynching. The grand jury, however, found insufficient evidence and brought no indictments. According to newspaper accounts, in discharging the jury, Daley indicated his "disappointment and disapproval."

MILE 90.8 (32.656320, -82.665555) Dude Sumner Road. This road bears the name of E. J. "Dude" Sumner (1874–1947), a prominent citizen around the turn of the twentieth century who ran a general store, turpentine still, sawmill, and cotton gin nearby. When the Georgia General Assembly created a county commission to govern Johnson County in 1902, it appointed Sumner among the county's initial three commissioners. Sumner's descendants continue to play a role in the community. William Sumner, the proprietor of MidWay Straw Company, gained notoriety in 2019 when he and his employees created a mammoth American flag from

RIVER BIRCH NEAR DUDE SUMNER ROAD, JOHNSON COUNTY

65 round hay bales. Stacked in the company's pole barn facing U.S. 319 west of Wrightsville, the unique flag has become a local landmark. Said Sumner after several years of displaying the flag: "I'd probably be kicked out of the county if I didn't paint it every year." The bridge spanning the river here has been known since the 1800s as Snells Bridge. Christopher Snell migrated to this part of Georgia in 1789. His grandson, James Christopher Snell, a Confederate war veteran, served as justice of the peace and as a state representative from the area in 1898–1899.

MILE 85.5 (32.617626, -82.612249) Pullen's Bridge Road. Historically a popular swimming hole, in 1895 this spot was the site of a grisly discovery when fisherman seining the river pulled up the body of Carrie Padgett. The *Savannah Morning News* reported on the apparent murder: "The men found her hands and feet bound securely by strong ropes and attached to the body was a huge rock. . . . The supposition is that several women residing in the neighborhood[,] assisted by some men, carried the girl to the river and pushed her in." The motive for the execution, according to the newspaper account, was the woman's affair with a local married man. Her sister, Ellen Padgett, was also missing according to news accounts, and a similar fate was feared for her, though her body was never found.

MILE 79.1 (32.545157, -82.577337) U.S. 80 & Adrian. One of the Ohoopee's oldest bridges, the span here dates to 1932 and is named for William H. Brantley Jr., a Department of Transportation employee who died in an accident while working on the bridge in 1982. A bridge has spanned the river here since the late 1800s, when the town of Adrian was experiencing tremendous growth. In 1899, a *Macon*

WILLIAM H. BRANTLEY JR. BRIDGE, EMANUEL COUNTY

*Telegraph* correspondent described the original wooden bridge as "1,780 feet long with "a dividing rail all the way through the middle, so that two teams can go over the bridge abreast. It is said to be the longest double bridge in the state, and it is another monument to the liberality and progressive spirit of Capt. James." In its early years, Adrian was the fiefdom of Captain T. J. James, the builder in the early 1890s of the Wadley Southern Railway, a short road that lived and died with the harvesting of the region's vast longleaf pine forests and the tapping of trees for rosin and turpentine. In 1890, not much other than the railroad existed in what is now Adrian, but within ten years, it was an incorporated town of 1,200 people with twenty-two stores, two churches, schools, and, as our *Macon Telegraph* correspondent described it, "an agreeable social life." Captain James operated a large sawmill in town, along with a grist mill, a rice mill, a cotton gin, and a syrup mill, while also cultivating thousands of nearby acres in sugarcane, sweet potatoes, tobacco, and rice, as well as staples such as corn and oats. His business, however, was built on the peculiar Reconstruction-era practice of leasing state convicts. Around 70 convicts worked the sawmill in Adrian, and James's railroad construction projects depended heavily on convict labor. Now often referred to as "slavery by another name," the state's convict lease system consisted mostly of Black prisoners and was criticized at the time by progressives, who saw it as a threat to "free labor" and as an institution that in practice was often more oppressive than slavery. The convict lease system was eventually abandoned in 1908 following outcry over abuses of the imprisoned workers.

When the timber played out, so too did the towns along the Wadley Southern; by the 1920s the road had ceased operation, and today you'll find no tracks in the town that rails originally built. The still-incorporated town is unusual in that the county line between Johnson and Emanuel Counties zigzags through the middle of town. This anomaly can be traced to an 1800s-era feud between Burrel Kea and Joe Hutcheson over where a bridge over the Ohoopee River would be built. Each man wanted it built on his own property, but Kea, a leader in Emanuel County, prevailed. Hutcheson, expressing his earnest desire not to live in the same county as Kea, petitioned the General Assembly to remove his property from Emanuel County. The legislature complied, resulting in perhaps the most bizarre county line in Georgia.

RIVERSIDE GROWTH, JOHNSON COUNTY

MILE 72.5 (32.499782, -82.493491) McLemore Bridge / U.S. 221. A bridge has spanned the river here since the 1820s. In 1827, the Georgia General Assembly authorized Howell McLemore to establish a toll bridge over the river at this spot. The act further set the tolls that McLemore could charge for the use of the bridge: 44 cents for a four-wheeled wagon, 19 cents for a two-wheeled cart, 6 cents for each horse and rider, 2 cents for each head of cattle, and 1 cent apiece for each hog, sheep, or goat. McLemore, in addition to building what was perhaps the first bridge across the river in Emanuel County, also established the county's first post office . . . largely so he could have a newspaper delivered to his doorstep. Reported the *Savannah Morning News* in 1878: "The first citizen of Emanuel County to subscribe for a newspaper was Mr. Howell McLemore. . . . There was then not a post office in Emanuel, and Mr. McLemore's nearest office was Dublin . . . 25 miles distant, and to this office was the paper sent. Mr. McLemore sometime afterwards succeeded in having a post office established at his place of residence which was on the stage line from Dublin to Savannah." The bridge that presently spans the river dates to 1998.

141

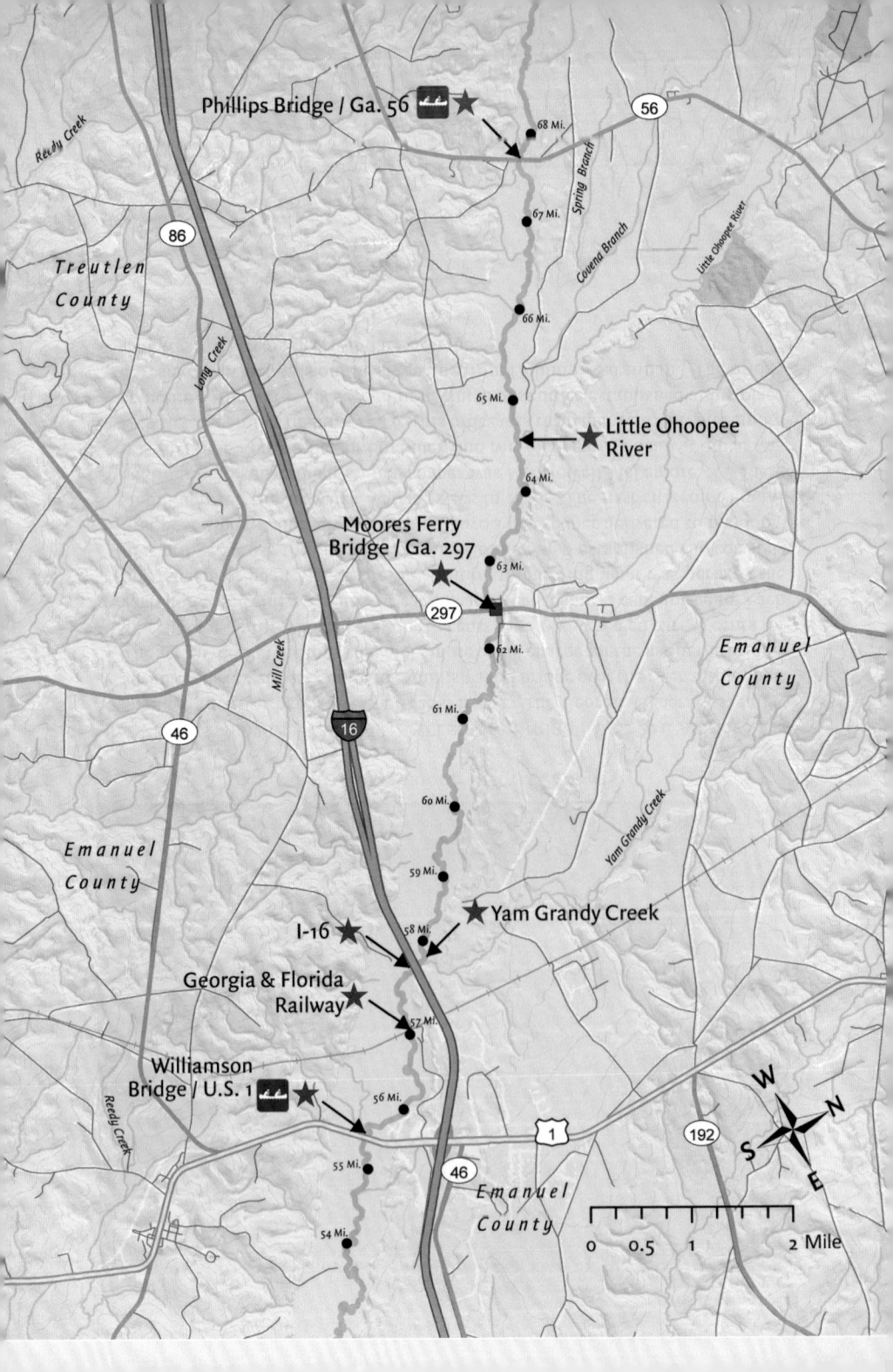

Phillips Bridge / Ga. 56

86

Treutlen
County

68 Mi.

56

67 Mi.

66 Mi.

65 Mi.

Little Ohoopee
River

64 Mi.

Moores Ferry
Bridge / Ga. 297

297

63 Mi.

62 Mi.

Emanuel
County

46

16

61 Mi.

60 Mi.

Emanuel
County

59 Mi.

Yam Grandy Creek

I-16

58 Mi.

Georgia & Florida
Railway

57 Mi.

Williamson
Bridge / U.S. 1

56 Mi.

1

192

W
N
S
E

55 Mi.

46

Emanuel
County

0    0.5    1          2 Mile

54 Mi.

Reedy Creek

Long Creek

Mill Creek

Reedy Creek

Spring Branch

Covena Branch

Little Ohoopee River

Yam Grandy Creek

# Yam Grandy

**Length**   11 miles (Ga. 56 to U.S. 1)

**Class**   Flatwater/I

**Minimum Level**   A gauge height of at least 10 feet and flows of 250 cubic feet per second (cfs) at the Ga. 297 gauge are needed to render this section navigable. Cross-river strainers can be expected at all water levels, but especially at lower water levels.

**River Gauge**   The nearest river gauge is located at Ga. 297, 5 miles downstream from the launch site for this section: https://waterdata.usgs.gov/ga/nwis/uv?02225270.

**Launch Site**   There is no developed access point at this launch site, but the river can be accessed via the right-of-way on the north and upstream side of the bridge.

DIRECTIONS   From Exit 78 (U.S. 221) on I-16, travel north on U.S. 221 1.7 miles. Turn right onto Ga. 56 and travel 3.1 miles to the river.

**Take Out Site**   The take out site is located on river right beneath the U.S. 1 bridge, with unpaved access and limited parking.

DIRECTIONS   From the Ga. 56 bridge, travel south 1.2 miles. Turn left onto Holton Chapel Road and proceed 4.2 miles. Bear hard to the left, continuing on Holton Chapel Road 0.9 mile. Turn right onto Ga. 297 and proceed 1 mile to I-16. Take the eastbound ramp and proceed 5 miles to Exit 90 (U.S. 1). Take the exit ramp, turn right onto U.S. 1, and proceed 0.8 mile to the bridge. The entrance to the river access is on the right, immediately south of the bridge.

NEAR MOORES FERRY BRIDGE, EMANUEL COUNTY

Alternative Take Out Site    It is possible to take out at Ga. 297 to create a 5-mile journey. There is no developed access point at this location, but the river can be accessed via the right-of-way on the north and downstream side of the bridge.

DIRECTIONS    From the Ga. 56 bridge, travel south 1.2 miles. Turn left onto Holton Chapel Road and proceed 4.2 miles. Bear hard to the left, continuing on Holton Chapel Road 0.9 mile. Turn left onto Ga. 297 and proceed 0.8 mile to the river.

Description    This section stretches the upper limits of the Ohoopee's navigability and is best attempted at water levels above 11 feet and flows above 400 cfs at the Ga. 297 gauge. At these levels, the river begins to leave its banks, opening up the low-lying and scenic floodplain to exploration. Though the river passes beneath I-16 and is occasionally fronted by riverside fish camps and cabins along this route, it maintains a remote and wild feel. At all water levels, expect frequent strainers, some of which may block the river's path, requiring portages.

## Points of Interest

MILE 67.8 (32.471031, -82.446747) Phillips Bridge / Ga. 56. Where Ga. 56 crosses the river is the haunt of the Phillips family. Mark Phillips, a Revolutionary War veteran, moved to the area in the early 1800s. He died in 1812, but by the early 1900s, his progeny populated much of the land south of the river here between what is now Ga. 56 and Ga. 297. The cemetery at Boiling Springs Baptist Church, located approximately 4 miles south of the bridge, is the final resting place for more than 200 Phillips family members. Immediately north of the bridge is Palm Beach Island, a privately owned spring-fed swimming destination open to the public during the spring and summer. The facility features a water slide, diving boards, beach, concession area, and pavilion. 2970 Ga. 56, Soperton, Ga. 30457, 912-562-3643.

MILE 64.5 (32.453502, -82.405071) Little Ohoopee River. On river left, this major tributary joins the Ohoopee's flow, improving the river's navigability. Downstream from this confluence, the river widens and at higher flows becomes more suitable for canoes, kayaks, and small motorized vessels. Though the Ohoopee (or Great Ohoopee, as it has historically been called) and Little Ohoopee take divergent paths to this one spot, they both rise within 3 miles of one another southeast of Tennille. Some 14 miles upstream along the Little Ohoopee, near Swainsboro, is the state-owned Ohoopee Dunes Wildlife Management Area and the Nature Conservancy's Ohoopee Dunes Preserve. The sand dunes were created between 15,000 and 30,000 years ago when westerly winds transported sands exposed on river bars onto the north and northeast banks of rivers and streams. The Ohoopee Dunes parallel the Little Ohoopee and Ohoopee Rivers for more than 35 miles, and in places the sand deposits are 70 feet deep. The quartz-based sand holds few nutrients and drains quickly, and thus it harbors unusual, elfin-like forests of oaks and pines. But the habitat also hosts many unique species, such as sandhill rosemary, woody goldenrod, and scarlet wild basil.

MILE 62.4 (32.440619, -82.381913) Moores Ferry Bridge / Ga. 297. James L. Moore, a soldier in the Revolutionary War, received nearly 300 acres of land along the Ohoopee River for his service and became one of the earliest settlers of what is now Emanuel County. According to Lucian Lamar Knight in *A Standard History of Georgia and Georgians,* Moore "became one of the most prosperous planters and largest slaveholders in this part of the state, and at one time was said to be the principal stock raiser of the community."

MILE 57.5 (32.408737, -82.335264) Yam Grandy Creek. This tributary, which drains much of Emanuel County, including large portions of Swainsboro, joins on river left immediately upstream of the I-16 bridge. It is the receptacle for the treated wastewater of Swainsboro residents. The Yam Grandy Creek Water Pollution Control Plant, regulated by the Georgia Environmental Protection Division, is permitted to discharge up to 3 million gallons of treated sewage into the creek daily. It is one of five sewage treatment plants in the Ohoopee River basin that discharge directly into the Ohoopee or one of its tributaries.

Swainsboro was the hometown of Larry Jon Wilson, a noted country-folk-blues singer-songwriter who cut four albums in the 1970s. Among his compositions was the tune "Ohoopee River Bottomland," an ode to the musician's homeland that begins: "This low rent land has turned to sand, and I done stood 'bout all I can, I'm leaving." Of course, the song ends with the wayward troubadour learning that pastures were, in fact, greener along his beloved Ohoopee River bottomlands.

I-16 BRIDGE, EMANUEL COUNTY

MILE 57.4 (32.408063, -82.334978) I-16. This 167-mile freeway runs from Macon to Savannah and along the way spans five major rivers, which can be memorized using the mnemonic COOOO—Canoochee, Ogeechee, Ohoopee, Oconee, and Ocmulgee. The highway was constructed between 1972 and 1978, and in 2003 the Georgia General Assembly named the road "Jim Gillis Historic Savannah Parkway" in honor of James L. Gillis, a former state senator and the first highway commissioner for the state of Georgia. Gillis's sons, Jim Jr. and Hugh, both served in the state legislature. Hugh was the longest-tenured member of the legislature when he retired in 2004, having served as a representative or senator from Soperton, with only a few interruptions, since 1941. In his farewell address at age 85, he told his fellow senators, "I'm going to miss you, but it's time to go fishing." In 2015, an average of 21,700 vehicles crossed these bridges daily, including many tractor trailers bound to and from the Port of Savannah.

MILE 57.0 (32.403710, -82.326393) Georgia & Florida Railway. A railroad has crossed the river here since the first decade of the 20th century, when the Georgia & Florida Railway was created by connecting existing rails with new construction such as this line. Once completed around 1911, the Georgia & Florida ran from Madison, Florida, to Augusta, and beyond into South Carolina. In 1927, the ride from Augusta to Valdosta was a nearly seven-hour proposition. The line is still in use today as the state-owned Heart of Georgia, or HOG, Railroad, which Genesee & Wyoming leases. It is part of the state's 4,600-mile rail system.

MILE 55.5 (32.391431, -82.313683) Williamson Bridge / U.S. 1. The U.S. 1 bridge that spans the river here was known as Williamson Bridge during the first century of Emanuel County's existence. Lemuel Williamson and his family set-

tled in this area in the early 1800s, and by the mid-1800s, one of his sons, Solomon Williamson, owned some 5,000 acres in the Oak Park area. Aside from the family name being associated with the bridge, parts of the family history are tragically linked to the Ohoopee River and the wildlife of the area. In the winter of 1857, William "Bill" Williamson died of hypothermia after attempting to swim across the river. Family history holds that he was impatient for the ferry and didn't wish to wait. He left behind four children under the age of 17, including John G. Williamson. In 1891, tragedy would strike John G.'s family when his 11-year-old son, Ira, died after being bitten by a rattlesnake. Rattlesnakes were—and still are—ubiquitous in South Georgia. Just four years prior to Ira's death, the *Savannah Morning News* reported that an F. M. Murray, while on his way to Williamson Bridge, had spotted a rattlesnake and followed it to a gopher tortoise burrow. Enlisting the help of a friend, the paper reported, Murray then killed 17 large rattlesnakes. Though the populations of both timber and eastern diamondback rattlesnakes have declined due to habitat loss and indiscriminate killing, they are still found throughout Georgia's Coastal Plain. On occasion, they can be seen on rivers. They are adept at swimming and when necessary will take to water. In fact, their internal organs include a bladder-like prolongation that they can fill with air, increasing their buoyancy. Thus "inflated," a rattlesnake can slither across the surface of the water.

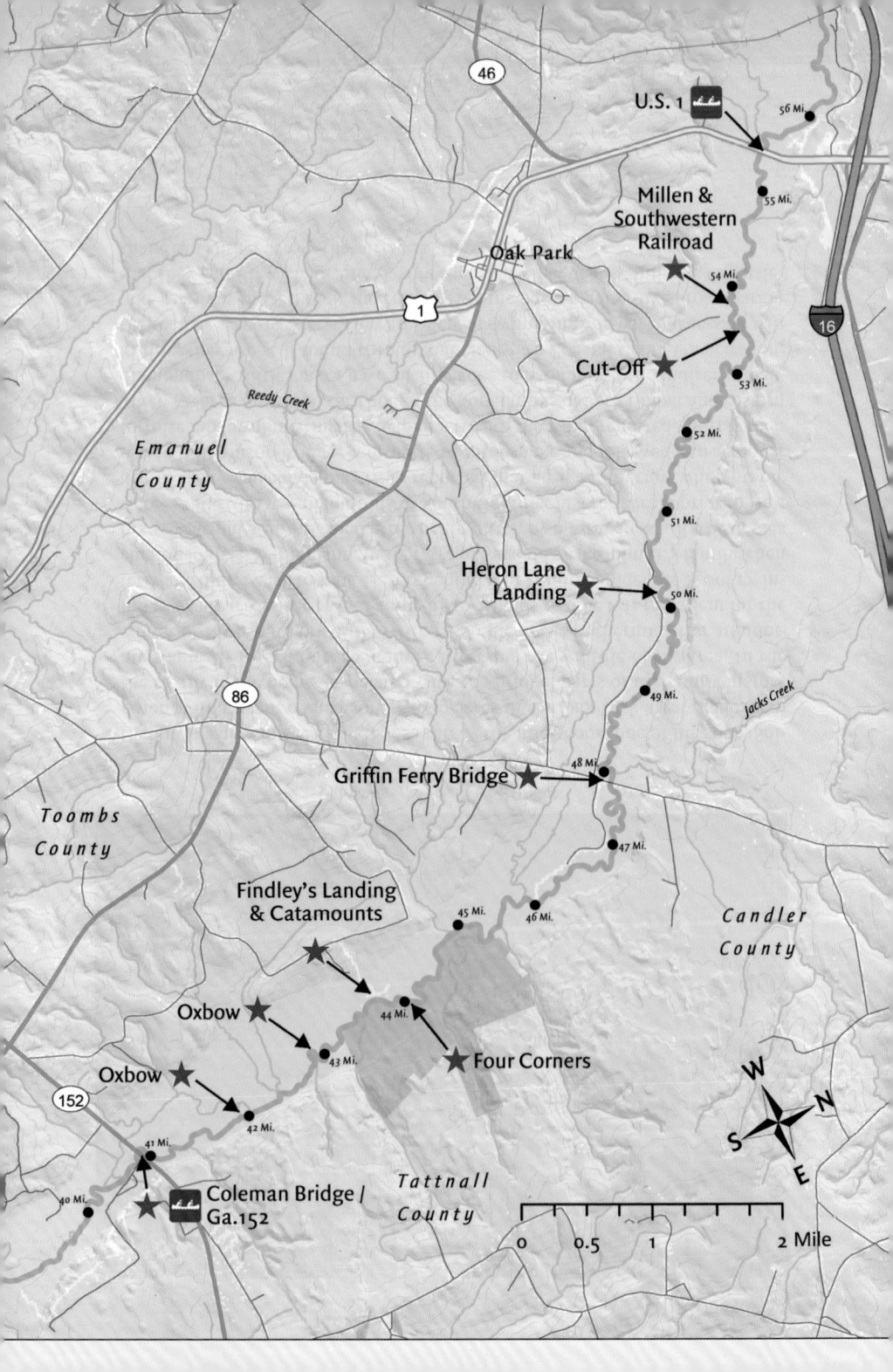

46

U.S. 1

56 Mi.

Millen &
Southwestern
Railroad

55 Mi.

Oak Park

54 Mi.

Cut-Off

53 Mi.

1

16

52 Mi.

Reedy Creek

51 Mi.

Emanuel
County

Heron Lane
Landing

50 Mi.

49 Mi.

Jacks Creek

86

Griffin Ferry Bridge

48 Mi.

47 Mi.

Toombs
County

Findley's Landing
& Catamounts

45 Mi.

46 Mi.

Candler
County

Oxbow

44 Mi.

Four Corners

Oxbow

43 Mi.

152

42 Mi.

41 Mi.

40 Mi.

Coleman Bridge /
Ga.152

Tattnall
County

W

N

S

E

0    0.5    1    2 Mile

# Griffin Ferry

**Length**   15 miles (U.S. 1 to Ga. 152 / New Cobbtown Road)

**Class**   Flatwater/I

**Minimum Level**   A gauge height of at least 10 feet and flows of 250 cubic feet per second (cfs) at the Ga. 297 gauge are recommended. Cross-river strainers may be encountered, especially at lower water levels.

---

**River Gauge**   The nearest river gauge is located at Ga. 297, 6 miles upstream from the launch site for this section: https://waterdata.usgs.gov/ga/nwis/uv?02225270.

**Launch Site**   The launch site is located on the south and upstream side of the U.S. 1 bridge and features an unpaved access and limited parking.

DIRECTIONS   From Exit 90 (U.S. 1) on I-16, travel south on U.S. 1, cross the bridge at 0.9 mile, and turn right onto the access road leading to the river.

**Take Out Site**   The take out site is located on river left along a large sandbar beneath the Ga. 152/New Cobbtown Road bridge. The site features unpaved access to the sandbar and limited parking.

DIRECTIONS   From the U.S. 1 bridge, travel south on U.S. 1 1.6 miles. Turn left onto Harrington Street (Ga. 86) toward Oak Park and travel 1.2 miles through Oak Park. Bear left on Ga. 86 and proceed 6.9 miles. Turn left onto Ga. 152 and proceed 1.4 miles. After crossing over the river, turn left onto the access road leading to the river.

**Alternative Take Out Site**   It is possible to take out at Griffin Ferry Road to create a 6-mile trip. However, there is no developed access point at this location; the river can be accessed only along the right-of-way.

DIRECTIONS   From the U.S. 1 bridge, travel south on U.S. 1 1.6 miles. Turn left onto Harrington Road (Ga. 86) toward Oak Park and travel 1.2 miles through Oak Park. Bear left on Ga. 86 and proceed 3.7 miles. Turn left onto Griffin Ferry Road and proceed 3 miles to the river.

BROWN WATER SNAKE WITH FISH, EMANUEL COUNTY

149

**Description**   This 15-mile run winds through the Ohoopee's wide bottomland forest. At high water levels, the river spreads into these bottomlands, providing off-the-main-channel exploration. At lower water levels, the river features numerous sandbars along its very sinuous route. Cut-offs and oxbow lakes are numerous. Though the route is wild and remote, clusters of riverside fish camps, cabins, and homes crowd the riverbanks in places. The river widens, but cross-river strainers can still be expected, with some requiring portages.

## Points of Interest

MILE 53.8 (32.381948, -82.296933) Millen & Southwestern Railroad. Near this location, between the late 1800s and 1930, the short-lived Millen & Southwestern Railroad spanned the Ohoopee, running 42 miles between Millen to the northeast and Vidalia to the southwest. Georgia's railroads reached their zenith in the 1920s, when more than 7,000 miles of railroads crisscrossed the state. The dawn of automobiles and better roads, coupled with the exhaustion of the longleaf pine forests of South Georgia (many railroads were built to haul lumber and naval stores), led to a steady loss of trackage. The Millen & Southwestern, after becoming part of the Georgia & Florida Railway, was abandoned in 1930. Today, Georgia boasts about 4,600 miles of rail.

MILE 53.5 (32.381438, -82.293918) Cut-Off. Here the river has cut a new path, beginning the process of isolating an oxbow to the northwest. The Ohoopee is a very sinuous river and is regularly changing its course through this section, carving more direct paths downstream and forever creating oxbow sloughs and lakes. Over the next mile, there are no fewer than three cut-offs. The straightline distance from U.S. 1 to Griffin Ferry Road is a little more than 4 miles, but the river's course between those two points is almost twice that distance. Two miles southwest of this location is the city of Oak Park, population 647. Incorporated in 1929, it made national headlines in 1934 when its citizens elected an all-female town council. When Oak Park's mayor, H. H. Strange, declined to seek reelection and no one stepped forward to fill the void, some of the town's men decided to enter a slate of women on the ballot. United Press International reported on what happened: "As the women came to town to do their shopping, they were asked whether they would be candidates. They were amused, and consented. One woman, however, didn't get to town that day and she didn't know she was a candidate until the day of the election." The election was accompanied by a fire at the jail and dynamite explosions that damaged several buildings, but the town's chief of police reported that there was no connection between the violence and the election. In 2022, two of the five seats on the Oak Park city council were occupied by women.

MILE 50.2 (32.361513, -82.267128) Heron Lane Landing. On river right is a private landing at the end of Heron Lane, a dirt road that parallels the river downstream for more than a mile, to Griffin Ferry Road. On the downstream side of

Griffin Ferry Road, another road, Egret Place, parallels the river for about a mile. Thus, over the next four miles there are numerous fish camps, cabins, trailers, and homes along the south bank of the river, though some have succumbed to the ravages of the river. All of these structures lie within what is known as the floodplain, that area that has a 1 percent chance of experiencing a severe flood in any given year, or the 100-year flood. Since the passage of the National Flood Insurance Act in 1968 and of subsequent related legislation, residents in such areas are required to purchase flood insurance. The 1968 legislation was passed because private insurers by and large refused to offer insurance for structures in such areas, thus escalating the costs of federal disaster relief following major flood events.

ALONG HERON LANE, EMANUEL COUNTY

While providing federally backed insurance to property owners, the law also requires local governments to adopt regulations intended to reduce future flood damage. Those regulations and the desire to get more favorable insurance premiums drive property owners to elevate their structures on stilts, as commonly seen in riverfront homes. Since 2000, more frequent flood events have put a strain on the federal program, with the costs of damage repair and replacement exceeding revenues from premiums. Increasingly, this has led to the federal government purchasing repeatedly flooded properties to permanently remove the risk . . . and the cost to taxpayers.

MILE 47.8 (32.348308, -82.247794) Griffin Ferry Bridge. Since the 1800s, when the Griffin family began operating a ferry here, this location has been an important river crossing. The current bridge, which dates to 1979 and spans more than 500 feet across the river, is, according to historic reports, a vast improvement over some of the original bridges. Accounts recorded by the Emanuel County Historical Society describe the original Griffin Ferry Bridge as a makeshift structure built of "mud, sticks, boards, and locally made bricks." Later wooden versions were notorious for loose boards that travelers were expected to return to their proper place after crossing.

MILE 44.1 (32.318877, -82.232937) Four Corners. At this spot on the river, the four counties of Emanuel, Candler, Toombs, and Tattnall converge. Tattnall County was created first, in 1801, and was followed by Emanuel in 1812, Toombs in 1905, and Candler in 1914. Only Texas, with 254 counties, has more county seats than

151

BEAVER CHEW, CANDLER COUNTY

Georgia's 159. Candler County, which borders the river for about four miles, lob-bied the state legislature for 10 years before finally gaining its independence. The driving force behind the movement was to bring development and improved roads to remote sections of Emanuel, Tattnall, and Bulloch Counties, from which Candler was drawn. It also provided Candler County voters with more power, thanks to the county unit voting system. At that time, statewide Georgia primaries were decided by which candidate secured the most votes in individual counties, rather than by the popular vote. This system gave rural voters outsized influence over statewide elections, diminishing the voting power of residents of urban counties. In 1945, the Georgia Constitution capped the number of coun-ties at 159. In 1962, under the direction of state and federal courts, Georgia did away with the county unit voting system.

MILE 43.7 (32.314945, -82.235388) Findley's Landing & Catamounts. On river right here is a clearing that marks the spot of this historic landing. The Findley family's roots in this area date back to the early 1800s, with branches of the fam-ily tree running on both the Tattnall and Toombs sides of the river. In 1914, an E. Findley made headlines in the *Tattnall Journal* when he brought to the newspa-per office the "forepaw of a large catamount" that he had killed in the Ohoopee River swamp near Collins (11 miles southwest of this location). This was the last account in local newspapers of catamounts, or cougars, in the area. In 1905, a cougar was killed in nearby Bulloch County, which prompted the editors of the *Tattnall Journal* to recount two prior cougar incidents: in 1872, a cougar weighing 144 pounds and measuring nine and a half feet in length was killed by Dr. F. M. Alexander and J. B. Smith near the Ohoopee, and in 1887, after much livestock was killed by a large predator in the eastern part of Tattnall County, a hunting party of 51 men and 23 dogs tracked down and killed four cougars. Less than four years later, Tattnall County surveyor Josiah Kennedy was attacked by a cougar near the river. His encounter was reported in riveting detail in the *Savannah Morning News*: "His attention was attracted by a screaming noise as it made its leap. It was fought back with the buggy whip. . . . As it made its second attempt, it was met by the surveyor's staff, which he broke over it. At this juncture his animal [horse] became frightened, threw Kennedy out behind the buggy, and then a general engagement took place; the broken staff was shifted, and the ball and socket was used to perfection until its brains were knocked out. The cat measures 5 feet in length, has very large nails, with teeth over two inches long."

Today, according to the Georgia Department of Natural Resources, there are no cougars in Georgia, the closest population being the Florida panthers of South Florida. Historically, cougars ranged from coast to coast in the United States, but due to indiscriminate killing and loss of habitat, cougars now occupy only a third of their original range. The Findley family fared better than the cougars. Between 1868 and 1888, William Elbert Findley and his wife, Elizabeth Ann Bazemore, produced eight children. Their grandson, James Emory Findley, served as a superior court judge in Georgia's Atlantic Circuit for nearly 20 years, from the 1970s into the 1990s.

MILE 42.8 (32.306195, -82.231429) Oxbow. On river right is an oxbow lake that is accessible in high water.

MILE 41.9 (32.296556, -82.228520) Oxbow. On river right is an extensive oxbow lake dominated by large stands of tupelo trees.

MILE 40.8 (32.284094, -82.229923) Coleman Bridge / Ga. 152. Known as Coleman Bridge since the 1800s, when Jeremiah Coleman was a large landowner in the area, this span was most recently rebuilt in 1990 and is named in honor of Jeremiah Coleman's grandson, James "Jim" F. Coleman, a prosperous postbellum farmer in the area. On a fishing trip near the bridge in the early 1900s, Jim's son Fred waded into a backwater covered in lily pads. Unaware of the depth of this hole, he soon went under and became entangled in the underwater stems of the lilies. His father rushed in to save him but suffered the same fate. Sadly, Coleman's two remaining sons also met tragic deaths. One died in a freak accident en route to fighting in World War I, and the other son was murdered.

As with most of the bridges along the Ohoopee, a sandbar beneath this bridge has long been a gathering place for nearby communities. In a column published in the *Statesboro Herald* in 2021, Dr. Roger Branch, a retired sociology professor at Georgia Southern University who grew up in the area, recounted meeting and falling in love with his future wife here. He called the place "a fixture on the social and geographical landscape" where locals came to "swim, fish, baptize, court, picnic and just visit," and he lamented the fact that over the years, river floods had reshaped the sandbars and eliminated the historic swimming hole. Typical of the gatherings held here during the 1900s was the Monroe family reunion in 1959; a notice in the *Tattnall Journal* announced that "[t]he family reunion of the late Dunken and Lucy Collins Monroe will be held at the Coleman Bridge on the Ohoopee River . . . at 10 a.m. Sunday. Relatives and friends are invited to attend and bring a basket for lunch."

153

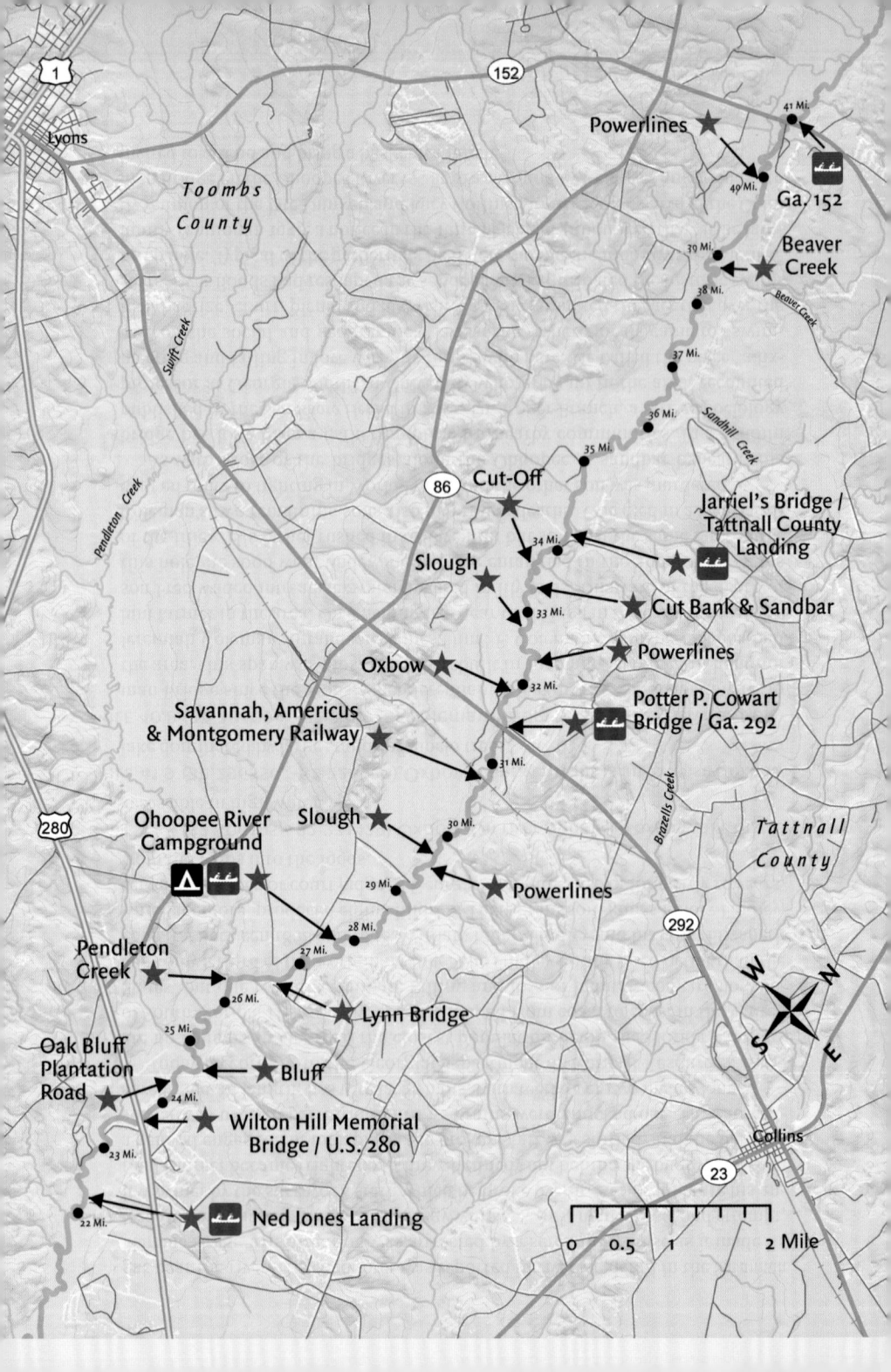

# Collins

**Length**  18 miles (Ga. 152 / New Cobbtown Road to Ned Jones Landing)

**Class**  Flatwater/I

**Minimum Level**  A gauge height of at least 4 feet and flows of 250 cubic feet per second (cfs) at the Ga. 56 gauge are recommended. Cross-river strainers should be expected, especially at lower water levels.

---

**River Gauge**  The nearest river gauge is located at Ga. 56, 4 miles downstream from the take out site for this section: https://waterdata.usgs.gov/ga/nwis/uv ?02225500.

**Launch Site**  The launch site is located on the north and upstream side of the Ga. 152 bridge and features unpaved sandbar access and limited parking.

DIRECTIONS  From the intersection of Ga. 152 and Ga. 292 in Lyons, travel east on Ga. 152 for 7.8 miles to the bridge. Cross the bridge and turn left onto the access road leading to the river.

**Take Out Site**  The take out site is located on river left 1.5 miles downstream of the U.S. 280 bridge. It features a concrete boat ramp and unpaved parking area.

DIRECTIONS  From the Ga. 152 bridge, travel west for 1.4 miles. Turn left onto Ga. 86 and proceed 11 miles. Turn left onto U.S. 280 and travel 2.4 miles. Turn right onto James B Toler Road and proceed 0.7 mile to the boat ramp.

**Alternative Take Out Sites**  Access points at Tattnall County Landing, Ga. 292, and Ohoopee River Campground will create trips of 7, 10, and 14 miles, respectively. Tattnall County Landing and Ga. 292 feature sandbar landings and unpaved parking areas. Ohoopee River Campground features a boat launch and an unpaved parking area (user fees apply).

DIRECTIONS TO TATTNALL COUNTY LANDING  From the Ga. 152 bridge, travel east for 3.4 miles. Turn right onto Conners Church Road and proceed 2.5 miles. Turn right onto Lynn-

CYPRESS, TATTNALL COUNTY

town Road and proceed 2 miles. Turn right onto Co. Rd. 127 and travel 1.7 miles to the boat ramp.

DIRECTIONS TO GA. 292    From the Ga. 152 bridge, travel west for 1.4 miles. Turn left onto Ga. 86 and proceed 6.5 miles. Turn left onto Ga. 292 and proceed 1.6 miles. Turn right onto the entrance road to the river access on the west side of the bridge.

DIRECTIONS TO OHOOPEE RIVER CAMPGROUND    From the Ga. 152 bridge, travel west for 1.4 miles. Turn left onto Ga. 86 and proceed 7.3 miles. Turn left onto John Trull Circle and travel 2.6 miles to the entrance to Ohoopee River Campground on the left.

Outfitters    Ohoopee River Campground offers boat rentals and shuttle service. Ohoopee River Campground, 1449 John Trull Cir., Lyons, Ga. 30436, 833-646-6733, www.ohoopeerivercampground.com

Description    This 18-mile run continues the Ohoopee's twisting course through Tattnall and Toombs Counties. At low water, cut banks and sandbars are numerous; at high water, the river spills over its low banks into the adjacent floodplain forest, offering off-river exploration. Oxbow lakes and sloughs with corresponding cut-offs are common. The river winds through a mostly wooded corridor, but riverfront fish camps, cabins, and houses are seen regularly. Cross-river strainers are not uncommon.

## Points of Interest

MILE 40.0 (32.276202, -82.224517) Powerlines. Downstream from these powerlines, on river left for the next mile, is a riverfront community located along Coleman Bridge Spur where cabins and docks crowd the riverbank in places. Since 1989, Georgia law has required a natural vegetated 25-foot buffer along all streams (or a 50-foot buffer on cold-water trout streams), within which no structures can be built. Of course, the law had no impact on existing structures. In the Coastal Plain, where waterways regularly change their course, a structure that was at one time well outside the "buffer" can find itself between water and a hard place. At multiple locations along Coleman Bridge Spur, one can see evidence of property owners' attempts to armor the riverbanks to keep the Ohoopee on its historic course.

MILE 38.6 (32.262339, -82.219965) Beaver Creek. On river left is the mouth of this creek that bears the name of Georgia's largest rodent family member. By the mid-1900s, beavers had nearly been eliminated from Georgia, but in the 1940s the Georgia Department of Natural Resources initiated a beaver restoration program. Today, thanks to those conservation efforts and to limited demand for beaver pelts, the state's beaver population is such that state game managers allow trapping year-round. That said, biologists believe that the total North American beaver population—an estimated 15 million— is about 10 percent of the population prior to European settlement. The ability of beavers to dam streams

and create massive wetlands that serve as a home for hundreds of other species and help protect water quality has earned them the status of "keystone species." A few other beaver notes of interest: it is believed that they are monogamous and mate for life; their incisors grow continuously throughout their lives and are worn down by chewing the tender wood that is the basis of their diet; and finally, beaver poo—as one might expect—has the consistency of sawdust.

MILE 34.3 (32.219871, -82.206913) Jarriel's Bridge / Tattnall County Landing. On river left is Tattnall County Landing, a public landing situated at the end of Jarriel's Bridge Road. On river right (the Toombs County side), Oaky Grove Church Road ends at the river. Dating to the 1800s, this bridge was ultimately abandoned in the mid-1900s. In 1941, commissioners in Tattnall and Toombs Counties agreed to spend $7,500 to rebuild the span, but before 1970 the bridge fell out of use. In its day, however, it was the site of many a gathering. In 1950, the *Tattnall Journal* reported on the Wren family reunion: "They gathered on the banks at Jarriel's Bridge on Sunday with a picnic lunch."

MILE 33.7 (32.213361, -82.207516) Cut-Off. At high water, the river cuts a direct path across the oxbow peninsula on river right. Ultimately, it may cut off the looping channel to the east to create an oxbow lake. As of 2022, however, at low water, the main channel of the river remained, and the cut-off was impassable.

MILE 33.4 (32.211420, -82.204350) Cut Bank & Sandbar. Here is a quintessential example of the principles of hydro-geomorphology (the study of the interaction between water and land) at work. On river left, the force of the water is slowly eroding a cut bank. On river right, where the water slows in the bend, heavy sands are deposited to form a wide sandbar.

157

MILE 32.8 (32.206114, -82.201536) Slough. On river right here at high water, a scenic slough reaches back into the floodplain forest more than 100 yards.

MILE 32.3 (32.202841, -82.196046) Powerlines.

MILE 31.9 (32.199016, -82.194854) Oxbow. On river right at high water, a remnant oxbow lake leads off to the west. Historic maps show the river forming a wide loop to the west here.

MILE 31.5 (32.194415, -82.191900) Potter P. Cowart Bridge / Ga. 292. The 800-foot-long Ga. 292 bridge currently spanning the river here dates to 1993; the original span was built in the early 1950s, when the Collins-to-Lyons road was constructed. In 1961, Tattnall Countians chose to honor longtime county commissioner Potter P. Cowart by naming that original bridge in his memory. In the category of "only in a small town . . .": in 1946, on a visit to Vidalia, Mr. Cowart found on the ground a unique coat button and brought it to his home in Collins, only to find out that his daughter had lost the button on a trip to Vidalia the previous week. The unusual occurrence was highlighted in an *Atlanta Journal* feature, "It Happened in Georgia." The river is accessible from both sides of the bridge.

MILE 30.8 (32.187085, -82.187562) Savannah, Americus & Montgomery Railway. A railroad bridge has spanned the river here since 1890, when this railway, known as the SAM, was completed between the Ocmulgee River at Abbeville to the west and Savannah to the east. The road later became part of the Seaboard Air Line Railway, and today it is operated as the Georgia Central Railway by Genesee & Wyoming. When the connection from Savannah to Lyons was completed

SAVANNAH, AMERICUS & MONTGOMERY RAILWAY, TATTNALL COUNTY

in 1890, the *Savannah Morning News* described the trestle here as "2,000 feet in length" and "as solid as a brick wall." Today the road carries primarily agricultural products, lumber and forest products, minerals and stone, and pulp and paper. On opposite sides of the river, the rails lead to towns that grew up around the SAM in the last decade of the 1800s—to the west, Lyons, which was incorporated in 1893; to the east, Collins, incorporated in 1905.

MILE 29.7 (32.172760, -82.185296) Slough. On river right is a scenic backwater slough that during high water is worthy of exploration.

MILE 29.5 (32.171970, -82.185383) Powerlines.

MILE 27.8 (32.155887, -82.187048) Ohoopee River Campground. On river right is the landing for this private campground that offers RV and tent sites, cabin rentals, restrooms with showers, a camp store, canoe and kayak rentals, and shuttle service. 1449 John Trull Cir., Lyons, Ga. 30436, 833-646-6733, www. ohoopeerivercampground.com.

MILE 26.6 (32.145710, -82.189533) Lynn Bridge. On river left is an unusual outcropping of sandstone. Though Georgia's Coastal Plain is predominantly sand and clay, underlying that sandy surface is a bedrock of hardened sandstone that in places—especially along riverbanks—rises to the surface. The outcropping also marks the approximate location of Lynn Bridge, an important river crossing and meeting place in Tattnall and Toombs Counties in the 1800s and early 1900s. During that period, the Lynn family operated Lynn Mill near the mouth of a small tributary here, and the community that grew up around the mill became known as Lynntown. The bridge that once spanned the river here was built

MORNING AT OHOOPEE RIVER CAMPGROUND, TOOMBS COUNTY

159

in the 1800s. In May 1903, high water severely damaged the bridge, but in June of that year, the *Tattnall Journal* reported that the span was back in service. By 1928, the county was paying for a rebuild of the bridge—this time with a steel span, at a cost of some $3,000. But by the mid-1900s, with the construction of Ga. 292 upstream and U.S. 280 downstream, historic Lynn Bridge had become obsolete and was abandoned.

Over the years, the bridge was the site of much rejoicing, as well as of much tragedy. In 1932, a Methodist minister from nearby Collins broke from the denomination's sprinkling baptism tradition to baptize 21 converts here by immersion in the Ohoopee (the unusual occurrence was noted in the *Tattnall Journal*); five years later, trustees from Collins High School entertained the school's faculty at the bridge with a "swimming party and chicken supper." In 1963, two men were arrested for the suspected murder of a third man at the bridge. Local authorities believed the victim, who drowned in the river, was knocked unconscious by a blow from a heavy chain before his death. And finally, in 1965, a 26-year-old local woman drove her vehicle off the by-then-abandoned bridge in an apparent suicide. Sheriff Romie Waters told the *Tattnall Journal* that the woman had disappeared the previous year and was estranged from her husband. The bridge, he said, had been gone for a number of years, "but in her childhood, she lived right close to there. I would say that she definitely knew where she was. She should have known the bridge was out."

MILE 26.2 (32.140853, -82.195363) Pendleton Creek. The wide mouth of this major tributary is accessible, especially in high water. From its headwaters in the northernmost reaches of Treutlen County, Pendleton Creek flows for more than 50 miles, draining significant portions of both Treutlen and Toombs Counties. Amazingly enough, this creek and the Ohoopee as far upstream as Emanuel County were used to float log rafts downriver to the coast. Typically, farmers would fell the timber and then wait for rising water (usually in the winter or spring), which would enable them to gather the logs in appropriately sized rafts and pilot the rafts downstream. A February 1892 note in the *Savannah Morning News* reported that "last Saturday between 75 and 100 rafts of timber were floating down the Ohoopee River for the Altamaha River, and thence to Darien. About 50 go down daily on an average." Water levels were critical not just for floating the logs but also for the safety of the crews that piloted them, as the heart-wrenching story of Kenyon Dickerson illustrates. A young farmer who lived along the Ohoopee, Dickerson cut timber and floated rafts to supplement his farm labors. One winter in the 1800s, the rivers didn't rise as they normally did, leaving his valuable lumber sitting worthless miles from the Darien market. When heavy rains finally arrived and raised river levels in June, he decided to make a summer run to Darien. He returned stricken with malaria and died soon after, leaving behind a wife and five children. Local historian and Ohoopee River lover Roger Branch recounted this family story, concluding, "My river bears in its bosom thousands of human stories, some glorious and some tragic."

MILE 24.6 (32.128661, -82.188233) Bluff. On river left is a scenic bluff that rises some 20 feet above the river and features outcroppings of sandstone, over some of which flow small waterfalls during wet weather.

MILE 24.3 (32.124921, -82.190772) Oak Bluff Plantation Road. On river right for the next half mile is a series of riverside homes along this road. Riverfront development continues on both sides of the river for half a mile downstream of the U.S. 280 bridge.

MILE 23.7 (32.117328, -82.189195) Wilton Hill Memorial Bridge / U.S. 280. First proposed in the early 1930s, the idea of U.S. 280 connecting Reidsville with Lyons finally became a reality in the mid-1940s with the construction of a bridge at the river feature then known as Hardens Reaches. The current span—a 960-foot-long structure consisting of 19 concrete sections—was completed in 1992, at which time the bridge was named in memory of Wilton Hill, who died at age 80 while still serving on the Reidsville City Council. Hill began his service to the community in 1948 when he was elected mayor, an office he held for 12 years. He later served as a state representative and senator from the area. Upon his death, the *Tattnall Journal* noted that, despite his many years of public service, Hill may be best remembered as the director of the Georgia School Bus Drivers Association, an organization he founded and served for more than 40 years. In that capacity, he led the fight in the 1960s to stop the Georgia General Assembly from adopting a plan to allow high school students to drive school buses instead of higher-paid adult drivers. Proponents said it would save state schools millions of dollars; Hill argued it was simply dangerous. His argument carried the day. Mayor Hill's son, Jack Hill, was sworn in as a state senator the year of his father's death and went on to be reelected 15 times, becoming in 2018 the senate's longest-serving member up until his unexpected death in 2020. Months before his death, his support as chairman of the powerful Senate Appropriations Committee was critical in restoring funding for the state's Hazardous Waste and Solid Waste Trust Funds, monies generated from various fee programs that are used to perform environmental cleanups around the state. There is no developed public access at this bridge; a public boat ramp is located 1.6 miles downstream on river left.

MILE 22.2 (32.103425, -82.186382) Ned Jones Landing. Like many boat ramps around the state, this landing was born out of cooperation between a private landowner, local government, and Georgia's Department of Natural Resources (DNR). In 1972, Ned Jones donated two acres of land at the end of James B Toler Road to the county; the state built the ramp, and Tattnall County now has primary responsibility for its maintenance. The landing features a concrete boat ramp and unpaved parking area.

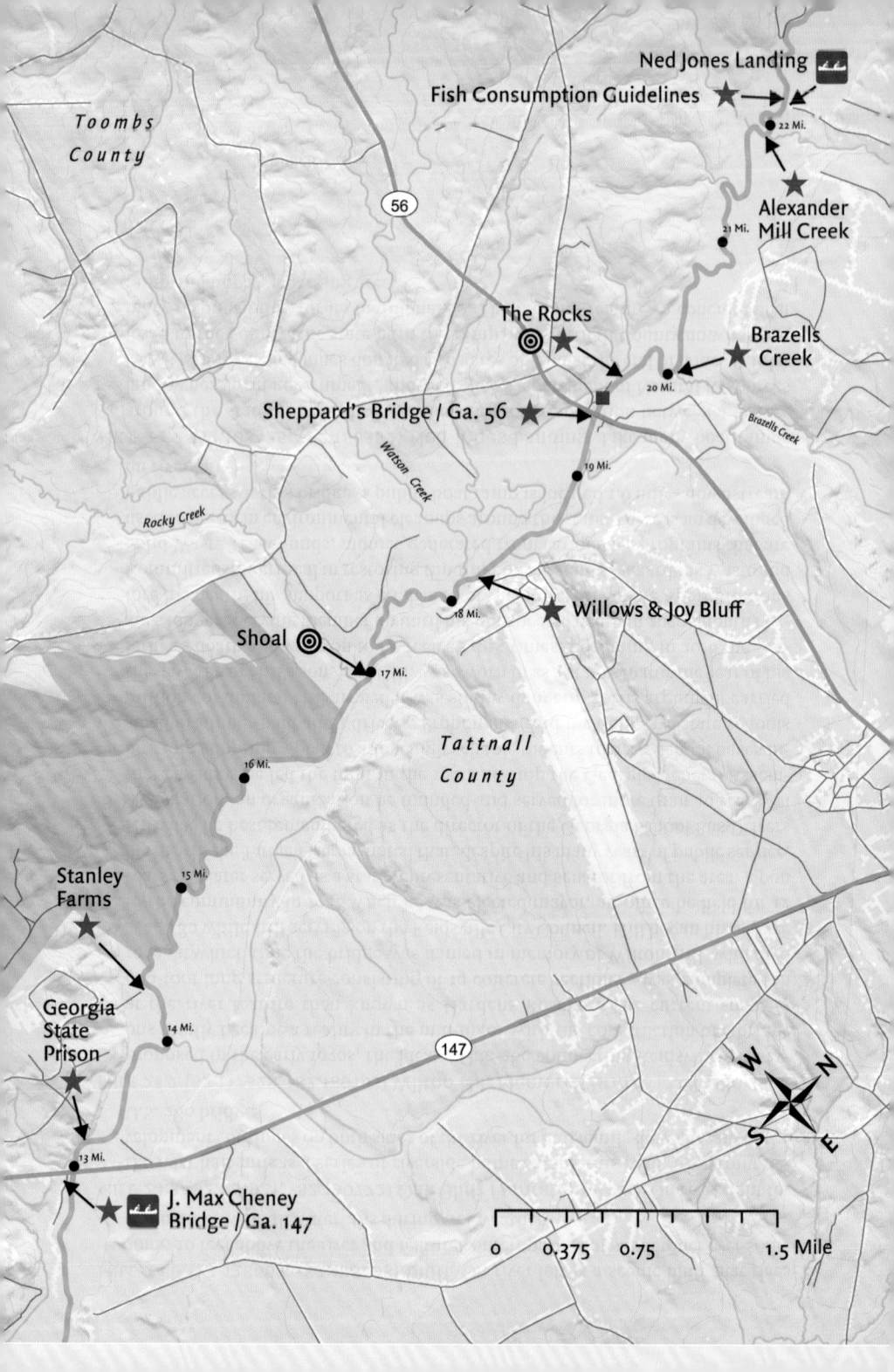

# Reidsville

**Length**   14 miles (Ned Jones Landing to Ga. 147)

**Class**   Flatwater/I

**Minimum Level**   A gauge height of at least 4 feet and flows of 250 cubic feet per second (cfs) at the Ga. 56 gauge are recommended. Cross-river strainers may be encountered, especially at lower water levels.

---

**River Gauge**   The nearest river gauge is located at Ga. 56, 4 miles downstream from the launch site for this section: https://waterdata.usgs.gov/ga/nwis/uv?02225500.

**Launch Site**   The launch site is located on the east side of the river at the end of James B Toler Road and features a concrete boat ramp and unpaved parking area.

DIRECTIONS   From the intersection of U.S. 280 and Main Street in downtown Reidsville, travel west on U.S. 280 for 4.2 miles. Turn left onto James B Toler Road (a dirt road) and proceed 0.7 mile to the boat ramp.

**Take Out Site**   The take out site is located on river right immediately downstream of the Ga. 147 bridge. It features a concrete boat ramp and unpaved parking area.

DIRECTIONS   From Ned Jones Landing, return to U.S. 280. Turn right and travel 3.6 miles. Turn right onto Smith Avenue and proceed 0.2 mile. Turn right onto

NED JONES LANDING, TATTNALL COUNTY

Ga. 147 (Tattnall St.) and proceed 5.2 miles. Continue across the bridge and turn left onto the entrance road leading to the boat ramp.

Outfitters   Stanley Southern Traditions, a lodge and event space, also provides canoe and kayak rentals and shuttle service on the Ohoopee River in the Reidsville area.

> Stanley Southern Traditions, 251 Bud Clifton Rd., Lyons, Ga. 30436, 256-684-6735, www.stanleysoutherntraditions.com

Description   Below the U.S. 280 bridge, the Ohoopee begins to widen and become more navigable even at lower water levels. This 14-mile run alternates between looping oxbows and short straightaways. With more straight reaches, the sandbars—so common on the river's winding course upstream—become less abundant. Traditionally, this section has been the play place for boaters and anglers from nearby Reidsville, and though it's only a short distance from the town, the river maintains a decidedly wild and remote feel, with little riverfront development. Banks crowded with willows stand out, as does "The Rocks," the site of a former hydroelectric power dam that, depending on water levels, should be approached with caution and scouted. Portaging may be necessary. The old dam is located a quarter mile upstream of the Ga. 56 bridge.

## Points of Interest

MILE 22.2 (32.103351, -82.186379) Fish Consumption Guidelines. In 2021, the Georgia Department of Natural Resources (DNR) maintained a fish consumption advisory for portions of the Ohoopee and Altamaha Rivers due to high levels of mercury found in the tissue of tested fish. The DNR recommends limiting consumption of some species of catfish, bass, and sunfish caught from these waters to one meal a week or one meal a month, depending on the species. While the consumption advisory specifies this section of the Ohoopee (U.S. 280 to Ga. 56), it should be noted that fish swim, and fish contaminated with mercury won't know not to travel outside the DNR's arbitrary boundaries! While mercury is naturally occurring, the U.S. Geological Survey (USGS) has determined that the predominant source of mercury in fish is the deposition of atmospheric inorganic mercury produced by coal combustion. The USGS estimates than humans have doubled the amount of inorganic mercury in the global atmosphere since the Industrial Revolution. The deposition of atmospheric mercury in blackwater streams like the Ohoopee is especially problematic because the chemical makeup of these blackwater streams contributes to the likelihood that the mercury will be taken up in the food chain. The state's fish advisories are particularly important for subsistence anglers who regularly catch and eat fish from the same locale and thus are at greater risk of accumulating toxins. Other top-tier fish predators like otters, minks, herons, and ospreys are also susceptible to exposure to mercury through the food chain. Mercury affects wild animals much as it affects us, making them more prone to disease and diminishing their reproductive ability.

MILE 21.9 (32.101154, -82.185575) Alexander Mill Creek. Though unnamed on maps, in the early 1900s this small tributary on river left was known by this name, owing to a mill that the Alexander family operated on the creek near Reidsville. In October 1929, along the river here, Tattnall County sheriff J. Henry Kennedy and deputies confiscated what at the time was reported to be the largest whiskey still ever found in the county—one capable of producing 500 gallons of whiskey a day. The secluded bottomlands along the Ohoopee were a favorite haunt of moonshiners during Georgia's prohibition era, which spanned from 1908 to 1935. During that time, other stills were busted near Sheppard's Bridge, Lynn Bridge, and Ryals Bridge (twice). The crackdown and scarcity of illicit alcohol must have prompted the following question posed in the pages of the *Tattnall Journal* in 1930: "Will a Ohoopee River fish fry be a real Ohoopee River fish fry without the usual keg of beer accompaniment?"

MILE 20.1 (32.084132, -82.174927) Brazells Creek. On river left is this tributary that drains portions of Reidsville. In September 1923, the land where Brazells Creek and the Ohoopee River meet was the site of a unique festivity, one that will likely never be duplicated. That year, the Rising Sun Masonic Lodge of Reidsville hosted a convention of local Masons and included in the proceedings a ceremony at "Decker Hammock," a bottomland forest by the Ohoopee. A firsthand account of the convention was reprinted in a 1965 issue of the *Tattnall Journal:* "We had cut out trees and underbrush to make a clearing large enough to set up the Lodge. Trees that were cut down served as the seats for the more than 700 who attended. . . . The stations were stumps of trees cut in the clearing process, and the altar was made of logs cut for the purpose. These were piled to the proper height and the finished altar was draped heavily with the gray moss so abundant about. The gavels used by the officers were 'lightard' knots cut for the purpose, uniforms used by the officers . . . were striped coveralls with knee-length boots. It was a most picturesque scene and made a lasting impression." The Brazells were a significant family in the early history of Tattnall County and Reidsville. The east–west thoroughfare in Reidsville also bears the family's name.

MILE 19.6 (32.080803, -82.177552) The Rocks. No other place has played a more significant role in the history of this area than this spot where the river once dropped over limestone shoals known as "The Rocks"—one of the only places within miles at which a natural fall creates enough power to warrant harnessing it for human endeavors. It was here in the late 1700s that Zachariah Cox began using the river to power his "Ohoopee Sawmill." The village that grew up around the sawmill became Tattnall County's first seat of government in 1801. In 1806, the Georgia General Assembly granted Ignatius Hall rights to operate a ferry at the site, and a year later James Hancock was granted a license to sell liquor and maintain a tavern for travelers. This river village served as Tattnall's seat of government until 1832, when a courthouse was built some 4 miles to the east in recently incorporated Reidsville. Though the government moved off the river, the people remained tied to it. Throughout the 1800s and well into the 1900s, the Rocks served as a gathering place for the community, perhaps reaching its ze-

165

THE ROCKS/NAIL'S DAM, TATTNALL COUNTY

nith in the 1920s after W. A. Nail erected a 6-foot-high dam at the Rocks and began producing hydropower that electrified the area. In 1924, as the hydro plant was under construction, Nail hosted a Fourth of July gathering at "Nails Park" for an estimated 4,000 people, who paid 25 cents each to attend. The affair featured drinks and food from area restaurants, a jazz orchestra, dancing in a large pavilion, a speech by gubernatorial candidate H. H. Elders, and, of course, swimming in the river. A shooting and murder marred the event; nevertheless, Nails Park became a favorite destination for a generation of Tattnall residents, as the Rocks had been for the previous generation. Typical of the reports on gatherings at the site was this one from the *Tattnall Journal*: "The principal feature of amusement was target shooting, both with pistol and rifle, and boat riding, bathing, and fishing. Young ladies prepared baskets and the dinner was very much enjoyed." This dam should be approached with caution. While high water levels eliminate the obstacle all together, at low-to-mid levels this lowhead dam can create strong and dangerous hydraulics and should be portaged with care. The safest route through the shoal/dam is on river left, as is the best portage route.

MILE 19.4 (32.077236, -82.176550) Sheppard's Bridge / Ga. 56. Due to its close proximity to Ohoopee Sawmill and the Rocks, this is likely the site of the first bridge to span the Ohoopee in Tattnall County. As late as 1829, records show that a ferry was still in operation here under the direction of James Drake. Eventually a bridge followed, and by the late 1800s it had become known as Sheppard's Bridge. The span that now stretches across the river was completed in 2010 at a cost of $2.6 million.

Since this bridge was the closest one to Reidsville, it was at this site—and at the Rocks just upstream—that the community most interacted with the river.

NEAR SHEPPARD'S BRIDGE, TATTNALL COUNTY

An excerpt from a 1905 issue of the *Tattnall Journal* paints a colorful (but perhaps disapproving) picture of a typical summertime scene at the bridge: "Any day you cross Sheppard's bridge on the Ohoopee you can see from eight to a dozen yearling boys and big strong negroes perched against a tree fishing, in other words, killing time and keeping out of the cotton patch." So popular was the swimming hole here that in 1945 the city of Reidsville established regular daily bus service to the bridge, in part to placate citizens who were clamoring for the city to build a playground and swimming pool for the town's youth. The city even provided adults to supervise the children at the river. Two years later, city leaders likely viewed the idea of a public pool more favorably after a murder victim was found, bound and weighted, at the river's bottom beneath the bridge. Nevertheless, the site continued to be a gathering spot for the community, hosting everything from picnics to political rallies. In 1957, gubernatorial candidate Lieutenant Governor Ernest Vandiver attracted a crowd of 250 to the banks of the river, where he railed against the Supreme Court's recent ruling ending segregation in public schools and vowed to fight integration. During his administration, however, integration began after Governor Vandiver refused to uphold a misguided law passed during the previous administration that would cut state funding to any school district that chose to integrate its classrooms.

In 1973, the Georgia General Assembly named the bridge here in memory of W. A. "At" Nail, a local farmer and country store merchant who developed the dam and hydropower project immediately upstream and gave the state land for the bridge right-of-way. A description of Nail's 329-acre farm along the banks of the river here, published in a 1917 issue of the *Tattnall Journal*, provides interesting details about a successful South Georgia farm of that day. Nail had some 60 acres of cotton planted, though boll weevils had infested much of it, while his

167

corn crop stood "seven to eight and nine feet high." In other fields he grew watermelon, sugarcane, peas, and potatoes, and surrounding his home were a host of fruit-bearing plants, including mulberry, apple, peach, and fig trees.

MILE 18.2 (32.062691, -82.172418) Willows & Joy Bluff. On river left is the Joy Bluff neighborhood, where numerous homes front the low bank of the river. The sandy white bluff that gives the neighborhood its name is just downstream. On river right is a bank of willow, a tree that becomes predominant as the Ohoopee nears the Altamaha. Lovers of wet soil and sunshine, willows flourish along stream banks and play an important role in stabilizing those banks. Willows are easily identified by their long narrow leaves that are somewhat curved, with a very tapered tip and finely toothed margins. In the spring and early summer, when the willows' pollinated seeds ripen and burst, a strong wind through a dense stand of willows will create the appearance of what looks like snow. Each seed is covered in a silky white down that allows it to drift through the air and find purchase. Lightweight and straight grained, black willow was once the preferred wood for artificial limbs. Traditionally, willow bark and leaves were used as a treatment for a variety of ailments ranging from rheumatism to headaches. In fact, the bark and leaves contain salicin, which is the basic ingredient in aspirin.

MILE 17.0 (32.051539, -82.172102) Shoal. In low water, a shoal and rocky river bottom are visible here.

MILE 14.4 (32.023312, -82.163297) Stanley Farms. On river right is a landing and fish camp owned by the Stanley family of nearby Lyons, one of the first families of Vidalia sweet onions. R. T. Stanley Sr. first planted onions in 1975, eschewing tobacco to gamble on what became one of Georgia's most famous vegetable crops. His son, R. T. Stanley Jr., would go on to become one of the most recognizable Vidalia onion ambassadors, playing a pivotal role in securing the 1986 passage of state legislation defining the 20-county production area. In 1989 he also helped gain a federal marketing order for the locally grown onions that protected the name and enabled producers to jointly fund research and promotional programs. The sweet onion industry began in the 1930s when a single farmer, Moses Coleman, accidentally planted sweet onions instead of hot onions. Low-sulfur soils in the area, coupled with abundant winter rain and mild temperatures, helped create a distinct, mild flavor that consumers loved, and over the next five decades, Vidalia sweet onions became a household name. In the days before interstate highways, Vidalia's location at a busy crossroads carrying tourists bound for the Florida and Georgia coast helped spread the fame of the onions. In the 1960s, the Piggly Wiggly chain began carrying the onions in its stores throughout the Southeast, and soon other supermarkets began demanding the onions. Today, some 12,000 acres of Vidalia sweet onions are planted annually in the area, including many acres in the sandy soils along the Ohoopee; the average annual farmgate value of the crop is $150 million. Unsurprisingly, in 1990 R. T. Stanley and others were successful in having the General Assembly designate the Vidalia sweet onion as Georgia's official state vegetable.

MILE 13.2 (32.011734, -82.156707) Georgia State Prison. On river right beyond the high rocky bluff is a 7,000-acre tract of land that holds both the Georgia State Prison, which opened in 1937, and the Rogers State Prison, which opened in 1983. Georgia State Prison is a maximum-security prison that houses some 1,500 inmates, while Rogers is a medium-security facility holding some 1,300 prisoners. The prisons are surrounded by farmland, where inmates from Rogers work to provide vegetables, meat, and milk for the facilities. Georgia State Prison is famous as the filming location for the 1974 Burt Reynolds movie The Longest Yard, and it is infamous as the site of Georgia's death row from 1938 until 1980. In 1945 Lena Baker, an African American maid from Cuthbert who had been wrongfully convicted of murdering a white man, was executed in the state's electric chair; she remains the only woman ever executed in Georgia. In 2005, the state granted Baker a full and unconditional pardon. The Ohoopee and its swampy bottomlands have played a part in the lore of the prison, as many escapees have made a run to the river in an attempt to outfox the prison's bloodhounds. The prison's link to the river extends to its wastewater treatment plant, which discharges up to 850,000 gallons of treated sewage into the river daily. The discharge is located on river right about 1,500 feet downstream from the Ga. 147 bridge.

MILE 12.9 (32.009927, -82.155333) J. Max Cheney Bridge / Ga. 147. A bridge has spanned the river here since 1937, when the original bridge leading from Reidsville to Georgia State Prison was completed at a cost of $61,122. When that span was built, it and the prison were heralded as a local economic renaissance in the midst of the Great Depression. The Tattnall Journal enthusiastically announced construction of the bridge: "'Ole Man Depression' may not be knocked out completely, as far as Tattnall County is concerned, but business has him groggy from consistent punching, and he is expected to be counted out before many more days." The current span, completed in 1996, came in at a cost of $6.5 million. It is named in memory of Judge J. Max Cheney, a Reidsville native son who died in 1974 at age 48. Cheney was a superior court judge at his death and also served as district attorney in Georgia's Atlantic Judicial Circuit. In Reidsville he was a Mason, commander of a National Guard unit, deacon at Reidsville Baptist Church, and a founding member of the Tattnall County Historical Society. A high achiever from an early age, he is noted as the first Eagle Scout from Tattnall County.

In August 1979, the bridge was the site of a clash between some 400 civil rights demonstrators and state patrolmen trying to prevent the crowd from reaching prison property. In this incident, 66 protestors were arrested, including the Reverend Hosea Williams, a well-known civil rights activist and then a state representative, and comedian Dick Gregory. The clash was the culmination of an 80-mile, multiday march from Savannah to the prison to protest the prosecution of six African American inmates implicated in killing a white prison guard and two white inmates during a riot at the prison in 1978. The unrest at the prison, coupled with other reports of poor conditions and the well-publicized protests, led to improvements at the facility during the early 1980s. Ultimately, two of the six prisoners were convicted in the slayings and received life sentences. The boat ramp here is located on river right immediately downstream of the bridge.

169

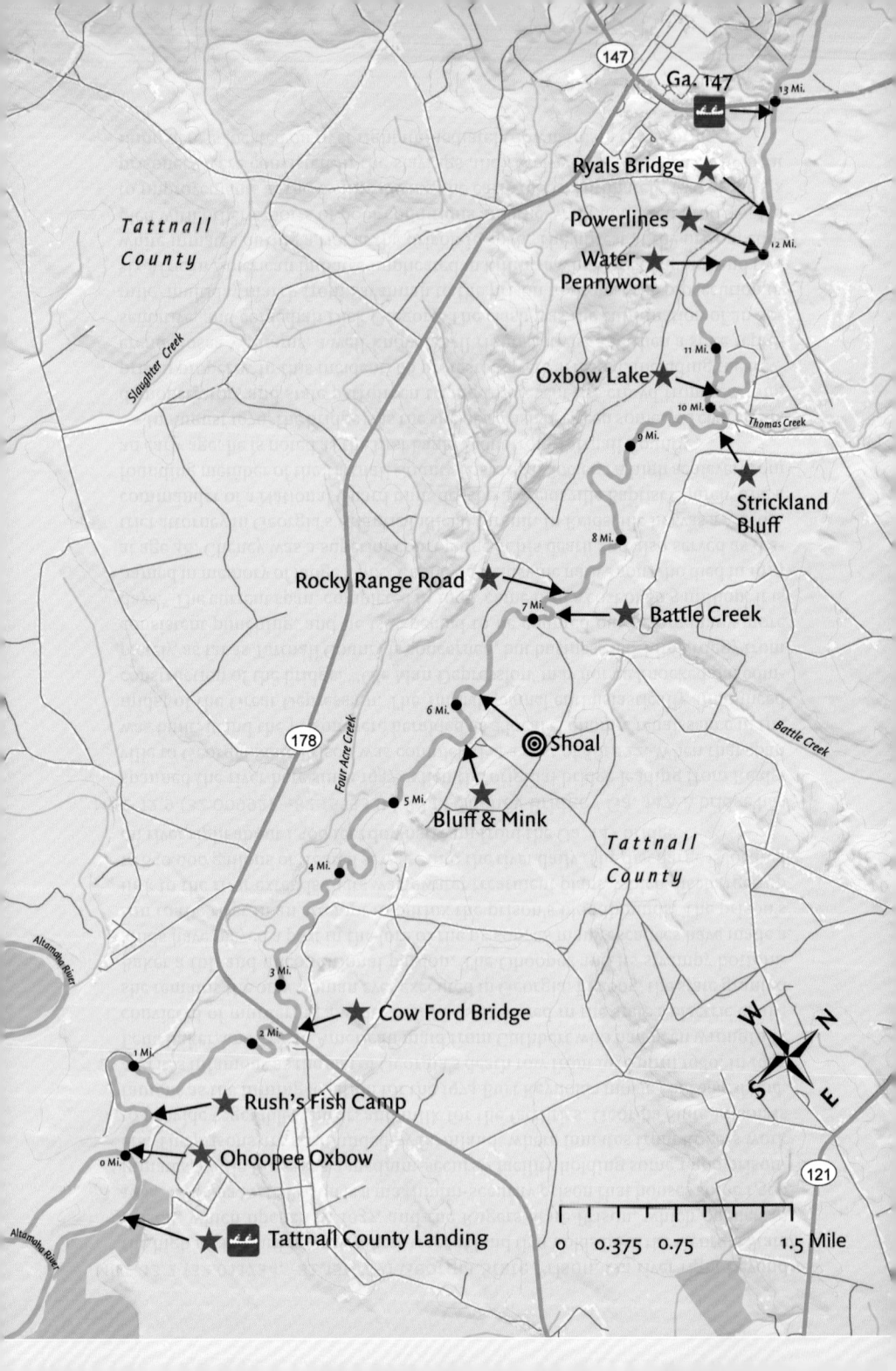

147

Ga. 147

13 Mi.

Ryals Bridge ★

Powerlines ★

Water
Pennywort ★

*Tattnall
County*

*Slaughter Creek*

12 Mi.

11 Mi.

Oxbow Lake ★

10 Mi.

*Thomas Creek*

9 Mi.

Strickland
Bluff ★

8 Mi.

Rocky Range Road ★

7 Mi.

Battle Creek ★

*Battle Creek*

178

*Four Acre Creek*

6 Mi.

Shoal ◎

5 Mi.

Bluff & Mink ★

*Tattnall
County*

4 Mi.

3 Mi.

Cow Ford Bridge ★

*Altamaha River*

1 Mi.

2 Mi.

★ Rush's Fish Camp

0 Mi.

★ Ohoopee Oxbow

N
W    E
S

121

★ ⛴ Tattnall County Landing

*Altamaha River*

0    0.375   0.75        1.5 Mile

# Cow Ford

**Length**   13 miles (Ga. 147 to Tattnall County Landing)

**Class**   Flatwater/I

**Minimum Level**   A gauge height of at least 4 feet and flows of 250 cubic feet per second (cfs) at the Ga. 56 gauge are recommended. Cross-river strainers may be encountered, especially at lower water levels.

---

**River Gauge**   The nearest river gauge is located at Ga. 56, 9 miles upstream from the launch site for this section: https://waterdata.usgs.gov/ga/nwis/uv?02225500.

**Launch Site**   The launch site is located on the west and downstream side of the bridge and features a concrete boat ramp and unpaved parking area.

DIRECTIONS   From the intersection of U.S. 280 and Main Street in downtown Reidsville, travel west on U.S. 280 for 0.2 mile and then bear left on Tattnall Street (Ga. 147). Travel 5.6 miles to the bridge, and after crossing the bridge, turn left onto the entrance road to the boat ramp.

**Take Out Site**   The take out site is located on river left 0.4 mile before the Ohoopee meets the Altamaha. It features a concrete boat ramp and unpaved parking area.

DIRECTIONS   From the entrance to the boat ramp, turn left onto Ga. 147 and travel 0.9 mile. Turn left onto Ga. 178 and proceed 7.5 miles. Turn right onto Oak Grove Road (Co. Rd. 296) and travel 0.9 mile. Turn right onto dirt County Road 537 and

SANDBAR CAMPING, TATTNALL COUNTY

proceed 0.4 mile. Turn left onto Tattnall County Landing Road and proceed 1 mile to the boat ramp.

Alternative Take Out Site    To explore the final 0.4 mile of the Ohoopee and enter the Altamaha, use J. E. Stanfield Landing, located on river left on the Altamaha 0.5 mile downstream of the mouth of the Ohoopee, or Carter's Bight Landing, located on river right on the Altamaha 2.5 miles downstream of the mouth of the Ohoopee.

DIRECTIONS    For J. E. Stanfield Landing: from the entrance to the boat ramp, turn left onto Ga. 147 and travel 0.9 mile. Turn left onto Ga. 178 and proceed 11.3 miles. Turn right onto Ga. 169 and proceed 4 miles to the entrance to Big Hammock Wildlife Management Area. Turn left onto the unpaved road, travel 0.1 mile, and then bear right, continuing on the dirt road beneath Ga. 169 and for 2.5 miles to the boat landing. The landing features a concrete boat ramp and unpaved parking area. For Carter's Bight Landing: from the intersection of Ga. 178 and Ga. 169, travel southwest on Ga. 169 for 5.9 miles. Turn right onto Ella Reddish Road and proceed 1.4 miles. Turn right onto James Stanfield Road and proceed 0.4 mile. Turn right onto Carter Bight Landing Road and proceed 1.5 miles to the boat ramp and parking area.

Outfitters    Stanley Southern Traditions, a lodge and event space, also provides canoe and kayak rentals and shuttle service on the Ohoopee River in the Reidsville area.

Stanley Southern Traditions, 251 Bud Clifton Rd., Lyons, Ga. 30436, 256-684-6735, www.stanleysoutherntraditions.com

Description    The Ohoopee reaches its climax on this 13-mile route that ends in a beautiful labyrinth of willow-lined channels and bottomland swamps, as the river flows into the Altamaha. The course is winding and remote, with limited riverside development, and features cut banks, sandbars, cut-offs, and several oxbow lakes and sloughs worthy of exploration, especially at high water. In places, particularly as the river nears Tattnall County Landing and the river's mouth, the course is narrow, with arching willow trees creating a tunnel-like effect. Where the blackwater Ohoopee meets the alluvial Altamaha, the contrast in water color can be striking.

## Points of Interest

MILE 12.3 (32.002659, -82.145950) Ryals Bridge. On river right, a concrete piling marks the location of this historic bridge that spanned the river beginning in the 1800s. The piling dates to around 1908, when the first steel truss bridge was built here, but that structure didn't last long; high water in 1911 toppled it, necessitating a rebuild in 1915 that cost Tattnall taxpayers $5,000. When the new bridge was completed, the *Tattnall Journal* predicted that it would "stand for generations." By the late 1940s, it was abandoned. Henry and Mary Ryals and their three children (Henry, Madison, and George Ann) farmed alongside the Ohoopee River in the mid-1800s. When Henry Jr. died in 1925, the *Journal* noted that he was "one of the oldest citizens of the county and at one time consid-

ered one of the most substantial." Aside from getting locals over the river, Ryals Bridge connected the community to it. It was a place for 4-H camps and school outings, one of which was dutifully recorded in the *Journal* in 1912: "Mrs. Cecil Woodcliffe, the attractive teacher of the Shiloh School near Reidsville, together with her pupils and a number of friends, enjoyed a delightful picnic on the Ohoopee River near Ryals bridge last Wednesday. . . . The merry school kids romped and played in the woods in a light-hearted, happy manner while many of the older ones spent their time fishing along the banks, and were greatly repaid by a bountiful supply of fish which were cooked in true "camp style" and ready to serve along with the sumptuous dinner which was spread 'neath the grand old shady oaks. . . . The day was one of pleasure and enjoyment to all present and will not be soon forgotten." Immediately downstream of the bridge piling is a cut for an Atlanta Gas Light pipeline.

MILE 12.0 (32.000585, -82.143971) Powerlines.

MILE 11.7 (31.997374, -82.145750) Water Pennywort. On river right here (as at many places along the Ohoopee) is a large floating mat of this aquatic plant that sports circular, deep-green, leathery leaves. During the spring and summer, it blooms with small clusters of star-shaped flowers that can be white, yellowish-green, or purple. On the opposite bank is a clearing and fish camp. For the next 1.5 miles on river left there are numerous trailers, cabins, and fish camps.

MILE 10.2 (31.988432, -82.135844) Oxbow Lake. On river left is an entrance to an extensive oxbow lake. It is the remains of a 0.6-mile oxbow that the river cut off during the last half century. The willow and cypress-filled slough is rife with

173

duckweed and other aquatic plants and fronted on the east by a high sandy bluff (the abandoned cut bank of the original channel).

MILE 9.7 (31.987156, -82.132126) Strickland Bluff. On river left is this high (for the Ohoopee) bluff that bears the name of one of Tattnall County's early leaders, Henry Strickland, who in the antebellum period owned some 5,000 acres along the river here. Documents show that in 1860 he farmed this land with 38 enslaved workers. He was elected to the state senate in 1840, and in 1861 he represented Tattnall County at the Georgia Secession Convention, at which delegates voted to secede from the Union, leading to the Civil War. Though Strickland was among the largest landowners and enslavers in the county, he feared that war would ruin Georgia. Both he and Benjamin Brewton, Tattnall's other delegate to the convention, argued against secession. Strickland died less than a year later, never to see his dire prediction come true. For all the cotton that Strickland undoubtedly grew, his largest "crop" might have been his children. He married three times, producing 20 offspring in his 70 years. His last wife died in 1859, and at the occasion of her death he penned a poem, the first verse of which read: "On the Ohoopee banks I stand== / My Tears are falling to the sand. / For my companion is called away, / On, never, never to return."

MILE 7.4 (31.966756, -82.129132) Rocky Range Road. On river right is a river access at the end of Rocky Range Road. This is the southernmost point of state-owned property associated with Rogers State Prison and Georgia State Prison and as such is frequented by the fishing (and other) public. The Ohoopee is especially known for its panfish fishery—redbreast, bluegills, and redear sunfish—and through the years state and local game laws have attempted to manage and preserve this fishery. In addition to setting daily creel limits specific to species (anglers can take up to 50 panfish daily), the state prohibits the taking of fish through the use of electronic devices, explosives, poisons, or firearms. It is further illegal to take game fish (with the exception of hickory shad, channel catfish, blue catfish, or flathead catfish) by any means other than pole and line. Along this section of the Ohoopee in the mid-1900s, local authorities had their hands full rooting out "dynamiters." In 1948, local law enforcement officers caught three "anglers" with 25 pounds of fish and a dozen sticks of dynamite. Each of the three offenders was ultimately sentenced to a fine of $300 (the equivalent of $3,500 in 2021 dollars). The hefty fine is a reflection of the affection the local community held for the Ohoopee fishery. Local newspaper accounts throughout the past century are filled with references to the pursuit of the "finny tribe," including this humorous account from a 1903 issue of the *Tattnall Journal*: "The Ohoopee River still remains too full for fishing [high water], consequently Dr. Alexander, Henry Beasley, Remer Hendricks, Judge Alexander, and Dr. Rogers have all been confined at home to their great discomfort and inconvenience."

MILE 7.2 (31.963464, -82.128722) Battle Creek. On river left is the mouth of this creek, whose name reflects a conflict that took place near this location during the Revolutionary War. It was here that patriot troops under the command of Captain William Cone attacked an outlaw band of Tories led by Colonel Daniel

McGirth, a onetime patriot who had defected to the British side and spent much of 1781 raiding and stealing from homesteads along the Altamaha. After one such raid, McGirth and his troops, laden with the spoils of war, camped near here, unaware that Cone's force of 140 men was in close pursuit. As recounted in *Heritage of Tattnall County*, "As the Tories were preparing for camp a rain set in and made conditions difficult. Wishing to preserve the element of surprise, Cone sent forward a scout, who noiselessly killed the Tory sentry. Cone then ordered his dragoons to charge McGirth's camp. . . . A fierce skirmish ensued, during which the British were defeated, 12 or 13 enemy troops perished, with the remainder being driven into and across the Ohoopee." The battle put an end to McGirth's raids.

MILE 6.3 (31.953379, -82.128883) Shoal. At low water a small shoal appears here.

MILE 5.7 (31.949496, -82.124737) Bluff & Mink. On river left is a high, wooded bluff, but it is highly unlikely that any mink will be seen at this picturesque site. The sleek, dark brown, long-tailed weasels grow to a length of about two feet and a weight of 2–3 pounds and can be found throughout Georgia, and while they are common along coastal marshes and sand dunes, they are less so in this part of the Coastal Plain, though at one time their numbers might have been more abundant here. In 1903, the *Tattnall Journal* reported on two minks that were killed along the Ohoopee: "These little animals are destructive to chickens, one mink has been known to kill a half dozen chickens in one night. They were a few years ago very numerous in the county and gave the farmers a great deal of trouble, but we are glad to learn that they have about disappeared and it is very rare that one is ever captured now." Indeed, mink populations have de-

175

clined nationwide since the mid-1900s; wildlife biologists attribute that in part to the presence of industrial pollutants. As an opportunistic, top-tier predator that feeds heavily on fish, crayfish, and frogs, minks are susceptible to accumulating toxins, such as mercury, which are known to contaminate fish in the Ohoopee and Altamaha Rivers. Mercury is a neurotoxin that can impede reproductive success, and it has been detected in high levels in mink carcasses examined from this part of the state.

MILE 2.5 (31.920408, -82.112999) Cow Ford Bridge. Humans (and cows) have been crossing the river here at least since the 1700s, when colonial-era "ranchers" grazed cattle in this area. The Hencart Road, which crossed the river here, was an important trade road from Georgia's coastal settlements near present-day Richmond Hill to the Creek nation to the west. By the early 1800s, the crossing was well used. The current bridge was completed in 1964, and in 1965 the Georgia General Assembly dedicated the bridge in memory of native sons J. Cliff Kennedy and the Reverend Reed B. Purcell. Kennedy, who died in 1964, served as mayor of Reidsville and as a state representative and senator while also farming and running the Chevrolet dealership in town for 36 years. Purcell was a fisher of men . . . and fish. He was a well-known Baptist minister who served multiple churches in the area, as well as a noted shad fisherman. At one time, his family ran a restaurant at Cow Ford catering to anglers, especially during the shad season. In the 1800s and early 1900s, when American shad were still widely considered a culinary treat, and when they could be found in abundance on the Altamaha and Ohoopee Rivers, the run of the Ohoopee from Cow Ford to the river's mouth (then just 2 miles) was a center of activity during the early spring shad spawning runs. In 1934, the *Tattnall Journal* reported: "A half dozen or more boats are drifting constantly at the point known as 'The Fishery,' at the mouth of the Ohoopee River." At that time, shad brought 50 cents to $2 a fish.

MILE 0.5 (31.905154, -82.115787) Rush's Fish Camp. On river left here is the end of Tattnall County Road 537. The area surrounding the mouth of the Ohoopee was a locally popular fishing hole, especially in the late winter and early spring when shad made their annual spawning runs up the Altamaha and Ohoopee Rivers. Locals who owned land along this stretch took advantage of the fishery by opening fish camps. Among the best known was Dewey Rush's, which in the 1950s offered rental boats at $1 a day and sold crickets for one cent each. With frontage on the Ohoopee and the Altamaha, the camp provided free bank fishing. Rush, who represented the area in the General Assembly during the 1960s, dutifully used his position of influence to aid his community (and his business). In 1969, he convinced fellow legislators to extend the shad season 15 days because of "low water and extremely cold and rainy weather." "It would be a great help to shad fisherman," he told his colleagues.

MILE 0.0 (31.901434, -82.115045) Ohoopee Oxbow. Here the Ohoopee devolves into a labyrinth of narrow channels. This spot was once the true mouth of the Ohoopee, as the river met the Altamaha at the height of the northern end of a nearly 2-mile-long looping oxbow. The Ohoopee, for its part, seemed satisfied

WILLOW AT MOUTH OF OHOOPEE, TATTNALL COUNTY

with this relationship, but the Altamaha had other plans. During the latter half of the twentieth century, the big river began carving a new path, cutting across the spit of land forming this oxbow and creating a vast oxbow lake and wetland where a river once flowed through a well-defined channel. The results are spectacular and can befuddle river travelers. The narrow willow-and-river-birch-lined channels are enchanting, as they wind in multiple directions, leaving travelers to choose the best route. To reach Tattnall County Landing 0.5 mile downstream, bear left. To investigate the oxbow, bear right. At high water, the entire area can be flooded, opening for exploration a vast body of water that covers beautiful floodplain forests between here and the new mouth of the river.

MILE 0.5 FROM OHOOPEE RIVER MILE 0.0 (31.897296, -82.109734) Tattnall County Landing. Located on river left, this landing was gifted to Tattnall County by Georgia Pacific in 1964. After the donation, the county installed a boat ramp, a water well/pump, picnic tables, and grills, and the landing became a popular spot for anglers and community gatherings. In 1968, candidates in the Democratic primary election planned a community fish fry at the park and in the pages of the *Tattnall Journal* urged all "interested citizens, interested voters, and fish eaters" to attend: "Bring your pastor, your wife and children. There will be no alcoholic beverages on the premises and no political speeches." According to local reports, it was a huge success, attracting nearly 1,000 people. Beyond this landing, the Ohoopee continues to its mouth, where its blackwater contrasts dramatically with the sediment-laden water of the Altamaha. Along the way, the narrow channel winds beneath a canopy of willow and river birch. At high water, side channels lead into vast stretches of flooded bottomland forest. The public landing now features a concrete boat ramp and unpaved parking area.

177

# Animals and Plants along Georgia Rivers

Species are arranged, as best as possible, into groups similar to one another. Mammals move from aquatic toward terrestrial; birds from water birds to birds of prey and wild turkey; fish from cold-water to warm-water species; reptiles and amphibians from smallest (frogs) to largest (alligators), with snakes and turtles grouped together; and plants from largest to smallest, with large trees first, then smaller flowering trees, shrubs, understory vegetation (ferns, canes, wildflowers), and finally aquatic vegetation.

## Mammals

### Beaver (*Castor canadensis*)

Reaching lengths of up to 4 feet (including the iconic paddle-shaped tail) and weights of up to 60 pounds, beavers are North America's largest rodents. On Georgia rivers they usually live in burrows in the banks, rather than in constructed dens. They are rarely seen during daylight hours, but along the shore, "bleached" sticks that they have stripped of bark are a sign of beaver activity. Beavers are keystone species for clean water, as the wetlands they construct serve as natural filters that capture sediment and other pollutants and provide habitat for many other species.

### Muskrat (*Ondatra zibethica*)

This common aquatic rodent grows to lengths of 2 feet (including its foot-long, hairless tail). Though primarily nocturnal, muskrats can sometimes be seen foraging for food during the day. Its riverbank dens are concealed via an underwater entrance. Among its more notable attributes: lips that close behind its teeth to allow underwater feeding, and a prodigious reproductive cycle. They commonly bear four litters of five to seven young each year. They eat primarily plants but also consume mussels, frogs, and crayfish. If you come across a pile of small mussels, it's likely the site of a muskrat feast.

## Otter (*Lutra canadensis*)

Reaching lengths of over 4 feet (including its long fur-covered tail), river otters are long and slender compared to muskrats and beavers. They commonly commandeer abandoned muskrat or beaver dens for their homes, but unlike their aquatic neighbors they are carnivores, using their swimming skills to capture fish, crayfish, frogs, salamanders, snakes, and turtles. They also partake of mussels and even birds. Although they are rarely seen during the day, you sometimes hear their barks and squeals and see them in the early morning or at twilight.

## Groundhog (*Marmota monax*)

Often mistaken for an otter or beaver, groundhogs (also known as woodchucks) frequent areas where woodlands meet open spaces—like along rivers—where they forage on grasses, plants, fruits, and even tree bark. Yes, woodchucks do chuck wood. Though they are not aquatic, they do swim . . . and climb trees, but den in the ground, lending them their common name. Groundhogs grow to about 2 feet in length and have a short (7–9 inches) furry tail.

## Raccoon (*Procyon lotor*)

Known for its black mask and black-ringed tail, raccoons are riverside foragers. While they are highly adaptive and opportunistic, they prefer habitats near water (for food) that are filled with mature hardwoods (for shelter). The Latin *lotor* means washer—a reference to the raccoon's penchant for washing its food before eating. Theories abound about this practice, but to date scientists have not reached any conclusions. Raccoons feed on crayfish, fiddler crabs, fish, and even some snakes as well as fruits and acorns. They grow to lengths of 3 feet and can weigh as much as 20 pounds.

## Opossum (*Didelphis virginian*)

About the size of your average house cat, opossums are North America's only marsupial. After birth (following a gestation period of just 12 days), infants crawl into a pouch on their mother's abdomen, where they are suckled for about 70 days. They are unique for additional reasons . . . they have more teeth (50) than any other land mammal in North America, and they are immune to snake venom and kill and eat venomous snakes.

## Coyote (*Canis latrans*)

A nonnative species to Georgia, coyotes have filled the ecosystem niche vacated by the red wolf, which is a critically endangered species. In the late 1960s, coyotes were reported in only 23 Georgia counties, but in 2010 they could be found in all 159 counties. Their success in the state is attributable to their adaptability: they'll eat anything and live anywhere.

## Armadillo (*Dasypus novemcinctus*)

Originally restricted to Texas, nine-banded armadillos have pushed steadily east during the past century and are now found throughout Georgia except in the far north. Their preferred habitat is along streams, and they cross water either by swimming or by walking on the stream bottom while holding their breath. Their primary food is insects, which they forage from the ground, employing a sensitive nose, a sticking tongue, and feet adapted for digging.

181

## Gray Squirrel (*Sciurus carolinensis*)

The most commonly seen native mammal in Georgia, adaptable gray squirrels survive in many habitats but prefer hardwood forests, where nuts and acorns provide the bulk of their pound-a-week dietary requirements. Cracking the forest masts requires specialized equipment—namely incisor teeth that are continuously ground down but also continuously grow—up to 6 inches per year. Fossil records show that the gray squirrel roamed North America 50 million years ago.

## White-tailed Deer
(*Odocoileus virginianus*)

A species nearly lost to Georgia, white-tailed deer survive now because of restocking and wildlife management programs initiated during the mid-20th century. In 2002, Georgia's Department of Natural Resources estimated the state's deer population at 1.2 million. Hunting season in Georgia for white-tailed deer runs from September to January, depending on the area.

## Black Bear (*Ursus americanus*)

Prior to the 19th century, black bears were abundant in Georgia, but habitat loss and overhunting dramatically reduced their population. Restrictions on hunting and other management practices implemented during the 20th century have allowed the species to recover. Georgia's Department of Natural Resources estimates a population of more than 5,000. Their range is mostly restricted to the North Georgia mountains, the bottomland forests along the Ocmulgee River, and the Okefenokee Swamp. Reaching weights of up to 500 pounds, black bears are the state's heftiest land mammals, but their weight doesn't slow them down. They are excellent climbers, swim well, and can run at speeds up to 30 miles per hour.

## Red Fox (*Vulpes vulpes*) and Gray Fox (*Urocyon cinereoargenteus*)

The gray fox is Georgia's only remaining native member of the canine family, but along Georgia rivers you're more likely to encounter the red fox, a species introduced from Europe by early settlers. That's because the red fox is more common along forest edges, fields, and river bottoms, whereas the gray stays primarily in wooded areas. Grays are distinguished by a mottled gray coat, a black-tipped tail, and the unique ability (for canines) to climb trees. Reds have a rust-colored coat and a white-tipped tail.

# Birds

### Kingfisher (*Megaceryle alcyon*)

A slate-blue back, wings, and breast belt along with a white belly and crested head distinguish this patroller of riverbanks. Feeding mostly on fish, the kingfisher spends its time perched in trees over the water. In the spring, they construct nest burrows in riverbanks, and mating pairs produce five to eight offspring. Kingfishers, which have a distinctive cry (a loud, harsh rattle usually delivered in flight), are among the most common birds sighted along Georgia rivers.

183

## Great Blue Heron
### (Ardea herodias)

The largest North American heron, great blues grow to almost 4 feet in length and have a 6-foot wingspan. Silent sentinels along riverbanks, they wade slowly but strike with their bill with lightning quickness, feeding mostly on fish, frogs, and crustaceans, which they swallow whole. Herons engage in elaborate courtship displays and nest in colonies located high up in trees along rivers and lakes. When disturbed, they sometimes let out a loud, distinctive squawk as they flee.

## Green Heron (Butorides virescens)

A small, stocky wading bird reaching lengths of 18 inches, the green heron is one of the few tool-using birds. It commonly drops bait onto the surface of the water and grabs the small fish that are attracted. It uses a variety of baits and lures,  including crusts of bread, insects, earthworms, twigs, or feathers. It feeds on small fish, invertebrates, insects, frogs, and other small animals.

## Great Egret (Ardea alba)

Like the great blue heron, this large wading bird reaches lengths of close to 4 feet, but it is distinguished by its all-white plumage and black legs and feet. It is more commonly seen along the Georgia coast. It has the distinction of being the symbol of the National Audubon Society because when the society was founded in 1905, the egrets were being hunted into extinction for their plumes, which were used to decorate hats and clothing.

## Osprey (*Pandion haliaetus*)

Known as fish hawks because they feed almost exclusively on live fish, ospreys glide above open water and then dive-bomb their prey, sometimes completely submerging themselves to secure their quarry. Studies have shown that ospreys catch fish on at least 25 percent of their dives, with some kill rates as high as 70 percent. The average time they spend hunting before making a catch is about 12 minutes. Ospreys have a wingspan of 4–6 feet and can be confused with bald eagles because of their white head and brown wings. In flight, however, the white underside of their wings gives them away as eagle imposters. They build large nests of sticks in trees and artificial platforms high above open water.

## Bald Eagle
## (*Haliaeetus leucocephalus*)

The bald eagle has been emblazoned on the Great Seal of the United States since 1782 and has been a spiritual symbol for Native people far longer than that. Once endangered by hunting and pesticides, bald eagles have flourished under federal protection. Though regal-looking birds, their behavior is often less than noble. While they do hunt and capture live prey, they more often obtain their food by harassing and stealing it from other birds (like the osprey) or by dining on carrion. They can be found on rivers throughout Georgia.

## Turkey Vulture (*Cathartes aura*)

This large, black bird with a bald, red head can often be seen along Georgia rivers feeding on carrion that has washed onto sandbars or become stranded on strainers. Turkey vultures soar to great heights searching for food, and unique among birds, they have a strong sense of smell, which helps them locate it. They have a wingspan of 4–6 feet and are easily identified in flight by their two-toned wings—silvery to light gray flight feathers with black wing linings.

## Wild Turkey (*Meleagris gallopavo*)

Wild turkeys were almost hunted to extinction by the 20th century, but conservation efforts implemented after the 1930s have resulted in a dramatic increase in populations. Benjamin Franklin lobbied for the wild turkey to be featured in the national emblem instead of the bald eagle. He thought the turkey a more noble and beautiful bird than the thieving, carrion-eating bald eagle. Turkeys feed on nuts, seeds, fruits, insects, and salamanders and are commonly seen in floodplain forests along the river. And, they do fly . . . on wingspans of more than 4 feet.

# Fish

### Brook Trout (*Salvelinus fontinalis*)

The East Coast's only native trout species, brookies require cold, clear water to survive and as such are found only in the highest headwaters of the North Georgia mountains. Aquatic insects, like mayflies, caddisflies, and stoneflies, as well as fish and crayfish, make up the bulk of their diet. There are 5,400 miles of trout streams in Georgia. Nonnative rainbow and brown trout can be found in all those streams, but only 142 miles support native brook trout.

## Longnose Gar (*Lepisosteus osseus*)

This prehistoric fish is known for its long, cylindrical body and pointed snout filled with many sharp teeth. Little changed since the day of the dinosaur, its body is armored in thick hard scales that Native Americans employed as arrowheads. Its evolutionary longevity might be attributed to its unique ability to acquire oxygen from air. During summer months, when oxygen levels in water decrease, it can often be spotted just beneath the surface and surfacing to "gulp" air—a trait that makes it well adapted for surviving in warm, shallow water.

## Striped Bass (*Morone saxatilis*)

Easily identified by rows of dark horizontal lines on their flanks, striped bass are one of Georgia's native anadromous fishes, meaning they move from saltwater to freshwater to spawn. Female stripers can carry as many as 4 million eggs. Once fertilized by males, the eggs need at least 50 miles of free-flowing river to hatch. Less than 1 percent survive to adulthood. Dams have interrupted most migratory routes along the Atlantic and Gulf Coasts, but stocking programs maintain populations on inland lakes and rivers.

## Channel Catfish (*Ictalurus punctatus*)

One of 20 catfish species found in Georgia, channel cats are the most commercially important catfish species in North America and are commonly raised in large aquaculture operations. In the wild they are nighttime hunters, feeding on everything from small fish to algae and insects. They aren't fazed by low-visibility situations thanks to their dis-

tinctive whiskers and skin being covered in "taste buds." These external sensors help them locate food by taste rather than sight.

# Reptiles and Amphibians

## Green Tree Frog (*Hyla cinerea*)

Georgia's official state amphibian, the green tree frog primarily resides along South Georgia rivers. A green back, a white belly, and a white, yellow, or iridescent stripe down each flank distinguish this frog among the state's 30 native species. Protecting riparian vegetation along water bodies helps ensure the survival of this and other frogs.

## Snapping Turtle (*Chelydra serpentine*)

Snapping turtles are not commonly seen on Georgia rivers because they rarely bask. Instead, they spend much of their lives on the river bottom under cover of vegetation and mud, where they feed on aquatic vegetation and ambush fish, crayfish, frogs, and anything else that happens to cross their paths. They are most often spotted from May to June, when females leave the water to lay eggs in nearby sandbars or loamy soil. Young hatch out from August through October.

## River Cooter (*Pseudemys concinna*)

The consummate baskers of Georgia rivers, you may often spot river cooters sunning themselves on logs or rocks. At the first sign of danger, they plunge into the water, often creating loud splashes. They grow to 12 inches in length, feed mostly on aquatic vegetation and algae, and lay their eggs in sandbars along riverbanks. A pile of broken white shells on a sandbar in August and September is a likely indication of a cooter nest. Georgia limits the wild harvest of river cooters and other turtles that have come under increasing pressure due to demand in Asian food markets.

## Spiny Softshell Turtle
### (Apalone spinifera)

Sometimes described as a pancake with legs, the spiny softshell turtle sports a flat leathery shell. Males and young have dark spots on the shell that are absent in females, which can grow to lengths of 17 inches (males top out at 9 inches). Unique in the turtle world, softshells have the ability to obtain oxygen from adaptations on their throats and anuses, enabling them to remain submerged for up to 5 hours. They are carnivorous, ambushing unsuspecting prey while lying partially covered on the river bottom.

## Banded Watersnake
### (Nerodia fasciata)

The most common snake of Georgia's coastal plain rivers, streams, lakes, and wetlands, banded water snakes are often spotted basking on rocks, logs, and limbs overhanging the water's edge. They vary in color from light brown or reddish to black in ground-color with darker crossbands, and hunt for fish and amphibians in shallow water. A similar species, the northern watersnake (Nerodia sipedon), is restricted to North Georgia.

## Water Moccasin
### (Agkistrodon piscivorous)

Georgia is home to 11 species of water snakes; only the water moccasin is venomous. Unfortunately, five species of water snakes are similar in appearance to water moccasins, making positive identification of moccasins tricky. Moccasins are best differentiated from other snakes by their behavior and habitat preference. They are restricted to Georgia's Coastal Plain and southern portions of the Piedmont. In these regions, they bask on land, stumps, or logs near the water's surface and pre-

189

fer slow-moving streams, swamps, and backwaters. Common water snakes, on the other hand, bask on limbs and shrubs overhanging the water and prefer large, open reservoirs and rivers. Finally, swimming moccasins hold their heads above the water and their bodies ride on the surface of the water; water snakes swim below the surface. It is illegal to kill nonvenomous snakes in Georgia.

## Alligator (*Alligator mississippiensis*)

The largest predator in the state, alligators can grow to 16 feet in length and weigh as much as 800 pounds. They are found only in South Georgia, below the fall line running from Columbus to Augusta. Once a federally protected species, alligators have rebounded in population, and they are now common within their range. During warm weather, they can be spotted basking along riverbanks or patrolling the water with only their snouts visible above the water's surface. Since 1980, there have been only nine confirmed alligator attacks on humans in Georgia, only one of which was fatal.

## Macroinvertebrates

This group of animals includes mollusks (mussels and snails), arthropods (crayfish and sowbugs), and aquatic insects (mayflies, stoneflies, etc.). Though usually small, they form the base of the aquatic food chain and play critical roles in clean water. Their life cycles and adaptations are among the most interesting in nature, and their presence, or lack thereof, can be an indicator of the health of a water body.

## Native Freshwater Snails

Georgia is home to 67 species of freshwater snails that range in size from 0.1 inch to more than 1 inch in length. Easily overlooked because they dwell on the river bottom, they play an important role in river ecosystems. They scour rocks and other debris of algae, helping maintain healthy water and providing suitable habitat for aquatic insects. Snails, in turn, are an important food source for other wildlife.

## Native Freshwater Mussels

Historically, Georgia was home to 126 species of freshwater mussels. However, many have become extinct due to habitat changes wrought by the construction of dams and water pollution. The state is currently home to 14 federally protected species. Because they are filter feeders, meaning they remove nutrients from the water, they play a critical role in clean rivers. They come in various colors, shapes, and sizes, with some species growing to the size of dinner plates. Because their unique life cycle involves fish carrying young mussels on their gills, the loss of some fish species has contributed to declining mussel populations.

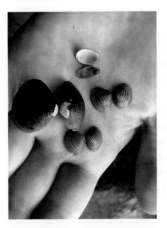

## Asian Clams (*Corbicula fluminea*)

This nonnative, invasive clam is the most commonly seen mollusk in Georgia rivers. Corbicula entered the United States in the Pacific Northwest and are now found in 38 states. Prolific reproducers and adaptable to many habitats, corbicula have flourished where native mussels have struggled. In doing so they have filled a food void. Numerous species of fish as well as crayfish, raccoons, muskrats, and otters feed on them. They are distinguished from native mussels by their size, rarely growing to more than 1 inch in length.

191

## Crayfish

Georgia is home to 73 species of crayfish, many of which are restricted to isolated populations in specific regions of the state. On Georgia rivers, you'll find them beneath rocks and debris on the river bottom, though some species create extensive burrows in the soil near wetlands areas. They are protected by a hard exoskeleton that, as adults, they outgrow and molt once or twice each year. In combination with diminishing stream health because of pollution, the introduction of nonnative crayfish used as bait by anglers poses a serious threat to Georgia's native crayfish.

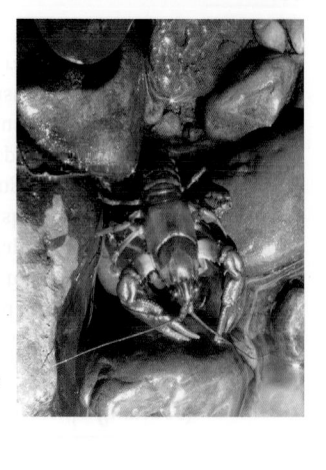

## Hellgrammite (Dobsonfly Larvae)

Flip over a rock in a healthy to moderately healthy stream in Georgia, and you'll find these frightening-looking creatures that are distinguished by two large mandibles. Reaching up to 3 inches in length, the hellgrammite is a predator of other aquatic insects and is a favorite food of popular game fish species. Dobsonfly larvae develop for one to three years in the water, crawl from the water, dig a cavity to pupate, and emerge 14–28 days later as adults. The adults survive just long enough to mate and lay eggs. The females deposit their eggs, encased in a white covering, on overhanging leaves, logs, tree trunks, or rocks so that when the larvae hatch they fall into the water.

## Dragonfly Nymphs

While adult dragonflies are always associated with water, by far most of a dragonfly's life is spent in the water, not hovering above it. Dragonfly nymphs live in the water for up to four years before crawling out for their final molts and becoming adults. The skin (exuvia) left on rocks and plants along the water can

be found long after the molt has occurred. Adult dragonflies generally survive less than two months. Dragonflies are appreciated for their efforts in mosquito control. Nymphs eat mosquito larvae from the water, while adults can consume hundreds of flying mosquitos daily, earning them the moniker "mosquito hawks."

## Mayfly Nymphs

Because all mayfly nymphs in an area commonly transform to adults at the same time, mayflies are known for their massive swarms that occur during the summer months. Their life underwater in Georgia rivers consists of clinging to the underside of rocks, where they feed mostly on algae. After a prolonged period (in some cases more than two years), they crawl out of the water to transform into adults. Nymphs are easily identified by their three hairlike tails (though sometimes only two). With fossil evidence confirming their existence more than 300 million years ago, they are believed to be the oldest living winged insects.

# Trees and Plants

## Sycamore (*Platanus occidentalis*)

A dominant deciduous tree of river corridors, sycamores are easily identified by their dark-brown to gray bark that peels and flakes, revealing a white inner bark. Sycamores also sport large, multilobed leaves that turn yellow and then tan in the fall, as well as conspicuous fruits—a round woody ball that in the winter breaks into many soft, fluffy seeds. Native Americans fashioned the large trunks of syca-mores into dugout canoes; beaver, squirrel, and muskrat eat the fruits; juncos and finches eat the seeds. They grow to 80–100 feet tall with a spread of 40–50 feet.

## River Birch (*Betula nigra*)

The deciduous river birch is known for its reddish brown to cinnamon-red bark that peels back in tough papery layers, giving the trunk a ragged appearance. In the winter, its fruits and flowers are conspicuous. Male flowers, dangling woody tubes (catkins) that are 1–3 inches long, can be seen on the ends of stems, along with the remnants of the previous year's fruit—1-inch woody cones. In the spring, the male flowers release pollen, fertilizing the emerging female flowers that produce the fruit. Growing to heights of 80 feet, birch play an important role in stabilizing stream banks with their extensive root system. Extracts from the tree are used in herbal treatments for gout, rheumatism, and kidney stones.

195

## Black Willow (*Salix nigra*)

The deciduous black willow is a dominant tree of Georgia's coastal plain rivers, especially along sandbars. Distinguished by its long, lance-like leaves, willows are perhaps most conspicuous in the midsummer, when their cottony seeds are borne on the wind, falling to the river and sometimes forming large floating mats of white fluff. Their fibrous roots play a critical role in stabilizing stream banks, and a compound derived from their bark is known for its fever-reducing and pain-killing effects. A synthetically produced variety is found in modern aspirin. Willows can attain heights of up to 60 feet.

## Black Walnut (*Juglans nigra*)

Because it thrives in full sunlight, the black walnut is often found in the open, well-lit spaces afforded by riverbanks. In the fall, after dropping its leaves it then drops its golf-ball-sized fruits, and it is not uncommon to find them floating down the river. After removing their husk (which stains hands and clothes), the hard, brown corrugated nut can—with considerable work—be broken to obtain the meat. Walnuts are high in antioxidants and beneficial fats and have more protein than any other nut—thus they are prized by squirrel, deer, and people. Walnuts typically grow to 60–70 feet, but specimens over 100 feet are common.

## Red Maple (*Acer rubrum*)

Aptly named because its buds, winged seeds, leaf stems, and leaves (in the fall) are all brilliant red, the red maple is one of the earliest flowering trees of the spring. Its buds sprout long before vegetation appears, and once pollinated, these buds mature to bright red, winged seeds that twirl off, helicopter-like, in the wind. Red maples also change color in the fall long before other trees have begun their transformation. Because of its tolerance for moist soils, it is commonly referred to as swamp maple.

## Water Oak (*Quercus nigra*)

A dominant oak of bottomland forests and riparian buffers, water oaks sport leaves that resemble a small kitchen spatula—narrow at the base and widening at a lobed end. Though deciduous, young water oaks are known to hold their leaves through the winter, while leaves on older specimens persist well into the winter. The tree's acorns are important food for squirrel, deer, and wild turkey. They commonly grow to a height of 50–80 feet.

199

## American Hornbeam (*Carpinus caroliniana*)

A tree of the bottomland forest understory, hornbeams grow to 20–30 feet in height and thrive in the shade beneath larger trees. Leaves are egg-shaped with distinct veins radiating from the main stem, ending in toothed leaf edges. The tree's fruit is conspicuous, as the nutlets are contained within a three-winged, narrow, leaflike bract. The leaves turn yellow, orange, and red in the fall and sometimes persist on the tree into the winter, causing confusion with the beech tree, which also holds its leaves in the winter.

## Tag Alder (*Alnus serrulata*)

Fibrous roots and flexible stems make this a favorite species for stream bank restoration projects. A shrub-like tree, it grows to heights of 8–12 feet and tends to form thickets along rivers and streams. Like river birch, during the winter months it is easily identified by the presence of last year's fruit (0.5-

inch woody cones) and dangling catkins, which though brown in the winter bloom bright yellow in the early spring. The bark and leaves of the alder have historically been used as an astringent to treat internal bleeding as well as external wounds.

## Catalpa (*Catalpa bignonioides*)

Perhaps the showiest bloomer of Georgia's river corridors, the catalpa produces large clusters of white bell-shaped blossoms with purple spots and two large orange markings at the throat. In the summer, these fertilized blooms produce long (up to 16 inches) bean-like pods that hang beneath the tree's heart-shaped leaves. The pods ripen and turn brown in the fall, eventually splitting to release paper-thin fringed seeds that float off in a breeze. Catalpas are best known as the sole host for catalpa sphinx moth larvae—a black-and-yellow, horned caterpillar highly prized by anglers as fish bait.

## Mountain Laurel (*Kalmia latifolia*)

A showy shrub of the Georgia mountains and Piedmont (and occasionally the Coastal Plain), mountain laurel produces abundant clusters of white-to-pink honeycomb-shaped blooms in the early spring. It is commonly seen along Georgia rivers at rocky outcroppings. Its evergreen leaves are conspicuous in the winter but can be confused with rhododendron, another evergreen flowering shrub. Rhododendron leaves are larger and more elongated. The leaves of the mountain laurel, as well as those of rhododendron and azalea, are toxic if consumed in quantity.

## Piedmont Azalea (*Rhododendron canescens*)

In 1979, the Georgia General Assembly designated wild azaleas as the state wildflower, and with good reason: Georgia is home to 10 of North America's 16 native azalea species. Almost all are partial to moist woodlands and stream banks, thus traveling Georgia's rivers you are likely to encounter many, from the hammock sweet azalea on the coast to the sweet azalea of the mountains. Piedmont azalea is among the most common. Its pink-to-white flowers appear from March through early May and emit a sweet, musky fragrance. Azaleas are considered shrubs and rarely grow taller than 15 feet.

## Dogwood (*Cornus florida*)

Perhaps the best known of North America's native flowering trees, dogwoods are common understory trees in floodplain forests along Georgia's rivers. The iconic four-petal, white flower blooms from March through April. In the fall the leaves turn scarlet red and the red berries become very conspicuous. Songbirds, wild turkeys, and a host of mammals—from chipmunks to bears—feed on these berries. Historically, humans have employed the root bark as an antidiarrheal agent, fever reducer, and pain reliever. Dogwoods grow up to 20 feet in height with a spread of up to 30 feet.

## Persimmon (*Diospyros virginiana*)

A lover of bottomland forests, persimmons can be found growing along streams and rivers in Georgia, and occasionally the prized fruit can be plucked from branches overhanging the water in the late fall. The plum-sized pulpy fruit filled with large seeds is very sweet, but only after it is fully ripe (usually after a hard frost). Unless the fruits are fully orange to black—and soft—avoid them. Unripe persimmons can leave you puckering and longing for a drink of water. Birds, deer, and hogs eat the fruits and thus help distribute the seeds throughout the forest. Persimmons can grow to 80 feet in height.

## Dog Hobble (*Leucothoe fontanesiana*)

Like its close relatives rhododendron and mountain laurel, this member of the heath family is an evergreen shrub, making it easy to identify during the winter. In the spring, it produces showy clusters of small, white bell-shaped blossoms that are often concealed beneath the leaves. Its common name is derived from its dense tangle of arching branches that make traveling through it a chore. Hunters say that bears run through stands of dog hobble to distance themselves from pursuing hounds. The leaves and flower nectar are poisonous to both humans and animals.

## Yellowroot (*Xanthorhiza simplicissima*)

A streamside dweller throughout the state, this unique shrub derives its common name from the color of its roots and inner bark. In the early spring before its leaves appear, it puts out 2-to-4-inch clusters of purple star-shaped flowers. The leaves are unique, their deeply toothed edges giving them a lacey appearance. In the fall they turn yellow, bronze, or red. It has long been recognized for its medicinal properties in treating ulcers of the mouth and stomach. It tends to grow in dense thickets and reaches no more than 3 feet in height.

## Elderberry (*Sambucus nigra*)

Common along streams, springs, and swamps, the elderberry is a favorite of songbirds and humans thanks to its abundant purple berries that appear in the late summer and early fall. More than 50 birds are known to feed on elderberries, and humans transform the berries into wines, jellies, and pies. The plant was an important food and medicinal source for Native Americans, who also fashioned the stems into flutes and arrow shafts. Elderberries tend to form thickets that commonly reach heights of 12–15 feet. The flower and berry clusters sit conspicuously at the top of the foliage.

## River Cane (*Arundinaria gigantean*)

*Arundinaria* is the only genera of bamboo native to North America. Growing in expansive, dense stands known as canebrakes, it was once the dominant plant along Georgia's rivers, but today scientists believe that it occupies less than 5 percent of its original range due to agriculture, grazing, fire suppression, and urbanization. It propagates primarily through rhizomes, with these spreading roots leading to the impenetrable canebrakes. The demise of river cane has likely contributed to the pollution of our streams, as it plays a critical role in slowing stormwater and filtering pollutants. Native Americans used the plant for nearly everything, fashioning it into spears, arrows, baskets, homes, mats, knives, torches, rafts, tubes, and drills.

## River Oats
### (*Chasmanthium latifolium*)

This 2-to-4-foot-tall native grass is distinguished by its seed head clusters that resemble flattened oats. In the summer, these clusters are bright green, but with the fall they turn brownish tan along with the plant's grasslike leaves. Like other riparian vegetation, it plays a critical role in stabilizing stream banks and minimizing erosion. It also serves as food for many songbirds.

## Sensitive Fern (*Onoclea sensibilis*)

This shade-loving fern is found in floodplain forests along rivers and streams as well as in swamps and marshes. To the untrained eye, the fronds of this fern may look very unfernlike because of the generous space between lobes. By late summer, fertile fronds arise that resemble an elongated cluster of dark brown beads on a stalk. Like many ferns, the leaves of the sensitive fern contain toxins that dissuade grazing by deer.

## Cinnamon Fern (*Osmunda cinnamomea*)

Cinnamon fern flourishes where its roots remain wet; thus it is a common fern along the river's edge. A large fern, it sends up several fronds in a palmlike whorl that reach 5 feet in length. The fertile fronds (cinnamon-colored stalks bearing the plant's spores) rise from the center of the whorl. In early spring, the young, hairy fiddleheads are a culinary treat for both humans and beasts, and hummingbirds are known to line their nests with the "hair" that covers this early growth. Fossilized fern specimens resembling cinnamon ferns date back 220 million years.

207

## Privet (*Ligustrum sinense*)

Next to kudzu, perhaps no other invasive plant has done more to alter Georgia's woodlands. A native of China, privet was introduced into the United States in 1852 for use as an ornamental shrub. By the mid-20th century, it had escaped domestic cultivation and spread throughout Georgia. It can grow to 30 feet in height and, owing to its ability to spread via seeds and sprouts, it forms dense thickets, outcompeting native species like river cane. Once estab-

lished, it is very difficult to remove. Its berries are eaten by many songbirds (which unfortunately further disperse the seeds), and beavers like the bark. Privet sports sickly-sweet-smelling white blooms in the spring and summer, which produce blue-black berries that persist on the plant into the winter.

## Cardinal Flower (*Lobelia cardinalis*)

From July through September, it is difficult to find a Georgia river that does not have the tall slender green stalks of cardinal flower topped by a cluster of brilliant red blooms along its banks. The stalks can grow to up to 4 feet in height and are common along the base of the riverbank. A lover of moist soils, some have even been seen growing in cavities of partially submerged logs. Their common name is derived from the colored vestments worn by cardinals of the Roman Catholic Church. That color makes the plant irresistible to hummingbirds, which, along with bees and butterflies, are the flower's primary pollinators.

# Aquatic Plants

### Riverweed/Threadfoot
### (*Podostemum ceratophyllum*)

This inconspicuous and highly specialized aquatic plant grows on rocks and boulders on the river bottom in swift-moving shoals, rapids, and waterfalls of Georgia rivers above the fall line. Its threadlike masses have an unusual rubbery, seaweed-like texture sporting many narrow olive-green leaves. It plays an important role in stream ecology by providing habitat and food for aquatic insects that form the base of a river's food chain.

## Water Willow (*Justicia americana*)

This perennial aquatic wildflower is common along river, stream, and lake margins and is often seen in large, dense colonies. Grasslike, its has leaves very similar to those of the black willow tree, but its white-to-pale-purple orchidlike blooms with purple streaks on the lower petals make this plant easy to identify. The blooms that appear throughout the summer are borne at the top of long (up to 3 feet) slender stems. Another important plant for the river's macroinvertebrate community, mammals also make use of it. Deer browse the leaves, while beavers and muskrats consume the plant's rhizomes.

## Pennsylvania Smartweed (*Polygonum pensylvanicum*)

There are more than a dozen native species of smartweed in Georgia, with Pennsylvania smartweed being one of the most important for waterfowl, songbirds, and mammals. Stands of smartweed provide cover for young waterfowl, and the shiny black seeds produced in the late summer provide food for those waterfowl and dozens of other birds. Muskrats, raccoons, and fox squirrels also feast on the seeds and the plants themselves. The white-to-light-pink blooms of smartweed are borne on spikes at the end of stems.

# Species of Special Interest in the Altamaha River

## Say's Spiketail Dragonfly (*Cordulegaster sayi*)

This state-threatened dragonfly measures 2 to 3 inches and
sports a long, narrow abdomen
that is striped in yellow and
dark brown. Magenta mark-
ings on its thorax also distinguish this dragonfly. When
adults emerge from the nymph
stage in the early spring, they
are partial to longleaf pine
and scrub oak forests, where
they feed on bees and wasps.

While they have a short life out of the water, surviving only long enough to breed,
as nymphs they spend up to three years inhabiting muddy seeps adjacent to hardwood forests, where they feed on other aquatic invertebrates. Say's spiketail dragonflies are found throughout the eastern Coastal Plain in Georgia, including sites
in the Penholoway Wildlife Management Area in Wayne County along the Altamaha and Gordonia-Alatamaha (Jack Hill) State Park near the Ohoopee River in
Tattnall County.

## Christmas Tree Crayfish (*Procambrus pygmaeus*)

Appropriately named, this 2-inch crayfish sports a greenish-olive body with red
highlights along its carapace, leg joints, and abdomen. In its Georgia range, no
other crayfishes have similar markings. Christmas tree crayfish can be found
among vegetation in flowing streams and in streamside burrows marked by mud
"chimneys" throughout Georgia's Coastal Plain between the Savannah and Alapaha
Rivers. They feed on live and decaying vegetation, larval insects, small fishes, and
dead animal matter.

## Altamaha Spinymussel
### (Eliptio spinosa)

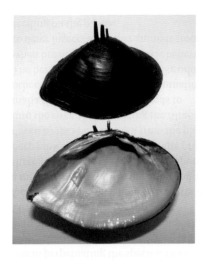

Federally protected, the Altamaha spiny-mussel is among the most unusual-looking mussels in Georgia, thanks to the spines or spikes that grow up to an inch long from the top of its 3-to-4-inch-wide shell. This feature makes it look something like an alien spacecraft. It is believed that the mussel survives only in the lower portions of the Ocmulgee River and the Altamaha River, and nowhere else on Earth. Like other mussels, it depends on host fish to carry fertilized young, known as glochidia, during the early stages of life. Thus mussel populations often depend on robust fish populations. The host for the spinymussel's glochidia is still unknown—determining its identity could help restore populations of this rare invertebrate.

## Rainbow Snake (Farancia erytrogramma)

This unusually colored snake thrives in the Coastal Plain, where it takes to blackwater creeks and rivers like the Ohoopee and others originating in the Coastal Plain. It is beautifully marked with three red stripes down its glossy black back; its psychedelic-colored belly is red to pink with rows of black spots, often with yellow

along the sides. Unfortunately, this stunning creature is rarely seen. Highly aquatic, the rainbow snake seldom leaves the water, where its favorite food is eels, lending it the nickname "eel moccasin." Populations of American eel, of course, have declined over the years as hydropower dams have disrupted their traditional migrations. That said, the rainbow snake is believed to be fairly common within its Coastal Plain habitat.

211

## Shortnose Sturgeon (*Acipenser brevirostrum*)

Included in the original Endangered Species Act of 1973, shortnose sturgeon populations declined throughout the 20th century due to overharvesting for meat and roe. The species viability was further hampered by the construction of multiple dams that blocked traditional migratory spawning routes along East Coast rivers. Undammed except on the upper reaches of its primary tributaries, the Altamaha is home to one of the most robust populations of shortnose sturgeon in the South Atlantic. This species features a shovel-like snout and, underneath, a fleshy, toothless mouth with which it forages the river bottom for insect larvae, crustaceans, worms, and mollusks. Its long, stout body is covered in rows of bony scutes along the sides and back; its heterocercal tail, characterized by a long, large upper lobe and shorter lower lobe, give it that distinctive sharklike look. The smallest of the East Coast sturgeons, it still reaches lengths of more than 3 feet and can weigh in at more than 50 pounds. By comparison, the Atlantic sturgeon, also found in the Altamaha, can reach lengths of nearly 9 feet and weights of up to 200 pounds. Both species can sometimes be spotted making great leaps above the surface of the river.

## Radford's Dicerandra (*Dicerandra radfordiana*)

This critically imperiled member of the mint family is found only along bluffs in the lower Altamaha River of McIntosh County—and nowhere else on Earth—and the Altamaha may play an important role in perpetuating the species. In late September and October, the 2-foot-tall herb blossoms into a riot of bright pink. The flowers cluster at the top of the stems; tubular, each bloom terminates in a mouth with a hoodlike upper lip and a three-lobed lip on the bottom that sports deep pink spots. The buoyant fruits produced by these blooms fall from the plant into the river, thus providing the Altamaha the role of dispersing seeds to other locations for possible germination. The herb gives off a cinnamon-like odor when brushed or crushed that is believed to deter insects and other animals from feeding on the plants.

# Protecting the Altamaha

If you have put this book to use by exploring the Altamaha and its tributaries, you can cite dozens of reasons to protect it. Aside from providing nearly 200 miles of recreational opportunities, the Altamaha and Ohoopee Rivers provide water for multiple uses, from cooling nuclear reactors near Baxley to assimilating pulp mill wastewater in Jesup. Countless businesses, industries, and farms depend on the river, which also supports a robust riverine ecosystem and contributes freshwater to important coastal fisheries. It is a workhorse of a river.

Unfortunately, like all of Georgia's rivers, the Altamaha faces challenges. Discharges from municipal and industrial facilities along its shores and tributaries and nonpoint source pollution from urban areas, farms, and silviculture all impact the health of the river, as does land development—particularly development within wetlands that feed the river. Meanwhile, plastic pollution plagues all of Georgia's rivers and our oceans.

You can protect the Altamaha River by getting involved with the Altamaha Riverkeeper, Georgia River Network, or one of the other organizations listed below. Make a contribution to support their efforts, volunteer as a water monitor, get involved in a river cleanup, learn about Georgia's laws protecting our rivers, report problems when you see them, engage elected officials in supporting laws that protect our rivers, and tell your friends and neighbors about the treasure that is the Altamaha and Ohoopee Rivers.

EDWIN I. HATCH NUCLEAR POWER PLANT INTAKE, APPLING COUNTY

Can one person make a difference? You bet, and the river teaches us how. While the Altamaha River ends as a wide, mighty river, it actually starts its life as tiny springs and streams in North Georgia. These springs and streams merge repeatedly, forming larger rivers like the Ocmulgee and the Oconee that ultimately merge to form the Altamaha. The cumulative force of hundreds of individual streams ultimately creates a mighty movement—Georgia's largest river, the Altamaha.

Similarly, the cumulative actions and choices of many individuals can create a mighty movement—one that cherishes and protects the Altamaha River and its tributaries.

Altamaha Riverkeeper
127 F St., Suite 204
Brunswick, GA 31520
404-985-9606
www.altamahariverkeeper.org

Georgia River Network
126 S. Milledge Ave.
Suite E3
Athens, GA 30605
706-549-4508
www.garivers.org

American Rivers (Atlanta office)
108 E. Ponce de Leon Ave.
Suite 212
Decatur, GA 30030
404-373-3602
www.americanrivers.org

Georgia Water Coalition
www.gawater.org

Georgia Sierra Club
743 E. College Ave.
Decatur, GA 30030
404-607-1262
www.sierraclub.org/georgia

Georgia Wildlife Federation
11600 Hazelbrand Rd.
Covington, GA 30014
770-787-7887
www.gwf.org

The Nature Conservancy
1270 Caroline St. NE
Suite D120 #357
Atlanta, GA 30307-2954
404-873-6946
www.nature.org

Georgia Conservation Voters
725 Ponce de Leon Ave. NE, Floor 2
Atlanta, GA 30306
404-955-7013
www.gcvoters.org

Georgia Conservancy
230 Peachtree St. NW, Suite 2275
Atlanta, GA 30303
404-876-2900
www.georgiaconservancy.org

Trust for Public Land
600 West Peachtree St. NW
Suite 1840
Atlanta, Georgia 30308
404-873-7306
www.tpl.org

Rivers Alive
Georgia Department of Natural Resources
2 Martin Luther King Jr. Dr. SE
Suite 1462, East Tower
Atlanta, GA 30334
470-524-0620
www.riversalive.com

Georgia Adopt-A-Stream
Georgia Department of Natural Resources
2 Martin Luther King Jr. Dr. SE
Suite 1462, East Tower
Atlanta, GA 30334
470-938-3341
www.georgiaadoptastream.com

# Photo Credits

All photos are by Joe Cook, except the following, for which the author thanks the photographers:

Brett Albanese, Georgia DNR: 186 bottom
R. D. Bartlett: 188 bottom
Steven J. Baskauf, http://bioimages .vanderbilt.edu: 194 left and right; 195 left and right; 196 left and right; 197 right; 198 right; 199 left and right; 200 left and right; 201 bottom right; 203 top and bottom right
Giff Beaton: 183 bottom; 184 top and middle; 193 top and middle
Alan Cressler: 209 top
EIC, used under Creative Commons license 3.0: 180 middle
Encyclopedia of Life, used under Creative Commons license 4.0: 210 top; 212 top
Kevin Enge: 189 bottom
Arlyn W. Evans: 209 bottom
Cris Hagen: 190
Ty Ivey: 184 bottom
John Jensen: 181 bottom
Steven G. Johnson, used under Creative Commons license 3.0: 187 middle
Phillip Jordan: 180 bottom; 181 top; 182 bottom; 185 middle and bottom; 186 top; 197 left
Thomas Luhring: 188 top
Linda May, Georgia DNR: 201 top and bottom left
Sturgis McKeever, Georgia Southern University, bugwood.org, used under Creative Commons license 3.0: 211 bottom

James H. Miller: 205 bottom
James H. Miller and Ted Bodner: 202 top, middle, and bottom; 204 bottom; 206; 208 top and bottom
Naturalis Biodiversity Center, used under Creative Commons license 1.0 Universal: 211 top
Hugh and Carol Nourse: 204 top left, center, and right; 205 top; 207 top; 209 middle
Richard Orr: 192 middle; 193 bottom
Robert Potts, © California Academy of Sciences: 179 top
C. Joel Sartore / Photo Ark: 210 bottom
Todd Schneider, Georgia DNR, Wildlife Resources Division: 198 left; 203 bottom left; 207 middle and bottom
David E. Scott: 187 top and bottom
Terry Spivey, USDA Forest Service, Bugwood.org: 181 middle
David Stone: 192 bottom
Robert Wayne Van Devender: 189 top and middle
Jess Van Dyke: 191 top
Daniel F. Vickers: 179 bottom; 180 top; 183 top left and top right; 185 top
Whatcom County Noxious Weed Board: 191 bottom
Wikimedia Commons: 212 bottom
Tom Wilson: 182 top and middle
Jason Wisniewski: 191 middle
Robert T. Zappalorti: 188 middle